Right Radicalism in Party and Political Systems in Present-day European States

Right Radicalism in Party and Political Systems in Present-day European States

By

Natalia Eremina and Sergei Seredenko

Cambridge
Scholars
Publishing

Right Radicalism in Party and Political Systems
in Present-day European States

By Natalia Eremina and Sergei Seredenko

This book first published 2015

Cambridge Scholars Publishing

Lady Stephenson Library, Newcastle upon Tyne, NE6 2PA, UK

British Library Cataloguing in Publication Data
A catalogue record for this book is available from the British Library

ISBN (10): 1-4438-7274-1
ISBN (13): 978-1-4438-7274-4

TABLE OF CONTENTS

INTRODUCTION

The political system of a state is forever evolving. This evolution is distinguished by ideological and political clashes and interactions between various political actors. Political evolution is a process influenced by society, political and economic institutions that respond to all kinds of challenges in their own ways. These challenges test the ability of the state to adapt to changing conditions and correct the system of governance by putting into the forefront certain political leaders who pronounce their ideas of the future of the state and the society. In periods of social, economic and political instability, radicalism becomes the main factor of party and political changes, thus forming a political trend. At the present time, right radicalism has become such a factor in the development of political systems of European states.

Right-wing radicalism, at the same time, is a rather vague conception. References to its vagueness are common since the development of the left-right party scale, differences between the right, the extreme right and ultra-nationalist parties, the impact of ideas propagated by Nazi and Fascist parties on the contemporary right-wing radicalism in Europe constitute hotly debated issues. Genetic and historical relationship between the extreme right of the pre-war period and contemporary right-wing radical parties often constitutes for scholars an obstacle for conceptual analysis of contemporary right-wing radicalism. A huge variety of opinions, outlooks and ideological views affect this task and prevent the scholars from attempting to create a single theory of extreme right political and ideological evolution that has not reached its end yet. It is obvious that certain ideological characteristics of extreme right-wing parties of the inter-war period are gone (such as the idea of physical extermination of people, since in the contemporary society in which knowledge and emotions have become a product and a merchandise having its own value, it is more effective to manipulate people's views and ideas than to destroy them), while new features have emerged (for instance, anti-immigration ideas and anti-Islamism). Does it mean that right-wing parties of the inter-war period and contemporary radicals are totally independent of each other and are different phenomena? How can we study them, what criteria should form the basis of such an analysis?

Some authors see a great political potential of the extreme right movement; others do not regard it as part of political establishment and relate the extreme right to marginal parties beyond the bounds of traditional political party scale of contemporary European states. Some authors study the motives of extreme right parties; some emphasize their political ambitions that are rooted in the shaky grounds of hate and fears. Some authors examine the extreme right vocabulary; others distinguish the ways to withstand these parties. Yet, practically every available scholarly paper on extreme right parties is political and concentrates on political ideas of the influence that right-wing radicals have on the society and the State, disregarding the legal dimension of the extreme right activities. Neither do authors agree on the significant issue if Nazi and Fascists are related to contemporary right-wing and ultra-nationalist groupings and parties.

Yet, if we fail to see the evolution and set ourselves to examine a party as it is, without historical examples and parallels to similar parties and political groups, we are incapable of understanding and imagining right-wing radicalism as a broad ideology with its own historical experience (while historical examples may provide material for comparison thereby helping to understand many aspects that are impossible to notice without this comparative analysis). If this analysis has not been made in the historical retrospective, right-wing radicalism will be nothing but a term, the name of a certain political activity, and it will not be able to stir anxiety or be recognized as an evident characteristic of the contemporary social development. The authors of this book tried to avoid such mistakes; they examine political philosophy (ideology in evolution) of right-wing radicalism and also depict political and legal dimensions of extreme right-wing parties.

The structure of the book correlates with interdependent aspects of the development of the contemporary European state and society, which allows for a consistent study of definitions, historical and ideological grounds of right-wing radicalism, extreme right parties in the geographic dimension, international and national law on sensitive issues of racism, xenophobia, nationalism, and ultra-nationalism, for determining the markers of neo-Nazism.

The authors tried to elaborate a diagnostics conception of right-wing radicalism that not only identifies the nature of extreme right parties but also discloses the socially dangerous nature of ultranationalist parties (neo-Nazi parties). The term "socially dangerous" applied to parties derives from the legal sphere and is suggested by the authors, since the scientific and political realms do not agree on the issue of definitions of extreme right parties (there are such well-known terms as anti-democratic, anti-establishment, anti-constitutional parties). Nevertheless, in spite of the terminological pluralism, these parties have one feature in common – they represent a threat to the development and the very existence of a society and state. So the term "socially dangerous" allows for distinguishing all risks (a crime is generally understood as a socially dangerous act) and for determining the criteria according to which these parties constitute a danger to the political system of the contemporary state. The examination of right-wing radicalism through the prism of legal and political trials allows the authors to have a better understanding of the genuine nature of right-wing parties. The legal approach to the study of social and cultural destabilization and conflicts allows for examining extreme right parties in the framework of law and beyond and for avoiding a discouraging uncertainty in the matter of what extreme right parties are and whether contemporary extreme right parties are distanced from the corresponding parties of the inter-war period or linked to them.

This book takes a fresh look at a wide spectrum of conceptions and approaches to the study of far-right parties and ultra-nationalist ideologies and examines the legal and political discourses in the framework of which they are formed. Proposing its ideas of the nature of far-right parties and their prospects, the book on the whole is a single, though complex multi-dimensional, conception of the evolution of far-right parties and their influence on the contemporary European party and political system, the society and the state.

Many issues were disregarded in various studies. Among those are the issues of legal and judicial mechanisms of influencing extreme right parties, as well as issues of practical and theoretical dimensions of extreme right activities. All these issues are closely related with one another and so must be examined in one study, but by all means in two dimensions – political and legal.

The book consistently builds up a vocabulary (legal and political); studies the interrelated nature of political, legal, cultural, social and economic processes that, taken together, elucidate the possibilities of extreme-right ideology and movement; it makes a comparative analysis of various far-right parties in Europe; it reveals intricate relations between ideas, political activity and election results; it puts forward juridical instruments that can be used to counter the extension of influence of extreme right parties.

The authors draw upon various conceptions and documents to enable them to continue the debate on the contemporary relevant understanding of right-wing radicalism and far-right parties. The need for a thorough analysis of conceptions and historical arguments relating to extreme-right ideology is beyond questioning, so the first two chapters (Chapters I and II) of the book examine the extreme-right ideology and evolution of parties in the context of conservatism, nationalism and social instability where they act as principles protecting “our own world” against the “attacks of an alien world”. Here the extreme right parties resort to the anti-immigration discourse as a key to many doors (various political activities) thereby articulating the ideas of conservatism and nationalism. These phenomena take on new overtones owing to globalization processes and globalizing threats that enabled the migration discourse to determine contemporary politics and become a fetish for far-right parties.

It should be emphasized that right-wing political radicalism is a new “old” trend in the political life of many states. Political radicalization frequently testifies to maladjustment of state institutions and power, and also traditional parties to various threats. New threats that every state faces (at least a short list of topical threats) are terrorism, financial and economic crises, huge flows of immigrants and ecological problems. Jumbled together owing to globalization, they testify to the crisis of traditional administration of government.

Globalization has also changed the nature of its self-identification in the society. For everyone, the cultural background is becoming more important than citizenship in a certain state, which is gradually yielding its position. Apart from that, European integration (as a regional example of globalization) also has an impact on the European society, stimulating migration movements and intensifying regional and national movements in member-state of the European Union, while the loss of common identity causes fragmentation of society.

No wonder that the globalization in many countries is accompanied by disintegration, constitutional decentralization, destabilization of relations between national and supranational governments, and division of citizens on local, regional, national and supranational levels[1].

In the context of integration, all these problems of controlling migration movements are becoming increasingly topical since they relate to positions and ambitions of states and the communitarian level and can affect the efficiency of their activities. So immigration and ethno-national problems, as well as political and public discussions of the question of how to integrate migrants and ethnic and national (historical) minorities, who have their own ideas about the future of the state, have become part

---

[1] Downs, W. M. 2002. Regionalism in the European Union: Key concepts and project overview, *European Integration*, 24 (3), p. 171.

of the political life in Europe. The most important question now is how to control immigration and other ethnics diasporas and communities within which people retain their traditions and the way of life and do not want to give up their culture in exchange of citizenship. Now this wish has been externalized as political demands. So the governmental power in many countries responded to this problem with a number of state acts on the integration of immigrants and immigration proper. But minor political parties, especially extreme right parties, profited by this and got a political key to the door of the political arena. Moreover, minor parties are always most active and quick to respond to the current topical issues by proposing their own solutions.

So at present it is political, social and cultural problems that opened up opportunities for far-right parties. Here we cannot help but mention that differences in cultural codes of different communities are the main source of political radicalism since, if we discuss far-right parties, it is the concept of "the culture of the Caucasian" that influences their actions and propaganda. Same goes for radical Islamic groups that set out on a campaign under the flag of their cultural peculiarities against the white Christian world. Moreover, if we remember ethnic, national (periphery) nationalism and separatism, we cannot help but note that cultural differences between the centre and the ethnic periphery are the perpetual motion machine fuelling the struggle of ethnic periphery for independence. It is important to emphasize that not only Western European countries but also countries of Central and Eastern Europe face the problems of cultural differences in their communities, and in many post-Soviet states (for example, Estonia, Latvia and Lithuania) Russophobia became a significant political trend in public fragmentation. Cultural barriers (or fault lines) kept springing up everywhere in Europe these past thirty years. They are conditioned by the growing complexity and fragmentation of the European community that bears the brunt of globalization, regionalization and even the emergence of new states (for instance, in Eastern and Central Europe).

The extreme right parties declare the need for restoring the link between the state and the society, while political, economic and cultural threats contribute to the growth of political extremism aimed against immigrants and certain ethnic (national) groups of population. These parties have become the vehicles of radical nationalism and xenophobia, which distinguishes them from other parties and groups. But at the same time this allows far-right parties, which call themselves the only true defenders of the state and society, to restore the faith of the population in the need for a powerful state. Extreme right parties present themselves as a "new" political alternative to traditional parties, though in many aspects such as anti-constitutionalism and anti-democratism they cannot help but resemble fascist and neo-fascist parties. Nevertheless, since contemporary far-right parties are institutionalized, they have a legitimate image.

Thus, contemporary Europe provides certain favourable conditions for ultra-nationalism and the development of extreme right concepts. The authors of the book do not restrict themselves to the analysis of successes attained by far-right-wing parties, they aim at explaining these successes exemplified by far-right parties in Northern Europe (Denmark, Latvia, Lithuania, Norway, the United kingdom, Finland, Sweden, Estonia), Western Europe (Belgium, Germany, the Netherlands, France), Eastern and Central Europe (Bulgaria, Hungary, Poland, Russia, Romania, Slovakia, Ukraine, Croatia) in Chapter III of the book (it should be noted that this is the official classification of regional division of Europe established by the United Nations). These examples constitute a vivid picture of general factors that have influence on right-wing radicalism and allow us to distinguish peculiarities of various far-right parties in different states.

When analyzing the political success of far-right parties, we should take into consideration that the feebleness of the national state and traditional parties indicates the ongoing transformation of political system in many European countries. Such conditions afford opportunities for minor radical parties to become the engine of political and public changes. Far-right parties, the principal proponents of the concept of unity of the state and the nation, now have a special political potential. Far-right parties were the first to voice protests against the policy of multiculturalism. They were the first to relate all social, economic and cultural problems to the growth of immigrant communities.

The European success of far-right parties is also a sign of ongoing transformation of political systems of European states. Far-right parties transform the political system and, at the same time, constitute a threat to it. Many European states, even those that do not have a massive far-right movement, have nonetheless provided conditions for the shaping and growth of right radicalism[2]. This situation demand full attention since changes in the political system encourage the emergence of far-right extremism[3].

---

[2] Eatwell, R. 2000. The Extreme right and the British exceptionalism: The primacy of politics, *The politics of the extreme right*, ed. by P. Hainsworth, London, pp.172-192.

[3] Ignazi, P. 2006. *Extreme right parties in Western Europe (comparative politics)*, Oxford.

Far-right parties have become an integral part of political establishment. No longer do they behave like marginal parties, nor do they perceive themselves as such. They win elections and gain support of the electorate at different national levels and even beyond (European Parliament elections). Their political strategies are definitely aimed at political success and winning seats in the Parliament.

All European far-right parties have elements of ideology and activity that unites them. For instance, we can say that nativism (nationalism and xenophobia) is the most evident element of all far-right parties. Since these parties, according to their nature and origin, are anti-system parties, such elements as authoritarianism and populism may be regarded as markers of these political groups. Political practice of far-right parties is based on their intolerance of immigrants, largely of those of Muslim origin and some ethnic (national) minorities. Their interrelations with a "non-civilized" society (for example, football fans and the so-called skinheads), acts of aggression, as well as their work in coalitional governments together with the traditional actors substantiate the idea that in the near future they will be able to further consolidate their position[4].

Since the contemporary far-right concepts are embodied in the calls to traditional common values under the umbrella of authoritarianism, populism and ultra-nationalism, of special scientific interest is a study of constitutional ways of the penetration of far-right ideology into the political and public life. This study allows for defining markers of ultra-nationalism (neo-Nazism) and methods to combat it. Unfortunately, the problem of nationalism penetrating into constitutional texts has never led to a study of the potential of far-right parties in public politics. This problem is dealt with in Chapter IV.

Chapters V, VI, VII and VIII examine the complex and controversial nature of international and national legal "Great Walls of China" put up to ward off and crush in the bud political radicalism and ultra-nationalism. These chapters devise and evaluate the techniques that will enable such counteraction and also they test the ability of the existing legal mechanics to adapt to the developing problems, threats and circumstances. In the framework of the legal study of threats far-right parties pose to contemporary national and public development, these chapters can be brought together to define the perspectives of far-right radicalism and the methods to combat it.

---

[4] Eremina, N. 2014. Radical Right Parties in Political System of State: Theoretical and Practical Aspects, *International Relations and Diplomacy*, 2(2), February, pp.102-110.

The key feature of these chapters is a deep and scrupulous analysis of the boundaries of the prohibited and the permissible for parties in international and national law, which allows the authors to see the dividing line between the "ordinary" right-wing parties and their ideas, and ultra-nationalist (neo-Nazi) parties and their ideas. This boundary line is useful as an instrument of identifying socially dangerous parties. This is nothing but an attempt to determine the true nature of such parties, which allows for solving the task of sustainable social development. The examination of legal norms and principles reveals the deeply buried roots of far-right ideology and helps us understand how and when a far-right party turns into an ultra-nationalist party that constitutes a threat to the society. Political and legal dimensions are used in this paper with a view to diagnosing and liquidating socially dangerous and banned parties.

The problems of xenophobia and racism in far-right ideology are often exemplified in numerous research papers that describe practical political activities of far-right parties, but these problems must be studied in the framework of law and legal practice. The book relies on the most important international instruments (Durban Declaration and Programme of Action, UN Declaration on the Elimination of All Forms of Racial Discrimination, etc.) and national law (Constitutions) in its analysis of socially dangerous parties, parties that intend to undermine the foundations of the constitutional order. A new examination of contemporary far-right parties is made possible by studying certain aspects of their activities in the legal dimension, for example, the use of Nazi symbols and attributes; relations between party members with other extremists right-wing and neo-Nazi organizations, paramilitary and military historical organizations; party responses, responses of allied parties and party internationals; responses of law-enforcement bodies; populism and populist provocations, etc.

These aspects act as constructing elements of legal discourse to show the actual international and national practice in this sphere. The analysis made in the book demonstrates that practical methods of liquidating neo-Nazi parties (ultra-nationalist, socially dangerous parties) have not been developed at the national level. The involuntary interest the United Nation showed in constitutional norms of participating parties was caused by the deadlock in the corresponding national law and the absence of political will. Moreover, neither international nor national law provides a definition of ultra-nationalist (neo-Nazi) party and threats that it constitutes to the state and the society. Examination of racist declarations is not sufficient to understand a true radical nature of a party. We must also analyze a party's funding, its relations with allied parties and organizations and consider the judgments passed on the party and activities of its members. Only in this case can comprehensive diagnostics of a party be performed. This is especially important now that far-right parties can form international groups which are engaged in the diffusion of power (for example, in the European Parliament, in bodies of the European Union) and the fragmentation of the society.

Thus, we realize that the far-right party is only the top of the pyramid whose base conceals an ideological layer (the so-called esoteric level)[5] from the public. But the main threat posed to the state and the society is attempts made by far-right parties (rather successful at times) to become the key actors in the contemporary political system. They provide instruments, mechanisms and political will to solve the existing problems; they try to gain power to create a new society and even new normative structures; they turn Europe into a laboratory to test new "old" forms and methods of administration of government.

The research into the declared questions is further pursued in the Annex.

Ultra-nationalism, serving as an umbrella for various far-right parties and groups, may be examined in various ways and in different contexts. The study of far-right ideology heavily relies on the interdisciplinary debate conducted by political scientists, jurists and historians. Yet, since there is a compelling need to learn to identify socially dangerous (neo-Nazi) parties and then to liquidate them, the judicial and legal dimension becomes the most important task set in this book. It should be noted that since there is no consensus of opinion about what a far-right party or a far-right extremist party is, a more important task is to solve the problem of what a socially dangerous party is, without classing it as a certain type of a far-right party. Especially when we see that the relation between leaders' statements and far-right parties proper differs from country to country in Europe.

The authors put forward a practical solution pattern. The diagnostic test for a neo-Nazi party is run on the All-Ukrainian Svoboda Union in accordance with the definition of the nature of Fascism given by P. Griffin. The party's activities, declarations and manifestations are subjected to

---

[5] Shehovtsov, A.V. 2008. Novyi pravyi radikalizm: k voprosu ob opredelenii, *in Vestnik SevNTU, Zbornik nauk*, Vyp. 91, Sevastopol', pp. 141-144. (Shekhovtsov, A.V. 2008. New right-wing radicalism: definition issue, *in Vesnik SevNTU, Collection of sciences*, Vol. 91, Sevastopol, Published by SevNTU, pp. 141-144). (in the original: Шеховцов, А.В. 2008. Новый правый радикализм: к вопросу об определении, *Вісник СевНТУ: Зб. наук. праць*, Вип. 91, Севастополь: СевНТУ, с. 141-144).

intense scrutiny by means of palingenetic markers ("golden age", national tragedy, "cleansing", rewriting of history, continuity)[6], ultra-nationalism and populism, as well as certain additional markers (Lebensraum, territorial claims, external enemies, militarism, glorification of Nazism, Nazi attributes).

Right radicalism has become the main challenge in the European political system. Yet it still remains a somewhat vague and murky phenomenon, since the far-right movement and ideology constitute a mix, a confusion of political views, ideas and instruments. So to understand the role of right radicalism in the development of state, party and political system of Europe we should first of all determine what far-right parties are. It is important to emphasize that the main aim of the book is to identify these parties (to perform diagnostic tests) and to prove their public danger (to define ideological views of far-right parties that constitute a certain risk to the society and the state).

To answer the question of what far-right parties are is possible if we cope with four interrelated tasks: to examine far-right evolution by analyzing the right end of the left-right party spectrum and ultra-nationalist ideology; to draw dividing lines between right, far-right and neo-Nazis; to adduce opportunities for the extension of influence of far-right parties on the society by analyzing legal systems of European states and gaps in international law on prevention of right radicalism; to determine markers of a socially dangerous (neo-Nazi) party.

A significant part of conceptual novelties of this book consists of several catalogues that were made up to examine far-right parties and ideology by means of specific markers.

First of all, it is a catalogue of distinguishing features of constitutional nationalism (explaining what markers can identify the potential and the extent of nationalist sentiments and internal ethnic and national conflicts, opportunities for the growth of far-right parties and the degree of ultra-nationalism in a society); second, it is a catalogue of features of the socially dangerous party, which was made up by virtue of the demarcation line drawn between right, far-right and ultra-nationalists in accordance with the boundaries of the prohibited and the permissible as defined in international and national law; third, the authors have made up a catalogue of threats posed by the far-right parties to the state and the society and showed the absence of legal instruments in international and national legal systems to prevent those threats; fourth, the book proposes a tentative

---

[6] Griffin, R. 1991. *The Nature of Fascism*, London.

algorithm (the principles and sequence of actions) for indentifying neo-Nazi parties.

The authors hope that on the whole the research will be interesting not only for scholars and students but also it will be sought after by all those who are concerned about right radicalism.

CHAPTER I

FAR-RIGHT PARTIES: TERMINOLOGICAL AND CONCEPTUAL APPROACHES

1.1 Ideological mutations: from fascism to right-wing radicalism

Present time has recorded the existence of different approaches to the definition of what a far-right (also extreme-right or ultra-right or right-wing radical) party is and the way it is associated with right-wing parties, fascist, neo-fascist, neo-Nazi parties and the whole post-fascism era. The academic and political circles hotly debate on whether certain parties are *genealogically (historically)* fascist and how and to what extent contemporary right-wing radicals ideologically retain the historical connection with National Socialism and fascism. However in the minds of many representatives of right-wing radicalism as well as in the minds of the political establishment and even ordinary voters the idea of direct continuity of these parties with Nazism and fascism is not always expressed. These groups and movements are quite heterogeneous and their political radicalism is caused not only by a variety of current challenges but is also based on the political experience of fascist and Nazi organizations.

Thus, when analyzing extreme-right radicalism the following aspects should be taken into account.

First, none of the political ideologies is always constant and unchangeable. Any ideology is mobile and flexible by its nature and capable of mutations in a new environment.

Second, the interpretation of the contemporary far-right ideology should be based on historical retrospectives which allow to accurately evaluate the genealogy and history of ideologies, i.e. their evolution.

Third, the existence of small parties with extreme-right beliefs creates complications in the political ideology interpretation. Yet the lack of clear historical links between various parties and fascist and Nazi parties should not confuse the researchers. First of all, it is necessary to pay attention to the extent of radicalism in their political statements and actions, as fascist and Nazi ideology demonstrates a diverse range of methods and techniques, some of which are in the arsenal of the new extreme-right groups.

The fourth aspect indicates that the most of far-right parties striving to become equal and full participants in the party political struggle reject any affiliation or ideological proximity to fascist and Nazi movements.

Fifth, it seems especially valuable to analyze the way far-right parties interact with their electorate and also review the nature of their public statements.

And, finally, for the parties offering the radical scenario of political activities it appears to be particularly crucial to take advantage of the patterns of public thinking and to form a corresponding associative symbolic set in the minds of potential voters, i.e. reliance on certain social and cultural attitudes of the population. It is also important to consider that the extreme-right ideology gains support in the traditional right-wing conservative values, so when the population voices discontent with the leading parties (usually conservative parties predominate in the party political development of the European states) the extreme-right groups seize this additional opportunity to strengthen their position.

1.1.1. The right wing of the party political development: towards the edge

The right wing of the party political spectrum is traditionally a leading sector in the development of political systems of many European countries. The leading parties which usually bear the name of Christian, national or democratic are, as a rule, conservative right-wing parties positioning themselves as the guardians of the existing state system and social stability. The dynamic development of these parties is historically justified by a complex of philosophical and ideological attitudes and values in the European society. In fact, these parties derived from so-called elitist societies and are committed to the traditional approaches in the interpretation of any events. Thus, conservatism, the significance of the state system and the preservation of the social hierarchy for maintaining order in the country provide essential support for the progressive development of the right-wing ideology.

With the passage of time a sharp division of all political ideologies into the right and left ones was critically reinterpreted as the political attitudes of both wings underwent a major transformation, though, in fact, the right wing constantly continued to strengthen. As a result, liberalism, in the historical course of time, gradually shifted from the left to the right wing leaving a niche for new parties of social democratic orientation which, in their turn, gave way to the Communists into the extreme-left wing.

This process provided the ideological interchange, especially, among Conservatives, Liberals and Social Democrats which allowed them to become the leading political force in many European countries while the liberal ideology, in essence, was shared between Conservatives and Social Democrats. After Liberals lost their distinctive features they factually dropped out of the political competition, although it affected only party organizations whereas the liberal ideology maintained its position and now fully belongs to the right party political sector in terms of left-right party division. Disputes and solutions to emerging problems, including those of global nature, stimulated the appearance of new ideological resources and tools. Moreover, those issues, which the centre-right and the centre-left did not dare to address, were eagerly proposed for debates by various radical groups acting at the both ends of the left-right party political scale. At the same time, extreme-right parties showed the most substantial growth of political influence. Focusing on the existing traditional and conservative values and partly recognizing market liberalism, right-wing extremists increasingly draw attention to themselves and begin to act as a serious political participant and rival recognized by the whole political establishment.

The right-wing ideological platform can serve as a reliable basis for the formation of new parties and political attitudes where the right-wing radicalism is one of its branches. New social problems require new policy prescriptions mostly associated with an iron will and a firm hand which are believed to restore order in the society and state. In particular, the disagreement in perception of the proper socio-political state structure has separated various right-wing parties from each other while the most radical views in Europe today belong to the far-right wingers. Over time they have largely succeeded in their political goals and got the opportunity to influence the formation of the political agenda which should motivate to take a thorough look at these parties as at the major contributors to the party political system development and decision-making process at the highest state level.

1.1.2. The far-right: scientific disputes

Gradually, far-right parties gained new features through expanding and advancing their policy tools.

There exist multiple approaches and definitions of far-right movements and groups: far-right extremism, far-right radicalism, far-right populism, populist radicalism, new right-wing radicalism, ultra-nationalism and other. Debates about overcoming the cultural crisis and creating new opportunities for a modern state caused a number of new terms associated with fascism and Nazism to appear: ethno-fascism, monarcho-fascism, glamour fascism, global fascism and other. But these terms, regardless of any names these or those far-right parties bear, share one and the same semantic set with such concepts as: xenophobia, Nazism, anti-Semitism, anti-Islam and radicalism. It is also obvious that such labels as the far-right, the extreme-right, right-wing radicals can be used as synonymous with each other.

However, it is necessary to consider that the terms meaning far-right parties and movements cannot apply for absolute support and are a product of scholars as far-right parties often do not refer themselves to right-wing radicals and what is more do not identify their parties with neo-fascist or neo-Nazi which creates difficulties in the interpretation of these movements. Therefore in the majority of studies their authors reveal intrinsic ideological views of the ultra-right which distinctly mark them out among all other parties of the right wing. It is obvious that all researchers emphasize that the ideology of the extreme-right, by its definition, is aimed against the existing state and social system, i.e. it is factually anti-constitutional as it opposes "undesirable" or "unwanted" elements in this system. These "unwanted elements" are presented by different ethnic groups which mainly practice Islam.

So, Elisabeth Carter reveals features of the extreme-right ideology through the negative characteristics common for the far-right ideological views: anti-democracy and anti-constitutionalism[1]. Cas Mudde suggests that far-right parties should be defined as the parties proclaiming the unity of the nation-state as the highest ideological value, where groups of other ethnic origin are deemed to be a potential threat and where nativism, authoritarianism and populism are the key components[2]. According to Roger Griffin, ethnocentrism also represents the central link in the interpretation of the extreme-right ideology[3].

However, while studying the distinctive features of right-wing radicalism it is essential to determine how these characteristics correspond to fascism and Nazism.

---

[1] Carter, E.L. 2005. *The Extreme Right in Western Europe: Success or Failure?* Manchester.

[2] Mudde, C. 2007. *Populist Radical Right Parties in Europe*, Cambridge.

[3] Griffin, R. 1991. *The Nature of Fascism*, London.

For example, the Russian researcher Nikolay Myazin does not observe neo-fascism as a true successor to fascism and Nazism as neo-fascists are focused on racial questions, but not economic, and the integral elements of neo-fascist ideology, according to N. Myazin, are neo-paganism, irrationalism and the Third Reich idealization. It also separates neo-fascists from ultra-right parties. The ultra-right ideology, from his point of view, represents the nationalist ideology supporting traditional values and rejecting Hitler's Germany legacy. The new ultra-right, as N. Myazin writes, advocate western but not Christian values and the core element of their ideology is anti-jihadism[4].

Paul Jackson, on the contrary, states a certain common reason for all similar movements and political organizations and proposes to divide all ultra-right parties into three categories: neo-fascists, i.e. far-right extremists who try to achieve their objectives in the violent way; the more moderate far-right which, though having the same purposes, employ political methods; and "the new far-right" which instead of biological racism operate with the concept of cultural racism[5].

It is evident that the author emphasizes similar purposes, revealing only a difference in tool approaches. But it still remains unclear to what extent all these far-right movements are successors to the fascist ideology. Also, it should be noted that researches quite often avoid linking ultra-right radicalism with inter-war fascism and Nazism and so break the ideological links between the ultra-right of the inter-war and post-war periods.

Most likely, these fears can be dictated by the recognition that certain parties are genetically and historically linked to fascism and Nazism (though many of them openly celebrate A. Hitler's birthday) which motivates to call these parties socially dangerous and consequently involves lawsuits and their expulsion from the political life.

---

[4] Myazin, N.A. 2014. *Islamskoe soobschestvo I islamizm v Anglii v XX – XXI kak factory transformatsii britanskikh pravyh dvizheniy ot neofashizma k antidjihadizmy*, Kaluga. (Myazin, N.A. 2014. *Islamic community and Islamism in England at the end of XX – the beginning of the XXI centuries as transformation factors of the British right-wing movements from neo-fascism to anti-jihadism*. The abstract of dissertation for the first level of postgraduate degree, Kaluga) (in the original: Мязин, Н.А. 2014. *Исламское сообщество и исламизм в Англии в конце XX – начале XXI вв. как факторы трансформации британских правых движений от неофашизма к антиджихадизму*. Автореферат диссертации на соискание ученой степени кандидата наук, Калуга).

[5] Jackson, Paul. 2011. *The EDL Britain`s «New Far Right» Social Movement*, Northampton: The University of Northampton, Radicalism and New Media Research Group.

Anton Shekhovtsov puts forward other solutions to handle the difficulties with defining the new extreme-right activists who, unlike the extreme-right parties of the inter-war period (it is clear that fascists and Nazis were on the extreme-right wing of the party political scale), are not able to openly and publicly express their true ideological ambitions and therefore hide them. A. Shekhovtsov highlights two levels of the new far-right ideology: "exoteric" (official party programs) and "esoteric" (the true purposes and ideology known to a limited number of party members). Also, he offers his own definition to this phenomenon describing it as the ideology which is based on the idea of preservation, realization and reproduction of the ethnically and culturally homogeneous type of the society within the liberal-democratic system[6].

It is obvious that the changing circumstances, which these parties pass through, profoundly influence the perception of the ideological continuity issue. Changes of the statehood concepts and principles of the national sovereignty and also failures in the decision-making system provoke a search for new solutions including the right-wing political spectrum. Since the beginning of the XX century far-right parties have adopted the leading position in the debate concerning the state role viewing their own state as the main actor in the formation of a new picture of the world.

It cannot be expected that after the Nuremberg trials and condemnation of fascism and Nazism, these movements definitively and irrevocably disappeared. Any ideology is subject to changes (mutations) allowing it to survive and remain relevant. In the era of post-fascism these forces chose two strategies for survival. The first strategy is a partial transformation of "historical fascism". The movements which follow this strategy have no ample opportunities for recovery and development. The second strategy is based on preserving party appeal to the voter by decreasing spirit of revolutionary demolition of the existing statehood and adjusting the party rhetoric within liberal democracy[7].

Thus, anyway, it is clear that the far-right demonstrate certain continuity with "historical fascism" which should be closely monitored in

---

[6] Shehovtsov, A.V. 2008. Novyi pravyi radikalizm: k voprosu ob opredelenii, *in Vestnik SevNTU, Zbornik nauk*, Vyp. 91, Sevastopol', p 143. (Shekhovtsov, A.V. 2008. New right-wing radicalism: definition issue*, in Vesnik SevNTU, Collection of sciences*, Vol. 91, Sevastopol, Published by SevNTU, p. 143). (in the original: Шеховцов, А.В. 2008. Новый правый радикализм: к вопросу об определении, *Вісник СевНТУ: Зб. наук. грацъ*, Вип. 91, Севастополь: СевНТУ, с. 143.)

[7] Shehovtsov, A.V. 2008. Novyi pravyi radikalizm: k voprosu ob opredelenii, in *Vestnik SevNTU, Zbornik nauk*, Vyp. 91, Sevastopol', p. 300.

each separate case and their programs and actions are to be subjected to the careful analysis in accordance with concrete life conditions.

Such authors as Alexander Galkin, Alexander Yefremov, Boris Lopukhov speak about similar circumstances which, emerging in different configurations in different periods, create optimum conditions for the activity of the far-right[8]. Some of these conditions include parliamentary democracy crisis, economic and social complications and pre-election rhetoric of the leading parties which is now deemed to be common. These factors inevitably generate the desire of citizens to return the strong state possessing political will and resources for taking tough and even unpopular decisions.

In Herbert Kitshelt's monograph the extreme-right show political force in specific conditions: advanced post-industrial society and political rapprochement of the right and left wings. In addition, far-right wingers offer to unite the liberal views on the economy development and the ideas about political authoritarianism[9].

Thus A. Galkin specifies that, despite the “true opposition” status, the extreme right indicate that they are ready to cooperate with conservative forces[10].

Also, E. Carter presents an interesting idea which proves that electoral progress of far-right parties depends on how moderate the political positions held by mainstream conservative right-wing parties are: the more moderate views they adhere to, the more potential the extreme-right possess[11].

It is important to notice that now far-right wingers really reflect the need for the cooperation and loyalty of mainstream conservative parties as they propose to establish a public order, to return to traditional religious values, to support a family and culture and to counteract threats received from the immigrant expansion.

---

[8] Galkin, A.A. 1971. *Sociologia neofashizma*, Moskva. (Galkin, A.A. 1971. *Neo-fascist Sociology*, Moscow) (in the original: Галкин, А.А. 1971. *Социология неофашизма*, М.); Yefremov, A.E. 1970. *Korichnevaya ugroza*, Moskva. (Yefremov, A.Y. 1970. *The Brown PlagueThreat*, Moscow). (in the original: Ефремов, А.Е. 1970. *Коричневая угроза*, М.); Lopukhov, B.R. 1985. *Neo-fashizm: opastnost' dlya mira*, Moskva. (Lopukhov, B.R. 1985. *Neo-fascism: the World Threat*, Moscow). (in the original: Лопухов, Б.Р. 1985. *Неофашизм: опасность для мира*, М.).

[9] Kitschelt, H. and McGann, Anthony J. 1997. *The Radical Right in Western Europe: a comparative analysis*, Michigan.

[10] Galkin, A.A. 1971. *Sociologia neofashizma*, Moskva.

[11] Carter, E.L. 2005. *The Extreme Right in Western Europe: Success or Failure?* Manchester.

B. Lopukhov is of the opinion that the reliance on these (traditional) values helps extreme-right parties to strengthen their position. However, their ideology, anyway, goes beyond the existing liberal-democratic system and actually rejects it. Therefore, neo-fascists and modern right-wing radicals, as B. Lopukhov states, are often terminologically interchangeable labels though are not absolutely homogeneous[12].

It must be noted that the word "traditional" is quite frequently used in the researches of this kind whereas Piero Ignazi's research comes up with totally contrary ideas.

P. Ignazi points out that after 1980s far-right parties have no relation to neo-fascist parties any more. They operate in the new environment and provide new (auth.: nonconventional?) solutions to the emerging problems, and in doing so they do not aim at implementing the idea of a great nation-state. Thus, according to P. Ignazi, neo-fascism was eventually transformed into new post-industrial right-wing extremism. P. Ignazi also believes that the progress far-right parties have achieved lies in the field of polarization of political systems and derives from a general crisis of political system legitimacy[13].

At the same time, denying any connection with fascism and neo-fascism the far-right cause perplexity, though, certainly, not all extreme-right parties can be probably correlated with neo-fascism. Nevertheless, it is perfectly clear that the extreme-right ideology in the form of fascism and Nazism, which arose during the inter-war period, made up an extensive bank of ideas, methods and techniques, while the fascist and Nazi ideology itself encouraged a tendency for development and mutations so far. As a result, it shows to be true that fascism, Nazism and the modern extreme-right are closely interlinked.

For instance, Michael Minkenberg proves the continuity of right-wing radicalism with fascism by analyzing fascism, nationalism and conservatism concepts[14].

As a matter of fact, Adolf Hitler and Benito Mussolini did not leave any definitions of "fascism" and "Nazism". They are known to favour all political technologies (both of left-wing and right-wing political spectrum) that could considerably strengthen their position in the political arena. For this reason, there are dozens of interpretations of these phenomena within the academic dispute, ranging from their psychological characteristics

---

[12] Lopukhov, B.R. 1985. *Neo-fashizm: opastnost' dlya mira*, Moskva.

[13] Ignazi, P. 2003. *Extreme Right Parties in Western Europe*, Oxford.

[14] Minkenberg, M. 1998. *Die neue radikale Rechte im Vergleich*, USA, Frankreich, Deutschland, Opladen.

(Erich Fromm[15]) to the analysis of their historical basis (Wolfgang Wippermann[16]). Apart from that, Professor R. Griffin introduced an original approach to this phenomenon labeling it as "revolutionary palingenetic ultra-nationalism" where the revival of the nation-state is emphasized and fascism is presented not only as a political but also as a cultural phenomenon[17].

Factually, fascism can change with the time and assume various forms in social and political life of the state still preserving certain fundamental principles related to the concept of the state, nation and race[18].

Besides, it should be stressed that in general ultra-right parties are tolerantly treated in former authoritarian states and also in those states where radical parties have achieved success before[19].

Nevertheless, far-right parties are sometimes associated with fascism and Nazism, for example, in mass media and in journalistic circles. In this case this evaluation impedes their political activities as in modern society people hardly ever feel nostalgic about the inter-war fascist experience, i.e. about ultra-right parties which exhibit opened or veiled intolerance towards foreigners or immigrants, express mistrust of parliamentary institutes and a multi-party system, uphold the principle of cultural and national identity of the indigenous population. Furthermore, in the modern European society these ideological schemes are mainly given a shape of a legal not extremist protest[20] and far-right parties started to display more enthusiasm for declaring their views. Thus, possessing more moderate attitudes, the right-wing UK Independence Party (UKIP) was more

---

[15] Fromm, E. 1994. *Escape from Freedom*, Henry Holt and Company LLC.

[16] Wippermann, W. 1983. *Europäischer Faschismus in Vergleich 1992-1982*, Frankfurt am Main: Suhrkamp.

[17] Griffin, R. 2002. The Primacy of Culture: the Current Growth (or Manufacture) of Consensus within Fascist Studies, *Journal of Contemporary History*, Vol.37, N1 January, p.42.

[18] Paxton, O.R. 1998. Five Stages of Fascism, *Journal of Modern History*, Vol.70, N1 March, p. 3.

[19] Duck, R.M., Gibson, J.L. 1992. "Putting up with" Fascism in Western Europe: a Comparative, Cross-Level Analysis of Political Tolerance, *The Western Political Quarterly*, Vol.45, N1 March, p.267.

[20] Veugelers, J.W.P. 1999. A Challenge for Political Sociology: the Rise of Far-Right Parties in Contemporary Western Europe, *Current Sociology*, Vol.47, N4 October, p.80-81.

successful than the British National Party (BNP) in the elections to the European Parliament[21].

So, the emergence and development of extreme-right parties require appropriate circumstances which are embodied in a certain set of the social, economic, political and cultural problems faced by the society and state.

Currently, the far-right ideology, being a part of the global world, is living through certain permutations. And if previously one of the main indicators of the political status of the extreme-right was their attitude to a socio-economic policy[22], nowadays their general ideological statements include protection of their own ethnic (national) identity on the one hand and posing obstacles for all those elements which can contribute to their destruction and loss on the other. As a rule, these threats, in the eyes of the extreme-right movement, are connected with a massive immigrant flood.

For example, in the monograph "Varieties of Right-Wing Extremism in Europe", published in 2013 by the Routledge publishing house, it was claimed that anti-Islam became a key appeal of right-wing radicals and accelerated the growth of those extreme-right wingers who preach religious extremism. So, it is clear that discussions about immigration and religious and cultural (national) identity turned to be sufficient for the extreme-right to noticeably improve their position in the political arena. Because of this, in those countries where Muslims are very hard to integrate into the host community, the far-right movements occupy stronger positions. Among those countries, first of all, are Austria, France and the United Kingdom. The authors of the monograph specify that these extreme-right ideas, having gained a foothold in the countries mentioned above, can easily enter other countries also due to the common European area. Moreover, the extreme-right influence is constantly stimulated not only by mass media, but also by the Internet and even by music and literature. All the authors point to the rise of populism, and even racism in the statements of extreme-right political leaders which inevitably revitalizes the ideas of fascism. In particular, one of the authors of the monograph, Jim Wolfreys, traces the revival of fascism in the Front National's (FN, a far-right party in France) growing political impact. Fascism, being a flexible doctrine, has notably mutated since the inter-war

---

[21] Voss, K. 2007. Support for the Far Right: the Desire for Cultural Preservation in an Increasingly Globalized and Multicultural Europe, Spring, p.4. Available at: http//www.icpsr.umich/edu/ICPSR/prize/winners.html

[22] McClosky, H., Chong, D. 1985. Similarities and Differences between Left-wing and Right-wing Radicals, *British Journal of Political Science*, Vol.15, N3 July, p.342.

period. Thanks to the alliance between the extreme-right and right-wing conservatives such movements and groups were also subjected to certain mutations which, undoubtedly, prevented them from calling themselves fascist any more or leaving their political program unchanged[23].

According to C. Mudde, the intensive integration process between Western and Eastern European countries can be defined as the crucial factor in the new far-right's evolution. The researcher considers a modern extreme-right trend, first of all, as the revival of nativism and insists on its centrist orientation in the economic policy provoked by the political flexibility[24].

Some scholars appeal to the fact that the extreme-right movements which rose in the 1990s in Europe were also encouraged by the collapse of the Soviet Union. Particularly, this refers to the political life in Russia, Ukraine and Belarus portrayed in the book "The Revival of Right Wing Extremism in the Nineties"[25].

Now fascism and Nazism represent general categories which form a certain ideological framework for new far-right parties, including those parties which openly deny their association with the ideology of fascism or Nazism (though, judging by the activities and statements of the leaders of the British National Party, the German People's Union, the National Democratic Party, they do not deny the genetic linkage with fascism). Not only political tools but also radical rhetoric and judgments about their nation's role in the world can serve as a determiner of the far-right's pro-fascist background.

The unity of the nation and strengthening state capacity are vitally necessary to implement the extreme-right ideas which correspondingly involve confrontation with other political movements and the far-right separation from any other groups. Currently, however, it would be futile to seek for an external enemy in order to unite the nation and the major threat, in the opinion of the far-right, comes from big ethnic communities and cultures of other origin. So, the belief in the rule of law and order becomes basic and the only one capable of maintaining the unity of the nation-state[26].

The progress of extreme-right parties derives not only from specific current circumstances but it is also rooted in the emotional coincidence of

[23] *Varieties of Right-Wing Extremism in Europe*. 2013, ed. by Andrea Mammone, Emmanuel Godin, Brian Jenkins, London.
[24] Mudde, C. 2007. *Populist Radical Right Parties in Europe*, Cambridge
[25] *The Revival of Right Wing Extremism in the Nineties*. 2013, ed. by Peter H. Merkl, Leonard Weinberg, London.
[26] Mudde, C. 2003. *The Ideology of the Extreme Right*, Manchester, p. 173.

voters' requirements and party's statements. Since the end of the 20th century extreme-right parties have represented a powerful political force. They won seats in parliaments, regional and local governments, and even could establish their own group in the European Parliament. The essence of fascism in the modern world, its interpretation by far-right parties are becoming the key aspect for an ordinary voter.

In this regard it is important to explore how seriously far-right parties threaten the whole political system or if they are becoming or even have already become its integral component?

Most of the researchers, studying this issue, have unambiguously shifted far-right parties from the marginalized to the so-called mainstream politics.

Thus, Pippa Norris claims that recently these parties have moved from the margins to the mainstream[27] and also Herbert Kitshelt and Anthony J. McGann interpret right-wing radicalism as the core feature of the modern political process where ethnocentric, authoritarian and racist statements of the far-right are employed as a quite convincing strategy[28]. C. Mudde views the extreme-right as a well-established political force and even points to their links, in this way or another, with the parties of the political mainstream[29]. The authors of the monograph "Mapping the Extreme-Right in Contemporary Europe: from Local to Transnational" also proved that far-right parties are no longer marginal political activists and over the past few decades have adapted to the existing requirements and rules of the party political fight. Despite the rhetoric of national or racial superiority, far-right parties share common political vision. Extreme-right radical groups actively cooperate with each other and possess similar views about the future of Europe, insisting on a homogeneous state concept. What is more, as the researchers see it, extreme-right radicals are united by a number of distinctive features: the spread of the rhetoric of threats, disdain for egalitarianism, "ancient" culture defence, rehabilitation of war criminals. For this reason the extreme-right, as the researchers show, are able to influence not only politics, but also culture and education, using massive propaganda of other patterns and ideals as well[30].

---

[27] Norris, P. 2005. *Radical Right: Voters and Parties in the Electoral Market*, Cambridge.

[28] Kitschelt, H. and McGann, Anthony J. 1997. *The Radical Right in Western Europe: a comparative analysis*, Michigan.

[29] Mudde, C. 2007. *Populist Radical Right Parties in Europe*, Cambridge.

[30] *Mapping the Extreme Right in contemporary Europe. From local to transnational*. 2012, ed. by Andrea Mammone, Emmanuel Godin, Brian Jenkins, London.

Politically, these parties are already integrated into the existing party political system as favouring traditional conservative values they have eventually obtained steady voters' support. Although, it is still quite difficult to provide a single portrait of a far-right proponent, as nowadays alongside the debates about citizens' discontent with social and economic situation there are also the debates about the pursuit of national superiority and state power manifestation. These ideas demonstrate immense potential to bring together representatives of different social groups. Therefore, in some cases, the label "far-right charismatic parties" can be justified as extreme-right parties use striking statements to appeal to the voter[31].

Robert Ford and Matthew J. Goodwin made an attempt to analyze the social basis of the extreme-right movement taking the UK Independence Party as an example. The researchers specify that gradually there has appeared a sector of population which has no access to new opportunities, unlike the prosperous middle class which enormously benefits from the liberalized and globalized economy. For this reason, the electorate of right-wing radicals shares three aspects: opposition to the European Union, anti-immigration issue and mistrust of the political establishment[32].

Terri Givens however stresses out that right-wing extremists will inevitably face and are facing difficulties increasing voters' loyalty and their success and achievements in certain countries only indicate crisis tendencies and the way the crisis is handled by local population and political actors. In this regard, according to T. Givens, an electoral system, traditional voting and electoral positions of the population remain prevailing factors in the political choice of the voter[33].

On another point, neo-fascist and neo-Nazi projects which emerged after World War II are deemed, in a way, to be thirst for order and combat against the communist ideology and realization of Western European elite's idea seeking to regain the lost positions. Specifically, in the monograph edited by Roger Eatwell and Cas Mudde, it seems quite persuasive that far-right parties have made a dramatic, though inhomogeneous, impact on political systems of the Western European countries. In such countries as Italy, Austria and the Netherlands these parties have entered the government, however, always relying on criticism of current politicians and taking advantage of public protests. Additionally, the political establishment, in one sense, can welcome far-

---

[31] Pedahzur, A., Brichta, A. 2002. The institutionalization of extreme right-wing charismatic parties: a paradox?, *Party Politics,* Vol.8, N 1, p.31.

[32] Ford, R. and Goodwin, Matthew J. 2014. *Revolt on the Right: Explaining Support for the Radical Right in Britain (Extremism and Democracy)*, London.

[33] Givens, Terri E. 2005. *Voting Radical Right in Western Europe*, Cambridge.

right wingers as they are able to update a lot of political issues[34]. Thus, extreme-right radicals are gradually strengthening their position in order to provide the ground for loud statements and radical actions. It is not surprising that many far-right parties in Europe today openly acknowledge their ties with fascist or Nazi organizations and their members during World War II.

The fact that extreme-right political movements are already integrated into party political systems of different countries is clearly demonstrated by national political leaders' statements. For instance, it looks quite remarkable that the official statements of the British authorities concerning the immigration issue and national security meet the statements of the British National Party and the English Defence League. Similarly, Nicolas Sarkozy's judgements about the crash of the multiculturalism policy played straight into the hands of the National Front in France.

Thus, immediately after World War II Europe was flooded by neo-fascist extreme-right groups whose core ideology was and is still comprised of hatred for ethnic minorities, racial purity concept, anti-Semitism and opposition to the government. However, modern extreme-right movements tend to avoid making radical claims for racial purity and gradually accentuate more positive ideas of maintaining cultural identity. Also, the electoral success of right-wing radicals can be explained by their ability to dispose of neo-fascist or neo-Nazi ideas and dismiss historical links with fascism and Nazism. Focus on cultural identity concept forced far-right activists to find new enemies. As a result, Islam became a primary target for the extreme-right attacks as Islamic values considerably differ from traditional western ideals. In contrast to this, in the countries of the former socialist camp Islamophobia is substituted for Russophobia as these countries are not preoccupied with Muslim immigration flows. Here far-right parties try to formulate an idea of the national superiority opposing it to the Russian world which, from their point of view, is a true successor to the imperial and Soviet past. All extreme-right parties also express hostility towards multiculturalism and reject an idea of the unity in variety. So, right-wing radicals specify that the fight of some ethnic minorities for their civil rights can establish a new political order. Therefore, Islamophobia (and, in some cases, Russophobia) is favorable to the far-right: the more considerable this phobia is, the stronger they are.

Apart from that, the official position of many West European states also confirms the fact that Islamic radical groups pose a real threat to the

---

[34] *Western Democracies and the New Extreme Right Challenge*. 2003, ed. by Eatwell R. and Mudde C., London.

existing order, which, in its turn, is the key concept promoted by right-wing radicals and due to which they managed to get closer to mainstream parties. For this reason, no wonder that extreme right groups and parties began to position themselves as defenders of the Western European values against the foreign culture influence. For the extreme-right the main indicator in this intercultural dispute is whether these values are shared by other national groups or not. As a rule, according to ultra-nationalists, groups of other ethnic and cultural origin cause cultural disorder in a society since they cannot be fully integrated into it.

1.2. Investigation of the Far-Right parties: methodological approaches

1.2.1. Methodology of social sciences in the application to the research issue

In the analysis of the right-wing political radicalism it is necessary to rely on significant researches of party political development of the modern European states. To start with, it is vital to conduct comparative research of the existing approaches and methods applicable to the analysis of party political systems and radical parties, primarily, far-right parties taking into consideration the following theoretical and conceptual framework.

Harold D. Lasswell's conceptual approach examines strategies certain political groups and individual politicians undertake to perform in the political arena and how fruitful and rewarding this performance is. The research emphasizes that political solutions fail to act as universal. Indeed, no matter how fair or objective one and the same solution is, it will definitely cause harm or appear unacceptable for certain population sectors. Clearly, all this creates the basis for the opposition to the key players[35]. Accordingly, none of the governments and none of the current political parties participating in decision-making process are able to stabilize and consolidate the population of the country, being initially deprived of this ability. Therefore, in the society staying in the context of permanent disunity there are always sufficient grounds for marginal political groups' activity.

With reference to the political analyst John P. Bradley it can be specified that considering the volatility of the political environment, parties make it possible to exert pressure on the population or, on the

---

[35] Lasswell, H.D., Kaplan, A. 1950. *Power and Society: A Framework for Political Inquiry*, New Haven.

contrary, secure public support. Certainly, political values in this approach, no matter shared or not by the representatives of parties and the population, carry out an important function[36]. However, it should not be neglected that centralized Western European states are not a model of the unity of political visions and ideals while multiculturalism policy effectively contributed to the preservation of diverse views and values in social, ethnic and regional dimensions.

In this respect, election promises, made to the public by the politicians participating in an electoral campaign, deserve special attention. These promises, however, have been increasingly viewed with skepticism due to the nature of powerful politicians to break them once in office. And their political manifestos are nothing but political deception which is not trusted by a voter whereas the number of gullible voters is rather variable (from 10% and above)[37].

Richard I. Hofferbert and Ian Budge's theory, in terms of right-wing radicalism, accentuates ideological and election program convergence between the main political game players which prevents a voter to make a rational political choice[38].

Incidentally, this convergence stems from the exchange of policy instruments to address emerging social and national issues and also is due to ideological party interpenetration. In these circumstances voters reveal a tendency to focus on the parties which hold their own views on tackling various challenges, do their utmost to show the proximity to a voter and his aspirations and act as true defenders of traditional values and ecological, cultural, social and economic well-being of the society. This advantage, provided by impersonal actions of all other political players and inherited by active minor parties as a "gift", helps them effectively perform for the last twenty years.

The ideas stated by Paul Jackson and Anton Shekhovtsov, the experts of the Research Centre for Radicalism of the University of Northampton in the UK, explicitly reflect cultural, social and political distinctions between extreme right-wing political parties and all other political movements.

---

[36] Bradley, J.P. 1969. Party Platforms and Party Performance Concerning Social Security, *Polity*, Vol. 1, No 3, pp. 337– 358.

[37] Schedler, A. 1998. The Normative Force of Electoral Promises, *Journal of Theoretical Politics*, Vol. 10, No 2,
pp. 191–214.

[38] Hofferbert, R.I., Budge, I. 1992. The Party Mandate and the Westminster Model: Election Programmes and
Government Spending in Britain, 1945–1985, *British Journal of Political Science*, Vol. 22, No 2, pp. 151–182.

Propaganda of so-called white culture, white race lifestyle and the like, as claimed by the far-right, put forward the idea that indigenous Europeans should be prioritized and multiculturalism policy should be dismissed as it provokes citizens' rejection or deepens public disagreement over this issue[39].

A significant role in exploring political radicalism is certainly fulfilled by such classical approaches as: 1) deviation from national and political targets; 2) consistent development of the state political system in Western Europe; 3) an outlook on the socio-economic framework of a capitalist society; 4) evolution of political parties within the civilization crisis[40]. Additionally, E. Fromm's approach can be also qualified as classical. The researcher investigates problems of human psychological alienation and a disruption to social communication which can encourage an individual to join an extreme right-wing radical party[41].

While analyzing political radicalism the populist theory inevitably pops up to add more features to the approaches mentioned above. Thus, for example, Paul A. Taggart views populism from the perspective of idealization and identification[42], Peter Worsley indicates the incompatibility between the inner and outer world which forces the population to make irrelevant decisions on these or those parties[43]. Apart from that, Max Weber's vision is worthy of attention who objectively evaluates the ability of charismatic politicians to be integrated into and exploit the existing party political system[44]. What is more, extreme-right populism witnesses internal division into new and regular critics of modern political strategies. This division presents a bifocal view on populism as beside its negative aspects, populism also embodies positive potential revealed by constructive criticism of the existing order.

---

[39] *White Power Music: Scenes of Extreme Right Cultural Resistance*. 2012, ed. by A. Shekhovtsov, P. Jackson,
Ilford.

[40] Griffin, R. 2000. Interregnum or Endgame? Radical Right Thought in «Post-fascist» Era, *The Journal of Political Ideologies*, Vol. 5, No 2, pp. 163–178.

[41] Fromm, E. 1992. *The Anatomy of Human Destructiveness*, New-York: Henry Holt and Company.

[42] Taggart, P.A. 2000. *Populism*, Buckingham.

[43] Worsley, P. 1970. The Concept of Populism, *in Populism: Its meanings and National Characteristics*, ed. by
G. Ionescu, E. Gellner, London, pp. 212–250.

[44] Weber, M. 1921. *Politics as Vocation*. Available at:
http://www.sscnet.ucla.edu/polisci/ethos/Weber-vocation.pdf

In critical debates about a political choice, an extensive list of political behavior theories occupies the central position. To evaluate these theories the following factors are to be harnessed: society and individual integration into the current political environment, political cultures and, also, human needs and motivations. Of particular interest at this point is the theory of political behaviorism in various aspects and the critical theory of society. The German philosopher Jurgen Habermas introduced his own version of the critical theory which modified the interaction between business and social relations as it ceased to relate many social problems to a formation type. It is important that today's society, according to the critical theory, failed to create the basis for monitoring and criticizing authorities. However, social communication forms the unity which does not depend on private groups and interests. As J. Habermas see it, criticism is on collision course with tradition and is able to neutralize its impact on the society, though, along with it, magnifies the importance of such factors as money and power which are social mechanisms themselves[45].

One of the essential components in the studies on right-wing political radicalism is the theory of small political party survival and its advantages over the main political players. Besides, within this matter several aspects merge into one another. Nowadays the significance of the social political movement gains momentum. Civil society and population, one way or another, strive to affect party activities, the political system in general and the decision making process. Therefore, being under pressure of mounting tensions in the society and call of time, the historical lag was bound to aim at radical reforming. First of all, major mainstream parties were compelled to pass through these reforms but as their political attitudes in application to the existing issues (mainly ignored by the rhetoric of these parties) were not subjected to considerable changes, small parties, which possessed more radical views, embraced the opportunity to occupy a vacant political niche. The electoral system applied in nation-wide elections is one of the crucial factors which determine the outcome for any party. In fact, only major political parties often enjoy tremendous success. Numerous small parties claim, in turn, that the existing system has nothing in common with the principle of equality and creates democracy deficiency which must be combated[46]. Also, it is necessary to mention a prominent role of social and

---

[45] Habermas, J. 1998. *The Inclusion of the Other: Studies in Political Theory*, Massachusetts.

[46] *Britain's Deficient Democracy*. Available at:

political development of the state. For example, in times of economic or political crisis only the party which is able to offer the program including all pressing issues can expect the population support, otherwise voters will confront a dilemma and would rather ignore any of the parties voting mostly for a coalition. The economic and social status of the population also affects party rhetoric and policy and is one of the dividing lines between parties, along with external conditions. Another point to be made is that in the circumstances of domestic and international political challenges small parties seize a good chance to strengthen their position taking advantage of the negative attitude to major parties which are traditionally responsible for decision-making activities. This process coincided with the process of losing credibility by major party leaders. Finally, it is necessary to consider the cross-party partnership. Currently, voter's choice is increasingly influenced by religious, national and historical factors. Moreover, sometimes these factors start prevailing over social and economic matters. So, the focus shifts towards interests and goals which are capable of uniting more people and forming large groups.

Indeed, while studying right-wing radicalism it is quite acceptable to rely on the broad scientific base created by the scholars viewing various aspects of a problem from many angles. Nonetheless, it is by now too obvious that the social studies should be prioritized as population's reaction, positions and attitudes most effectively reflect party political trends in the European states. However, the authors of this monograph decided to explore right-wing radicalism within the legal framework both national and international. Therefore, our research provides a new integrated approach which allows not only to determine evolution of the far right ideology but also to define its status and political potential in relation to the social, state and legal development.

1.2.2. New methodology: authors' view on the issue and approaches

When analyzing extreme right parties, primarily, it is necessary to define *ideological evolution of the new far-right which comes as the first scientific issue of this monograph.* For this reason, distinguishing between fascism and Nazism, the authors of the book qualify them as "an

http://www.centreforcitizenship.org/writ2.html (accessed: 22.12.2013); MacGarry, J., O'Leary, B. 2008. Must Pluri-National federations Fail?, *Ethnopolitics,* Vol. 8, No 1, p. 15.

ideological source" nourishing extreme-right movements in modern Europe.

This aspect allows you to identify a trajectory of their political pathway. Moreover, their political progress unambiguously demonstrates public control and supervision toughening which the extreme-right definitely carry out in case of coming to power or via other levers of influence, for example, through participation in party coalitions. In this regard it is critical to take a comprehensive look at the whole extreme-right sector starting from Nazism and fascism and stretching to modern right-wing radicalism which helps investigate the features of the new extreme-right ideology and gives evidence for their ideological evolution.

It is clear that political tools used by all far-right movements illustrate the rich diversity as it is aimed to draw maximum voters' attention. The far-right ideology is focused on all population sectors and for this reason far-right parties are always treated as populist parties. Also, right-wing radicalism has been always based on ideas of the fight against an alleged enemy of the nation (both external and internal) and it has always proposed one solution to all problems (e.g., land seizures or deportation of unwanted elements of certain ethnic groups). In addition, ultra-nationalism can be observed as a source and a union-maker for all parties and movements of the far-right family. Ultra-nationalism is the nationalism which appears in the most aggressive forms as it highlights the superiority of one's own nation meanwhile oppressing other ethnic groups declared, for example, wholly unworthy of being citizens of this or that country. Ultra-nationalism is a defining common characteristic of all far-right ideologies which actually states that the modern extreme-right border on Nazism even though they by all means declare the opposite.

The second scientific issue of this monograph is to study evolution of right-wing radicalism and its effect on the party and political system of various European states.

Firstly, especially fruitful seems the method of analyzing legal bases of the statehood through inspecting constitutional acts which can reveal the phenomenon of constitutional nationalism. Constitutional provisions adequately reflect the laid in volume of nationalism in the state and society and the degree of radicalism up to its ultra-nationalist form in case if constitution specifies the rights of the nation-state only whereas representatives of ethnic minorities are completely disregarded. Secondly, the extent of extreme-right influence can be easily detected by the analysis of electoral behavior of the population in different countries. In case this country is a European Union member, the data about elections to the European Parliament and their results are also subject to study.

For measuring the level of threat (direct or indirect) posed by ultra-right parties and movements it is required to involve the corresponding legal corpus of the United Nations (UN) (first of all, the provisions of the UN Convention on the Elimination of All Racial Discrimination, the Durban Declaration, the Programme of Action and the International Convention on the Elimination of All Forms of Racial Discrimination) as well as to appeal to the state legal framework concerning the activities of extreme-right parties (national constitutions, regular national laws and subordinate legislation).

Of vital importance is the third scientific issue raised by the authors of this research – to define and establish a formal boundary line between right-wing, extreme-right and Nazi parties likewise there is a demarcation line between the prohibited and the permissible as only this can give a proper definition for a socially dangerous party (neo-Nazi party).

The problem is that political scientists studying far-right parties draw this very line between right wingers, the extreme-right and neo-Nazis/neo-fascists but they seem to ignore the fundamental criterion of the social danger of the parties which are to be liquidated.

This monograph addresses all specified scientific issues: the ideological background of the extreme-right parties, identification of their political potential and political progress trajectory, definition of the criteria of a socially dangerous party and the analysis of a large corpus of various documents ranging from international to domestic legislation. Thanks to the research of the aforesaid aspects the authors pioneer the concrete criteria for labeling a party as neo-Nazi (and socially dangerous) and the techniques for diagnosing a party as neo-Nazi (the example of the Ukraine's Svoboda Party).

So, the diagnosis criteria to define a party as neo-Nazi and its liquidation perspectives make up the fourth scientific objective of this research.

CHAPTER II

IDEOLOGICAL FEATURES OF RIGHT-WING RADICALISM IN EUROPE

Being integrated into the modern society, right-wing radicalism should be observed only as a new "old" model of the ideology of counteraction and rejection of the existing political norms, practices and principles. In contrast to left-wing radicalism seeking to destroy the old world for the sake of the new one, right-wing radicalism means negation and destruction of the existing world for the sake of a certain former ideal preserved by historical memory and which is easy to exploit in periods of social and economic turmoil. Thus, for right wingers this vision functions as an effective instrument for restoring former "golden age". For this reason exactly, right-wing radicals exercise so-called "not-statements" proclaiming that a powerful nation can**not** be multinational, advanced society can**not** preach tolerance and prosperous future can**not** put at risk national interests and state sovereignty within supranational organizations. Therefore, in Chapter II our goal is to detect and study the sources of contemporary right-wing radicalism and how they are embodied and formulated in the statements of extreme-right leaders and program documents of extreme-right parties thereby projecting the image of today's right-wing radicalism.

2.1. Three pillars of right-wing radicalism

When arguing over the extreme-right ideology, we are inevitably drawn to the analysis of the nature of political thinking both of the ultra-right and the political establishment and of all political community as a whole. In this regard the understanding can be achieved through exploring the way these political groups perceive such traditional values as equality and inequality, individual and collective rights and freedoms, personal autonomy and distribution of political power which simultaneously serve as the ultra-right ideological basis.

The ultra-right ideology derives from nationalism and conservatism which, though, only provide the grounds for ultra-nationalism and the summation of all key factors (internal and external) fosters a favourable climate for emergence, growth and progress of the far-right political family. The fusion of conservatism and nationalism in many respects is highly beneficial for this sort of political movements and substantially contributes to their political success. For this reason, it seems logical to examine an ideological component of far-right parties from the angles of conservatism and nationalism.

2.1.1. The principle of conservatism

Conservatism (one of the crucial elements of the right-wing ideology) rests on the idea of order, law and tradition retained by the society and government. Throughout gradual complication of the socio-political interaction, traditions and laws come up as the core of a social order with restrictions, according to Edmund Burke, as a necessary instrument for order maintenance. Many conservative thinkers of 18th and 19th centuries, including Lous Bonald and Justus Möser with their philosophical treatises, believed it necessary for everyone to fulfill his obligations to the state within the monarchy-society-church framework, retain connections with the past and invest every effort in the state's greatness.

The revolutions, which swept the European countries in 1848-1849, posed a question of a new social order and a constitutional system and that was the time when conservatism captured ideas of nationalism and capitalism. In the opinion of right-wing ideologists a nation was to get the highest value (national socio-political order and statehood) and economic modernization became a tool for consolidating the national integrity of a nation-state. These thoughts assumed special importance in the German lands.

However, the absence of "pure" theoretical structure reveals certain complexity of the interpretation of conservatism as an ideology. The primary objective, pursued by conservatism, is to retain the existing social order, though the changes, aimed at the consolidation of the state, are quite acceptable. It is also worth emphasizing that conservatism, first of all, should be viewed as an idea of organicism which regards culture as a product of human interaction and the viability of a nation, being the unity of culture, directly depends on the life cycle of this cultural unity. Therefore, it is useless to transfer or import (export) elements of culture or political institutions from one state to another as it undermines the unity of national spirit, society and the state and involves plenty of negative consequences for statehood.

For this reason the main ideals of conservatism are religion (faith and church), a cult of property and a family, nationalism in its civil dimension (concern over national interests, protectionist policy, and counteraction to economic globalization). Also, of great value for conservatism is a concept of law presented, as a rule, by either the school of legal positivism or the historical school of law.

The historical school of law founded by a professor of law Gustav Hugo in Gottingen (also, one of the jurists who essentially contributed to philosophy of positive law) broached an issue of possibility of continuity between modern and historical law. Being influenced by the historical school of law, jurists ceased to perceive natural law as a universal model and tended to sustain historical views. Opposing these views, Karl Marx quoted this school as "one school of thought that legitimizes the infamy of today with the infamy of yesterday"[1].

Of special importance within this issue is the theory of the state as a legal entity, developed in the Weimar constitution (though, this theory is not much widespread) and borrowed in 1920 by Estonia. This theory means the formal unity of the state and the nation (people) in which the only mission the population is entrusted with is to provide the state with the parliament.

Nowadays Estonia does not conceal the fact of being influenced by the German school of law which profoundly affected the development of the concept of the state as a legal entity carrying out people's power and also made an impact on the followers of these principles in Estonia. So, it seems perfectly logical to trace the roots of the phenomena of Estonian statehood to the history of Germany[2].

Conservatism as a traditional and mainstream political ideology considerably strengthened its positions in the period of collisions between liberalism, social democracy and communism before and after the World War I. Despite some ideological losses during and after World War II, conservatism secured new levers of political influence within the neoconservative movement which combined the recognition of the leading role of the state with some market freedoms. So, over time conservatism,

---

[1] Marx, K., Engels, F. *Sobranie sochineniy*, 2 izdanie, Tom 1, pp.416. (Marx, K. and Engels, F. *The Works*, 2-nd edition, Vol.1, p.416). (in Russian: Маркс, К. и Энгельс, Ф. Соч., 2-е изд., Т. 1. С. 416);
https://www.marxists.org/archive/marx/works/1843/critique-hpr/intro.htm

[2] Schneider, Heinrich. 1998. Riigiteoreetilisi probleeme: miks nad on tekkinud ja kuidas neid lahendada?, *Juridica*, N 7.

being a flexible structure, collated an impressive bank of ideas borrowed from other movements of the party political spectrum and started acting under the label “neoconservatism”. However, social peace and harmony, continuity and order remained the fundamental political ideals for neoconservatives. Along with that, neoconservatives proceeded with the organic conception of society where behavior is subordinated to established traditions and legal regulations. Also, of major importance for political life of the state within this ideological framework were proclaimed stability and continuity which, however, do not mean stagnation and accept all necessary state reforms with any individual to participate.

Thus, conservatism as an ideology is always capable of certain transformations in accordance with the changing conditions. For this reason, it is no surprise that the right-wing party family is quite extended. Nowadays it is comprised of conservative, neoliberal and extreme-right groups of all possible kinds.

It is worth mentioning that the conservative ideology in the environment of escalation of social, economic and political problems can transform into radical forms of traditionalism, paganism and fascism (Friedrich Nietzsche, Oswald Spengler, Martin Heidegger). These ideological manifestations, as a rule, mean a look back to the past prosperity of people. Such factors as the appeal to the origins, denial of the present in the majority of its manifestations, the use of political categories of the past epochs, a vision of life as a fight for survival reflect a dislocation of political consciousness and inability of political community to propose a new way of social development. For this reason, shelter in these conditions can be found only in the past.

No wonder that soon after World War I the far-right ideology, fostered by representatives of conservative political values, emerged in those countries, such as Germany and Italy, where this dislocation was the most considerable. And eventually, all this led to the collapse of the entire global stability during World War II. In the post-war period conservatism gradually regained its positions within Christian and People's Democratic Parties. In the current political climate, in the period of aggravation of a political situation in different European states, conservative ideas can be easily transformed into radical right-wing populist ideas. So, conservative ideologists often view radical parties as the allies, especially in the countries of Central and Eastern Europe.

The right-wing ideology, being one of the steadiest and earliest ideologies in the political history, is fully associated with ideas of retaining power by those who already possess it. For this reason exactly, neoliberal, conservative and neoconservative ideas are hugely significant for understanding the extreme-right's attitudes towards power, freedoms and rights. Therefore, conservatism can be regarded as the first pillar of the right-wing political radicalism.

From the point of view of the social contract theory, the state is a major guardian of the established traditions and norms which implements reforms taking into account the peculiarities of its own political and legal development and the development of society, and determines the necessity of such reforms. All the above-mentioned ideas are believed to provide the national unity in the country. This very view was deepened within the extreme-right ideology[3]. With reference to the extreme-right, the state primarily requires population's support, also it should merge with people and become the state where cultural diversity is not welcomed. Multinational society, according to right-wing radicals, can result in the collapse of the state and nation. In this regard it is pertinent to quote Gaspar M. Tamas as saying that now right-wing radicalism has returned understanding of citizenship as a privilege, rather than a universal right belonging to every person by birth[4].

Furthermore, as the far-right parties see it, the state-government-nation (people) unity forms a configuration of vertical distribution of power where the nation is a principal constituent for supporting the state and government and, in fact, is dissolved in the state. In this structure there is no distribution of freedoms and rights as the nation is assigned the only mission - to contribute to the state's greatness being an integral part of it.

The modern far-right parties, formally falling within the legal liberal democratic framework and in every possible way emphasizing that they adhere to the idea of democratic elections, constantly destabilize society

---

[3] See: E.g.: The National Front Program. Available at: http://www.frontnational.com/le-projet-de-marine-le-pen/; The British National Party Program. Available at: https://www.bnp.org.uk/manifesto; The UK Independence Party Program. Available at: http://www.ukip.org/issues; The Flemish Interest Party Program. Available at: http://www.vlaamsbelang.org/files/20140318ProgrammaVerkiezingen2014.pdf; The Freedom Party of Austria Program. Available at: http://www.wien-konkret.at/politik/partei/fpoe/; The Swedish Democrats Party Program. Available at: https://sverigedemokraterna.se/var-politik/principprogram/; The National Democratic Party of Germany Program. Available at: http://www.npd.de/

[4] Tamas, G.M. 2000. O post-fashizme, *Konstitutsionnoye pravo: vostochno-evropeyskoe obozrenie,* N 3 (32), pp.6-14. (Tamas, G.M. 2000. On post-fascism, *East European Constitutional Review*, N 3 (32), pp. 6–14). (in Russian: Тамаш, Г.М. 2000. О постфашизме, *Конституционное право: восточноевропейское обозрение*, № 3 (32), С. 6–14).

from within, dividing citizens into those who belong to the nation and support the state and those who represent ethnic community endangering the unity of the state, government and nation.

Due to sustained efforts to rid themselves of any comparison with fascist and Nazi movements, far-right parties have cultivated quite tolerant attitude towards right-wing radicalism in the political community and in society in general. Moreover, the researchers lay stress on the statements of the far-right leaders who claim that they have no intentions to undermine the liberal democratic system. For this very reason, these movements are not always labeled "extreme-right" and sometimes they are treated as right-wing populist parties or simply right-wing parties close to mainstream Christian and People's parties of conservative orientation. Nevertheless, in this regard it should be always remembered that right-wing radicals have never attempted in advance to encroach on the existing state system until they seize power. However, the fundamental far-right idea about the complete unity of the nation and the state can be realized only by means of dismantling current political and public institutions.

2.1.2. The principle of nationalism

Nationalism, which is the second pillar of the far-right ideology, also deals with such aspects as the state, distribution of political power, freedoms and rights. It is through a prism of nationalism right-wing radicals view the concepts of democracy and personal freedom which can enjoy stability and be realized, in their opinion, only in a homogeneous community. Accordingly, cultural assimilation is deemed to be a perfect tool for creating homogeneous society which, in fact, represents the united nation. For this reason, the extreme-right parties declare the principle of "national preference".

For example, according to R. Eatwell, the right-wing radicals favour ideas of Christian integration and perceive other cultures as a severe threat to the state and European civilization in general[5]. Also, the German researcher Christoph Zuercher points out that hopes for the equilibrium effects of modernity (one of the main doctrines of modernization theories) failed and especially under the conditions of post-modernity, the differences between we-groups' diversity increased, the quest for

[5] Eatwell, R. 2000. The rebirth of the Extreme Right in Western Europe?, *Parliamentary Affairs*, p. 413.

collective rights also grew and added to the rise of their popularity[6]. The cornerstone of such differentiation is nationalism.

In modern society the concept of a nation-state and national identity have come under threat and the latter one, being surrounded by more powerful globalization processes, often appears to be a certain abstraction whereas the evident pluralization of identities is followed by the increase in violence and xenophobia.

Furthermore, alongside the recognition of cultural identity of immigrant population, indigenous citizens become aware of their own cultural identity which boils down to more complications and ethnoregional conflicts nullifying the efforts to unite society within one state. Moreover, as the researchers say, our social climate is facing a mounting crisis implying the destruction of social reality and leading to confusion about self-identification of a personality[7].

So, this evidence confirms the loss or crisis of the national unity in a modern state and the spread of movement "defence of identity" which originates from regional cultures of states. The growth of regional ethnonationalism can also be qualified as a barrier to immigration and loss of cultural identity. For instance, such regions in France as Normandy, Provence and other have never witnessed such a tremendous surge of interest in their roots like it has been for the last twenty years. Rene Monzat illustrates this phenomenon saying: "It is still possible to be a French Arab, but it is absolutely impossible to be an Arab and a Norman at the same time"[8].

---

[6] Zuercher, Ch. 1999. Multilulturalizm I etnopoliticheskyi poryadok v postsovetskoy Rossii: nekotorye metodologichskie zamechania, *Polis (politicheskie issledovania)*, N6, p. 5. (Zuercher, Ch. 1999. Multiculturalism and Ethnopolitical Order in Post-Soviet Russia: Some Methodological Remarks, *Polis (Political Studies)*, N 6). (in Russian: Цюрхер, К. 1999. Мультикультурализм и этнополитический порядок в постсоветской России: некоторые методологические замечания, *Полис (Политические исследования)*, N 6).

[7]Blyakher, L.E. 2005. *Nestabil'nye sotsial'nye sostoyania*, Moskva. (Blyakher, L.E. 2005. *Unstable social conditions*, Moscow). (in the original: Бляхер, Л.Е. 2005. *Нестабильные социальные состояния*. М.).

[8] Monzat, R. 2007. Region, natsia, Evropa: deistvuyuschie litsa istorii v konseptsiyakh frantsuzskih pravyh radikalov, *in Russkyi natsionalizm v politicheskom prostranstve (issledovania po natsionalizmu v Rossii)*, sostavlen M. Laruelle, Moskva, p.23. (Monzat, R. 2007. Region, Nation, Europe: Historical Actors in the Conception of French Right-Wing Radicals, *in Russian Nationalism in the Political Space (the Research on Nationalism in Russia)*, comp. by M. Laruelle. Moscow, p.23). (in Russian: Монза, Р. 2007. Регион, нация, Европа: действующие лица истории в концепциях французских правых радикалов,

In this regard, some governments, realizing the threat of social disunion, are still not able to discover an efficient means of opposing it. Therefore, the idea of acceleration of the European integration, supported by a number of states, can be interpreted, as the Russian researcher Aleksei Bogaturov specifies, as desperate attempts to narrow internal cultural and political disagreements with ethnic population which traditionally lives in this or that state[9]. European countries, fostering their supranational unity, devise and deliver appropriate strategies to curb radical self-determination. Particularly, these processes are a serious menace to Eastern Europe. It is here that ethnic divisions facilitate the rapid growth of extreme-right forces.

It should not be ignored that voting in favour of far-right parties always displays ethnocentrism. Being devoted to the concept of the nation-state, the far-right groups openly embrace certain ideas of radical nationalism. For the National Front, for example, such concepts as the state and France, the state sovereignty and national identity are directly interconnected.

Currently, political parties are being involved in fierce disputes over the integrity of the European culture. In this context, ethnocentrism and cultural unity are becoming the core values for extreme-right ideologists. The population of European countries is gradually losing the perception of its integrity that inevitably entails questions over the European way of development, causes revaluation of values and fear about the collapse of civilization. Today the European societies are compelled to deal with cultural barriers which appear to be even more formidable than economic and political ones. In the conditions of a "culture crisis" or the "collision of cultures" the adaptive abilities of an individual and society are maintained by certain ideological attitudes (stereotypes) established by long-lasting communication across generations.

Over time anxieties about national identity loss grow unconscious which provokes changes of social norms while the formation of new ones is stimulated by particular social circles and groups. Viewed from this perspective, the far-right rhetoric, both in the inter-war and post-war periods, is always the rhetoric of fear and aggression based on the feeling

---

Русский национализм в политическом пространстве (исследования по национализму в России), Сост. М. Ларюэль. М., С.23).

[9] Bogaturov, A. 1999. Sindrom pogloschenia v mezhdunarodnoy politike, *Pro et Contra*, N 4, p.35. Available at:
http://uisrussia.srcc.msu.ru/docs/nov/pec/1999/4/ProEtContra_1999_4_02.pdf (Bogaturov, A. 1999. The Syndrome of "Absorption" in International Politics, *Pro et Contra*, N 4, p. 35). (in the original: Богатуров, А. 1999. Синдром поглощения в международной политике, *Pro et Contra*, N 4, С. 35).

of threat of cultural identity loss. Thus, a role of the state, which is the only capable of resisting such threats, has become a dominant idea for extreme-right parties. It is to be emphasized that far-right ideological orientation has always reflected the statehood concept in preserving the nation where there should not be a place for cultural and language dissonances. In this regard any contemporary far-right party inherits the concept of the state which was formulated at the beginning of 20th century and gained a foothold in the form of fascist and Nazi ideology during the inter-war period. Moreover, it is necessary to perceive fascism and Nazism not only as a political phenomenon, but also to investigate it as a cultural (probably, even as national in a sense) movement that helps explicitly highlight crucial aspects in the nationalist ideology.

However, not only conservatism and nationalism but also socio-political instability constitutes the basis of right-wing political radicalism. It may serve as a third pillar in the foundation of the extreme-right ideology which can easily convert current challenges into catchy slogans. Far-right parties realize that now not only radical ideas or mitigation of their political position can affect the electorate but also immediate and correct reaction to the population's attitudes in present circumstances.

2.1.3. The principle of threats

Since the end of the last century the left wing's position has been slowly and gradually weakening which is reflected in the crisis of mainstream left-wing political organizations, their style of the political fight and in population's attitudes. By degrees the race for power and political processes started losing their balance which helped conservatives and right-wing conservatives, possessing the main financial and political resources, confirm their leading status in a new century.

According to Michel Foucault, power is concentrated not in political institutions but as a capillary network reaches each separate individual attaching him to hierarchical institutions[10]. Power is not a centralized system and, for this reason, it can enjoy stability and extension only when it is distributed to several institutions entailing abundant, mainly financial, resources. Thus, power means the multiplicity of power relations incarnated in state institutions, management strategies and laws. However, power is a moving part in the machine of political relations as power structure is practically always unstable. A typical problem of affecting the

[10] Foucault, M. 1982. *The Subject and Power*, Critical Inquiry, Vol. 8, No 4, pp. 777-795.

system locally is the criticism of social and political institutions, voiced by opposing political forces, in terms of social groups represented in them. If earlier in the first half of 20th century left wingers (social democratic) were deemed to be chief critics and participants in political interactions with right-wing (conservative) forces, nowadays the main disapproval of the system is expressed by the ultra-right groups.

Within the existing capitalist system new “territorialities” (the state, religion, morals, inclusion institutes) are being constantly created which means the process of reterritorialization, i.e. the recovery of similar schemes of management instead of the destroyed ones. Taking a retrospective look at the past, fascism can be viewed as the most terrible example of reterritorialization when actually within the capitalist environment the system of barbarity was revived and gave rise to the opposite process - deterritorialization - when social territories, collective identities, traditional value systems are subjected to collapse. Deterritorialization processes gradually spread from the center to the periphery breaking dependent territories[11]. As a matter of fact, this is the right-wing radicalism that has the most serious ties with these processes within the capitalist system as fascism assumes the complete recovery of the former schemes of government which are familiar to the population regarding the past as an instrument of its preservation and progress. Furthermore, this is the extreme-right ideology that is significantly able to influence the spread of values within the capitalist interdependence between countries. Therefore, any political destruction in one society or state is inevitably echoed in the other society or state.

Political parties and groups manipulate population and public opinion using them as a tool for political struggle which, in turn, also added to the active promotion of the fascist ideology in the tense inter-war period in Germany and Italy.

Fascism can evolve and flourish when it penetrates such parts of life as a school, a family, etc., when it can enjoy population’s support and public opinion and also, when we can observe a set of microfascism manifestations. According to Alvin Toffler's logic in the conditions of instability the influence of “decision-making minorities” is enormous[12]. Of

---

[11] Tomin, L.V. 2014. *Sovremennye konflikty: poststrukturalistskiy analiz*, Sankt-Peterburg, pp. 40-41. (Tomin, L.V. 2014. *Modern Political Conflicts: Post-structuralist Analysis*, Saint-Petersburg, pp. 40-41). (in the original: Томин, Л.В. 2014. *Современные конфликты: постструктуралистский анализ*. СПб., С. 40-41).

[12] Toffler, A. 1990. *Powershift: Knowledge, Wealth and Violence in the 21-st Century*, New-York.

special significance this thought is now when the focus is shifted from physical efforts to knowledge, intellectual opportunities, communicative abilities and even emotions. Therefore, it is right now that consciousness and political culture have huge impact on development of the political system. Moreover, it should be remembered that instability entails certain archaization and even criminalization of political culture and those political forces which take these changes into account appear more successful.

All far-right forces in the new circumstances pursue similar claims to the existing government system.

Far-right politics, as a rule, is in opposition to social equality and usually involves anti-immigration stances towards inferior masses. The far-right parties qualify this issue as a threat to the national identity, national security, social welfare system and as a reason for unemployment, indicating that they rapidly react to all modern threats.

According to the researchers, the modern mechanism of emergence or, more precisely, production of threats is quite simple. At the first stage something is declared a source, this source, being countable, fluctuates between "excessive" and "insufficient". Respectively, everything that displays direct or indirect, real or alleged insufficiency of the source is considered to be a threat. When general "state security" is already not enough for maintenance the level of threats, the ultra-right groups involve such resources as "energy security", "information security", "demographic safety", etc. However, general concepts of security will be examined in more detail below and from another angle, namely, in terms of the threat which the extreme-right ideology and movements may constitute.

As Aleksandr Galkin views, all threats existing in the present day can be divided into threats of primary and secondary concern[13]. Threats are becoming a determining factor in the evolution of the human community where primary threats comprise deficiency of non-renewable natural resources, lack of energy resources and climate changes. As a result, the increase in primary threats provokes the increase in the aggression level among various states and build-up of local military operations. Apart from that, the fruits of the progressing globalization provide grounds for manifestations of secondary threats which accentuate the everlasting opposition between poor and rich nations and considerably aggravate the fluctuating South-North contradictions. Furthermore, due to the retreat of left-wing ideas and the geography of poverty, religious fundamentalism

---

[13] Galkin, A.A. 2006. Protivorechia I ugrozy XXI veka, *Politia*, N 2. (Galkin, A.A. 2006. Contradictions and Threats of 21st Century, *Politia*, N 2). (in the original: Галкин, А.А. 2006. Противоречия и угрозы XXI века, *Полития*, N2).

displays a special dynamic which leads to the reciprocal action of Christian fundamentalism and initiates force-oriented solutions from both sides. The extreme-right groups are the only who explicitly declare the counteraction to Islamization overturning the European culture.

Additionally, secondary threats are also represented by migration flows which prompt substantial culture and civilization changes and aggravate problems of adaptation and integration of migrants into the European community. Consequently, far-right movements strengthen their political positions, ethnonationalism is in progress and citizens cease to trust "the big government".

Nevertheless, it seems relatively hard to depict a universal portrait of a far-right voter as nowadays alongside citizens' discontent with social and economic situation in certain countries there is an aspiration to national superiority and manifestation of the state power demonstrated by any number of citizens. These ideas are capable of uniting representatives of the most different social groups. The electorate of far-right parties is problematic to define due to its sluggish progress while an aspiration to superiority still remains its distinctive feature[14].

Thus, firstly, right-wing radicals submit the political views distinguishing them from other political parties. Effective integration of traditional views with nationalism against the background of social instability affords the extreme-right parties new political opportunities which, in turn, inspire them as the only alternative political force. Right-wing political radicalism rapidly reacts to all social changes and requirements and therefore can partly demonstrate necessary flexibility and adapt to various fluctuations in social and political life of the state, though being invariably loyal to the fundamental principles of the state and nation unity.

Secondly, the far-right's emergence and evolution derive from the combination of old and new social problems and the threat of culture loss by indigenous population. Addressing to nationalism, to cultural and ethnic national identity, far-right parties experience success and regard themselves as defenders of the long-standing traditions, values and

---

[14] Barygin, I. N. Kraine-pravye tendentsii politicheskoy zhizni v politiligicheskom I politicheskom diskursah, *in Pravoradikal'nye politicheskie partii I dvizhenia*, Sankt-Peterburg, p.24. (Barygin, I. N. 2011. The Far-Right Political Tendencies in Scientific and Political Discourse, *in Far-Right Political Parties and Movements in Modern Europe*, Saint-Petersburg, p. 24). (in the original: Барыгин, И.Н. 2011. Крайне-правые тенденции политической жизни в политологическом и политическом дискурсах, *Праворадикальные политические партии и движения современной Европы*, СПб., С. 24).

lifestyle. Their promotion campaigns are often accompanied by such words as "foreign" and "alien" bearing a certain clear-cut meaning to a voter and making an immigration issue a catalyst for the extreme-right socio-political development.

Thirdly, the far-right ideology in connection with concrete circumstances of state and global development is subject to certain alterations. If earlier one of the main indicators of the far-right's presence in the political arena was their vision of the social and economic policy, now their basic ideological attitudes stem from protection of their ethnic (national) identity on the one hand and from placing obstacles to all those phenomena which can add to its destruction and loss on the other. Mainly, these threats, in the opinion of the extreme-right movement, are sourced from extensive immigration flows.

And lastly, acting now within the legal field, far-right parties seek to realize their ideas by parliamentary and constitutional methods. Nevertheless, their rhetoric, one way or another, implicitly or explicitly, assumes radical activities as there is no alternative means to forge the proclaimed national unity. In this regard, the main ideas and methods used by the extreme-right parties in order to meet their goals can be put into the following classification:

(1) The concept of an enemy;
(2) Adverse criticism of the central government;
(3) Aggressive rhetoric and the "hate speech";
(4) Leadership;
(5) The use of mass media and Internet sources.

The first three points can be logically united by one common idea - preservation and protection of the state and nation while the last two points represent essential tools for political success.

(1) The concept of an enemy. This concept is strongly favoured by far-right parties, which is always possible in the conditions of radical transformation of political solutions to various problems such as immigration, integration, homeland (national) security. However, not every far-right party is ready to resort to extremist methods against "an enemy of the nation". Generally, the far-right groups seek to avoid accusations of extremism and prefer to employ democratic methods in their political strategy. Yet the members of these parties are periodically placed under arrest and can be subject to administrative prosecution. Besides, the rhetoric of far-right parties beyond any doubt promotes extremism and reveals radical nature of their intentions. For instance, the Hungarian party

"Jobbik" claimed to expel all the officials of Jewish origin from the government and parliament as they pose a threat to Hungary's national security. Clearly, similar statements against enemies are subsequently able to give birth to such criminal and violent acts like those of Anders Breivik. Anyway, the extreme-right parties seek to influence the growth of aggression in society that can lead to acts of terrorism. In 2007 one of the members of the British National Party was arrested for storage of explosive chemicals. Also, in 2012 a Polish nationalist inspired by A. Breivik's act launched an attack on the Polish parliament.

(2) Adverse criticism of the central government. Ultra-right parties are compelled to remain in opposition to the central government and other mainstream political movements as they do not propose comprehensive solutions to the existing problems. However, many of them were created on the basis of protest movements against taxes (The Danish People's Party) or the immigration growth (The British National Party) or demands for independence (The Vlaams Blok, i.e. Flemish Interest). Any far-right idea stems from the distorted understanding of national security which serves as a motive for accusations against the central government. Today, since public discontent with the central government policy is inexorably growing and far-right parties are reaping substantial benefits from that (with respective extreme-right electorate increase), it is possible to conclude that they are showing a trend in a sense and have already entered the political mainstream. Yet in any case this trend will result in pursuing oppression against ethnic minorities.

(3) Aggressive rhetoric and the "hate speech". The target, which far-right parties are keen to attain, is to spur the mounting concern of the population over existing problems and evoke the atmosphere of tension and threat including the threat of terrorism. For the extreme-right groups the major threat to combat is Islamization (in Eastern Europe and the post-Soviet states, as noted earlier, Russophobia is being implanted) and ultranationalists observe their parties as the deterrent force to the processes of Islamization. Therefore, it is no surprise far-right parties claim to restrict demographic growth of ethnic minorities and their influence on the government. Thus, all far-right statements are deeply implanted in ordinary people's hatred to aliens. Far-right wingers offer their own discourse on values which considerably differ from values of ethnic groups whilst far-right activists declare themselves crusaders in today's collision of civilizations. As the central authorities do not always relevantly react on arising and current challenges, the rhetoric of threats adopted by the extreme-right will both evolve and strengthen, and it is already functioning as a tool for transformation of the public policy.

(4) Leadership. Here, it is primarily to talk about the so-called charismatic parties based on a charisma concept, i.e. the appeal of the party leader that means formation of strong emotional communication between the leader and his followers. The researchers specify six traits to characterize a charismatic party: all party members' loyalty to the leader, which helps form the integral core pool of the party; a charismatic party is centralized but is not burdened with bureaucratic features; it is a group with blurred boundaries; the party leader's charisma is of a "revolutionary" nature; a distinction between the organization, its identity and the leader's political destiny[15]. However, contrary to expectations, these parties are not always successful in elections.

(5) The use of mass media and Internet sources.

Today, mass media and the Internet are often seen as influential forces on public opinion. The extreme-right parties have rapidly caught this trend having created a new public media world launching online magazines and directing much attention to the websites. They utilize a vast array of bright pictures and slogans to get their message out and attract people of various age and social groups. Internet resources provide them with mass audience and assist in the search for new financial support. Among the most effective means for influencing people's minds are Facebook, Twitter and YouTube.

Giving a brief overview of positions of all far-right parties, it appears reasonable to put them into two groups according to a conditional geographical division: Western European and Eastern European.

Thus, the Western European parties oppose immigration and defend cultural identity of the nation (such as the Danish People's Party, Swedish Democrats (Sweden), the Party of Progress (Norway), the National Alliance (USA), the Front National (France), North League (Italy), the Vlaams Blok / Flemish interest, the British National Party, the Republicans (acts as a far-right alternative to CDU/CSU in Germany). Also, the German national parties counteract the claim of Germans' moral guilt and oppose the discrimination of Wehrmacht soldiers.

The Eastern European parties can be represented by the following political forces: the Croatian Party of Rights, Confederation of Independent Poland, the Polish National Front, the Romanian National Unity Party, the Serbian Radical Party, the Slovak National Party. Similar to Germany, in this region the results of World War II and even World War I have had a huge impact on the goals and ambitions of ultra-right politicians. For example, Hungary can be called a political home for the

---

15 Panebianco, A. 1988. *Political Parties: Organization and Power*, Cambridge.

revanchist moods where the extreme-right parties actively advocate the revision of the Treaty of Trianon. On the whole, the common set of attitudes of all European extreme-right groups is comprised of the following components:

(1) belief in law and order;

(2) national (ethnic) identity protection;

(3) anti-immigration policy;

(4) anti-Muslim rhetoric (Russophobic rhetoric in Eastern Europe and the former USSR countries);

(5) social divisions.

These components are expressed through the state and culture perception and through the attitude towards cultural protectionism which is based on the protection policy of historical, cultural and language uniqueness of the nation and the whole state in general.

2.2. Four ideological constituents of the far-right

At the junction of conservatism, nationalism and the growing social tension generated by the loss of influence by mainstream political parties, the extreme-right movement and the right-wing radical ideology reinforce their position. Protection of national and state identity, which crowns all points of programs and ultra-right slogans, is viewed from the angle of four ideological constituents: racism, anti-Islam (partly anti-Semitism), xenophobia (Russophobia in the countries of the former Soviet camp) and anti-immigration discourse. The European Union (EU) is an object of full-scale criticism voiced by far-right activists and is the one to be blamed for the emergence of new threats faced by the European community. It should be specified, however, that in the countries of Eastern and Central Europe and in candidate countries there is no criticism of the European Union but there is disapproval of the European integration process. This fact is to be considered in the comparative analysis of various European far-right parties.

2.2.1. Racism in the extreme-right ideology

Racism of right-wing radicals is based both on thinking stereotypes and on the views of prominent philosophers, thus, resulting in a theoretical model of the biologization of public and political interactions. For example, Johann G. Herder believed that the state is able to exist and be "natural", i.e. not to raise any doubts in its viability, if only its population represents one single nation[16]. Apart from that, Joseph A. Gobineau and Gustave Le Bon regarded human races as different species, each with their own appearance, behavior, character, abilities and intellectual opportunities[17]. This approach drew a boundary line dividing races into so-called superior and inferior ones and stoking theories of racial superiority which became the central part of Hitler's Nazism. Nowadays, recognizing distinctive characteristics between various human communities allows the far-right groups to judge about cultural and national exceptionalism of certain nations or, on the contrary, about its absence and the threat which aliens pose to the host societies.

People's national consciousness is so deeply-rooted that an aspiration to separate from something alien is a natural feeling which can be shared both by an individual and a community in general. The key ultra-nationalist concept rejects other cultures and mutual cultural enrichment, calls for erasing intercultural distinctions, primarily, in the field of language and traditions and supports religious and cultural conflicts. If earlier for fascism and Nazism this combat meant resistance to cultural invasion of other communities which simultaneously spread their influence and cultural norms across other territories, now ultra-nationalism appeals, first of all, to preserve one's own cultural patterns instead of modifying and strengthening them. So, culturally modern ultra-nationalism welcomes static, rather than progressive vision ignoring the fact that in this day and age no culture is able to advance in the isolation from other cultures. An ambition to maintain so-called purity of nations, which embodies ideas of a great state, in reality means destroying one's own nation or simply reflects the fact that in cultural dimension this nation is unable to develop and offer the world anything new. It is obvious that vitality of a racial superiority idea, which survived after World War II in various parts of Europe and became the key idea of the cultural superiority issue, genetically and evolutionarily relates to the ideology of Nazism and

---

[16] Herder, J.G. *Idei k filosofii istorii chelovechestva*, perevod I primechania A.V. Mikhaylov, Moskva. (Herder, J. G. 1977. *Ideas for the Philosophy of History of Hum*anity, Translation and comments by Mihaylov A.V, Moscow). (in Russian: Гердер, И.Г. 1977. *Идеи к философии истории человечества*, пер. и примеч. А.В. Михайлова. М.)

[17]Gobineau de, J.A. *Opyt o neravenstve chelovecheskih ras*. Available at: http://www.e-reading.ws/book.php?book=108557 (Gobineau de, J.A. *The Essay on the Inequality of the Human Races*) (in Russian: Гобино де, Ж.А. *Опыт о неравенстве человеческих рас*); Le Bon, G. *Psikhologia narodov I mass*. Available at: http://lib.ru/POLITOLOG/LEBON/psihologia.txt. (Le Bon, G. *The Psychology of Peoples*) (in Russian: Лебон, Г. *Психология народов и масс*).

fascism. The ideology of cultural superiority is grounded in distortion of historical facts about this or that nation and nothing reveals such politicized interpretation of history and culture better than the extreme-right parties' declaration of their great mission to defend the civilization against barbarians' invasion. Naturally, sooner or later such activities can result not only in discrimination but also in genocide.

However, recently the influence of the extreme-right movement and ideology has been underestimated by population and political circles which are of the opinion that the mainstream political culture will never empower the ultra-right groups to take leading political positions. Many people wrongly believe that racism is there only when it is evidently manifested and neo-Nazism is not so problematic to identify. Nonetheless, the objective truth is that racism in the extreme-right ideology and policy is a multi-faceted, simultaneously covert and overt, complex framework. After all, in the course of time extreme-right movements have been subject to mutations and learned to disguise their radical orientation which is, factually, an imminent threat to the society. For example, in 2012 in the EU report on a terrorist situation and its trends (*EU Terrorism Situation and Trend Report*), the Europol recognized that A. Breivik's statements included a mixture of various ideologies without specifying anything in particular[18].

In this regard the far-right parties' attack has been mainly directed at the Muslim population which makes it possible to define anti-Islamism as the second ideological constituent of right-wing radicalism.

2.2.2. The anti-Islam policy of the ultra-right parties

With reference to the ultra-right parties, Islam and Islamic terrorism pose a severe threat to the progress and stability of the state, society and cultural identity. In debates, Islam is traditionally associated not only with terrorism but also with various hostile actions and impact on political, public and cultural life of the indigenous community. This, as the extreme-right groups claim, fuels the conflict of values making it vain for the Muslim population to integrate into the European life and culture. For this reason, since the policy of multiculturalism instead of solutions to the integration issues caused conflicts, extreme-right wingers offer another way out - the Muslim population has to be transformed and adopt the existing cultural norms or, alternatively, leave the country. This

[18] *EU Terrorism Situation and Trend Report*. 2012. Available at: https://www.europol.europa.eu/sites/default/files/publications/europoltsat.pdf

component of the extreme-right ideology is perceived as "normal abnormality" by the political establishment of many countries and is not deemed menacing to national security, as far as the extreme-right political efforts are not directed against indigenous population but turned against immigrants with extraneous religious and cultural beliefs. For example, in 2011 in a regular EU report on current terrorist tendencies[19], the Europol designated that incidents with the ultra-right groups involved, though cause some public concern, do not expose to danger political, constitutional and socio-economic structures of the member states of the European Union. In 2014 a similar report was also largely aimed at analyzing the situation in the European states in connection with the events of the Arab Spring, namely, its consequences[20].

The major concern is caused not so much by A. Breivik, who was arrested and imprisoned, as by activities of various neo-Nazi groups which in due course have not received objective evaluation. Indeed, a similar terrorist group, called "The National Socialist Underground", was operating in Germany for thirteen years and directly participated in a series of murders of immigrants (of Turkish and Greek origin, etc.). It is still unclear why such extremist-oriented groups have not been diagnosed as socially dangerous for a long time and regional and state authorities have not regarded them as destructive to the state's stability unlike jihadist movements which are known to be centralized, governed and well-funded organizations.

What is of equal importance is that right-wing extremists are able to affect public opinion, attitudes and behavior introducing events and situations in the manner that would serve their own objectives. Exploiting both real and alleged drawbacks of the immigration issue right-wing radicals reproduce and analyze this discourse taking advantage of any possibility to get public approval. Thus, the extreme-right parties are able to legitimize their political vision and view themselves as certain "defenders" of traditions. Such manifesto was made, for example, by A. Breivik who regarded Islamism as the totalitarian political ideology attacking the free European world. He stated that the European society was facing the ongoing process of Islamization which was provoked by the weak immigration control, tolerance and multiculturalism. As A. Breivik assumed, the European liberal values are incompatible with ideas of

---

19 *EU Terrorism Situation and Trend Report.* 2011. Available at: https://www.europol.europa.eu/sites/default/files/publications/te-sat2011.pdf

20 *EU Terrorism Situation and Trend Report.* 2014. Available at: https://www.europol.europa.eu/sites/default/files/publications/europol_tsat14_web_1.pdf

multiculturalism and as the Islamic world already put down roots in Europe, only violent acts could have changed the situation[21]. These attitudes are echoed by such parties as the English Defence League and the British National Party[22] which, adhering to similar positions and appealing to the most radical and aggressive-minded party members, resort to street racist protests.

Therefore, the anti-Islamist ideology preached by the extreme-right parties is not targeted simply against Islam and Muslims but is a complex arrangement of ideological views based on traditional values and on the state official narrative in the extreme-right groups' interpretation. Harnessing political innovations this ideology manages to avoid direct allegations of inciting national hatred and discord. Nonetheless, all ideological attitudes promoted by the far-right activists increasingly affect public minds and even the whole political establishment which occasionally takes up the challenge and plays by their rules.

Obviously, only after A. Breivik's twin terrorist attacks it became clear that the extreme-right ideology is the bulk of the threat. Since 1990 at least 249 people have been killed in the riots organized by the extreme-right in comparison with 269 killed in Islamist terrorist acts which proves that both threats are almost equally dangerous to Europe[23]. However, Islamist terrorism is becoming a matter of mounting public concern in many respects due to the extreme-right parties' political activities. In fact, extreme-right radicalism and Islamic fundamentalism have recently mobilized against each other having brought to life the phenomenon of "cumulative extremism".

Formally, the extreme-right parties defend traditional values, individual freedoms, freedom of speech and seek to avoid accusations of neo-Nazism. Nonetheless, they have already acquired a pro-Nazi reputation declaring the white civilization and the achievements of the white race to be dominant, thus, drawing a demarcation line between other races and cultures. Moreover, it is quite often that the members of far-right parties, who verbally distance themselves from other right-wing political

---

[21] A. Breivik zayavil o bor'be s islamizatsiey. Available at: http://www.bbc.co.uk/russian/international/2012/06/120622_breivik_court_last_day.shtml (A. Breivik said about struggle against Islamization). (in the original: A. Брейвик заявил о борьбе с исламизацией).

[22] *English Defence League*. Available at: http://www.englishdefenceleague.org/; *British National Party*. Available at: http://www.bnp.org.uk/

[23] Kundnani, A. 2012. Blind Spot? Security Narratives and Far-Right Violence in Europe, *in ICCT Research Paper*, June, p.4. Available at: http://www.icct.nl/download/file/ICCT-Kundnani-Blind-Spot-June-2012.pdf

radicals with overt views on the race and culture, in practice support them. For example, the activists of the English Defence League (Stephen Yaxley-Lennon and Kevin Carroll) are the former members of the British National Party and have been repeatedly accused of racism.

Indeed, anti-Islam has served as a catalyst for the theory of racism and stimulated its rebirth. The neo-Nazi interpretation of a race war, mentioned by A. Breivik, has become a keynote of the far-right ideology and the rhetoric of some extreme-right groups concerning culture wars does not eliminate the racial problem as along with the culture issue they advocate the idea of anti-miscegenation. Therefore, within the anti-jihad and anti-Islam framework the far-right manifest themselves as neo-Nazis convincing the population that it has reached the final point and so should move back.

The fascist (neo-fascist) ideology of far-right groups, analogous to the British National Party, has not only vented hatred of ethnic minorities but also exploited social issues to counteract left-wing parties which, according to the extreme-right, have created all these problems practicing indulgence and appealing to the future of the nation instead of its past[24].

It should be stressed that, added to anti-Islam, anti-Semitism also remains an essential component of the hostile extremism ideology. As David Edgar specified, the ultra-right radicals accused Jews of immigration flows across Europe as only the population of Jewish origin could perform as a secret source of economic and political power creating corruption problems in the European countries[25].

As it was mentioned above, in the countries of the former USSR and socialist camp Russophobia with a broad variety of its shades has occupied a strong position and is mainly initiated and maintained by the local government's official policy aimed at protecting ethnic minority's rights. It is necessary to note that in this case Russophobia does not derive from migration issues.

Thanks to anti-Islamic stances many parties such as the Front National are estimated in terms of Nazism and within the scope of the Nazi ideology which is the principle reason why the extreme-right groups have always sought to go beyond these allegations. For example, the aforementioned Front National, avoiding direct anti-immigration sentiment, has embarked on a new strategy forwarding the ideas of

---

[24]Kundnani, A. 2012. Blind Spot? Security Narratives and Far-Right Violence in Europe, *in ICCT Research Paper*, June. Available at:
http://www.icct.nl/download/file/ICCT-Kundnani-Blind-Spot-June-2012.pdf

[25] Edgar, D. 1977. Racism, fascism and the politics of the National Front, *Race and class*, Vol. 19, N 2 October, pp. 113-131.

defending the traditional culture and lifestyle. Thus, this provides a new narrative the far-right parties are riding on - it is impossible to build the equal opportunity society for people regardless of ethnic origin and background without sparking public controversy. For this very reason, ultra-right nationalists reject the concepts of internationalism preached by communists.

Since the beginning of 21st century, the far-right movement has politically matured. For example, since the year 2001 the British National Party has considerably advanced thanks to many factors, in particular, to attitude shifts in the hate ideology. Thus, party leader Nick Griffin has withdrawn the accusations against Jews controlling mass media in Britain and, following the Front National, addressed the ideas of cultural identity and its protection and the combat against immigration and Islamism.

Yet it should be noted that politicians, public activists and researchers cannot arrive at consensus on the nature of the extreme-right movement. Therefore, today's extreme-right groups should not be underestimated. Revealing the diverse, complex and volatile nature of right-wing political radicalism, the far-right parties are now not less dangerous than during the inter-war period. Researchers and the most of politicians commonly hold the opinion that as far-right parties go beyond the mainstream party political struggle, they can hardly count on considerable support and political success. Thus, mainstream parties, fallaciously underrating the scale of ultranationalist efforts, are close to yielding the ground.

2.2.3. Xenophobia in the ultra-right ideology

Xenophobia can manifest itself in many ways involving ostracism of alien cultural elements, other races, religious beliefs; an irrational fear of losing identity and desire to eliminate out-group presence to secure a presumed purity. Being a widespread social phenomenon, xenophobia not only mirrors the level of government policy effectiveness in terms of tolerance and multiculturalism promotion but to a great extent it also depends on human consciousness which within the rapidly changing world context unfavourably reacts to all changes threatening its own identity and, in fact, welcomes "us" and "them" division. In this regard xenophobia manifestations, which have become obvious to all European states, should be examined as an objective process or even as an expected public response to the metamorphoses on the global scale which have highlighted an enormous range of issues associated with understanding of ethnicity and nationality concepts.

The programs of far-right parties the most explicitly exhibit the ideas of xenophobia though the far-right groups' aggression is quite often hidden behind the mask of defence of European cultural values and civil culture which are rejected by immigrants[26].

Specifically, the successful Danish People's Party (Danish: Dansk Folkeparti), which in 2001 became the third in the country, favours the Danish traditions and anti-immigration laws[27]. Also, the Swedish Democrats (Swedish: Sverigedemokratern), having won the election in 2010, factually have the extremist past and display xenophobic sentiment and intolerance towards ethnic minorities. The Progress Party in Norway (Norwegian: Fremskrittspartiet) entered the government in 2009 and is entirely underpinned by the ideas of traditionalism. The True Finns Party (Finnish: Perussuomalaiset), now known as the Finns Party, came as a total surprise with the success in 2011 and protects the Finnish society and its traditions opposing immigrants. The Front National (French: Front National) is constantly strengthening thanks to the rhetoric of preservation of native in-group's interests and traditions in France and Europe-wide. The Party for Freedom (Dutch: Partij voor de Vrijheid) in the Netherlands, a steadily progressive party, made traditionalism and anti-Islamism the key points of its program. In Italy, North League (Italian: Lega Nord per l'Indipendenza della Padania), a member of ex- Silvio Berlusconi's coalition government, declares itself as a defender of the rich cultural heritage of Italians. The Freedom Party of Austria (German: Freiheitliche Partei Österreichs (FPÖ)), which repeatedly became a member of the government, actively advances neo-Nazi slogans underpinned by the ideas of Austrian traditionalism and patriotism. In Hungary, the Movement for a Better Hungary (Hungarian: Jobbik), having efficiently performed since 2012, resolutely defends traditionalism and national identity and is overtly hostile to the citizens (not only immigrants) of other ethnic origin, mainly to the Roma (or Gypsies). In Greece, Golden Dawn (Greek: Chrysí Avgí) gained popularity in 2012. This party has no fear about accusations of neo-Nazism and freely speaks about national uniqueness of Greeks.

However, it should be emphasized that mainstream European political forces do not consider far-right wingers as serious political rivals[28]. It

---

[26] *The Party Program of the "Flemish interest"*. Available at: http://www.vlaamsbelang.org/files/200806_programma.pdf

[27] Ivarsflaten, E., Gudbrandsen, F. 2009. *The Populist radical right in Western Europe*. Available at: http://www.nordic-populism.aau.dk/digitalAssets/43/43663_populistright_routledgeregionalsurveys11.pdf

[28] Putnam, R.D. 1993. *Making Democracy Work: Civic Traditions in Modern*, Princeton, NJ.

should also be remembered that right-wing extremists formally recognize the existing political system and claim that they are ready to play by its rules which always lulls into a false sense of security. The far-right parties seek to introduce their movement as anti-elitist and anti-party, exploiting society's disappointment at the political elite and mainstream parties. For this reason, they always act on behalf of all people and the whole nation without drawing any boundary lines between social groups.

2.2.4. Counteraction to the process of European integration

Another point to be made is that programs of the extreme-right political parties in the member states of the European Union contain anti-EU and anti-integration stances. In the opinion of the far-right groups, the European integration has opened borders for alien cultures and increasingly stirred up traditional societies jeopardizing the very advancement of European civilization. Indeed, the far-right anti-integration propaganda reflects the concept of the fight for racial purity and anti-Islam.

For the extreme-right ideologists the state and the nation are the core entities coinciding with each other. Therefore, any weakening of state (national) sovereignty would endanger national interests and undermine the social unity. No doubt, this threat is associated with the European Union which the European far-right leaders qualify as a trap for the candidates or potential candidate countries that no longer will be able to enjoy their independence. Moreover, many far-right activists pin the blame on the EU bureaucrats for the economic decline in Europe, rampant ethnic-motivated crimes among immigrants and threats of Islamic terrorism. Apparently, in many cases EU citizens perceive the criticism of the EU to be quite justified. Apart from that, not all EU citizens are aware of the real complexity of the EU structure and feel perplexed by the bulky legislative process and a huge bureaucratic apparatus, thus, regularly giving the far-right groups sufficient grounds for criticism. Far-right parties with reference to the law concept certainly advocate the supremacy of the national law that immediately puts them in the vanguard of the anti-integration movement as they present the principal theses of criticism of the European Union. For example, the EU member states are systematically to bring the national legal system into accordance with Community Law that inevitably encounters natural resistance in which the extreme-right groups voice their opinions the most distinctly.

The intense debate over the EU Draft Constitution in 2003, 2004 and 2005 inflicted a severe blow to Communitarian institutions culminating in deep mistrust of the population and governments of the EU member states. In fact, only 29% of respondents were familiar with the contents of the Draft Constitution[29]. Curiously, the majority (60%) of EU citizens were in favour of including a reference to the religious legacies of Europe in the Preamble of the Constitution with 25% of respondents favouring only Christian heritage[30].

The possible reasons why EU citizens voted against the European Constitution could include the following factors: Europeans' fear for the national sovereignty loss (37%), plus, citizens simply opposed the EU integration and the proposed Constitution due to mistrust of the Communitarian institutions (22%)[31]. In Spain, in February 2005 the first referendum on the Draft European Constitution resulted in the majority of Spanish citizens (76.72%) voting for and 17.24% voting against. However, this result was balanced by a low voter turnout[32]. In France, with 69.3% of respondents participating in the referendum, 54.7% voted against the new Constitution[33]. The reasons of rejection lied both in its contents (60%) and in the absence of information (49%)[34]. The population of France was especially anxious about the role of their country in the future EU and the lack of the social component in the Constitution's text[35]. In the Netherlands, in June 2005 the referendum showed that 61.6% did not vote for adoption of the Constitution whereas 38.4% favoured it. The Dutch expressed concern about the sovereignty loss (19%) and the burden of expenses (13%)[36]. Thus, the EU Draft Constitution in the referendums in France and the Netherlands was rejected, however, the analogous outcome, in case of vote, could have been also expected in such countries as the UK, Sweden, the Czech Republic and others. If the referendums had been held, the extreme-right parties of the EU member states would have

---

[29] Putnam, R.D. 1993. *Making Democracy Work: Civic Traditions in Modern*, Princeton, NJ.

[30] Intergovernmental Conference, *Flash Eurobarometer № 152*, Report, 2003, p. 27.

[31] The Draft European Constitution, *Face to Face Interviews, EU 25*, 2004, p. 6.

[32] The European Constitution: Post referendum Survey in Spain, *Flash Eurobarometer № 168*, 2005.

[33] La Constituion Europeenne: Sondage Post-Referendum en France Terrain 30-31 Mai 2005, *Flash Eurobarometer № 171*, Rapport, p. 2.

[34] La Constituion Europeenne: Sondage Post-Referendum en France Terrain 30-31 Mai 2005, *Flash Eurobarometer № 171*, Rapport, p. 30.

[35] La Constituion Europeenne: Sondage Post-Referendum en France Terrain 30-31 Mai 2005, *Flash Eurobarometer № 171*, Rapport, p. 31.

[36] *The European Constitution: Post Referendum Survey in the Netherlands*, 2005, p. 28.

been likely to strengthen their status immensely but, unluckily for them, at that time the extreme-right groups did not score their triumph owing to almost total refusal of parliaments to hold the referendums.

What is not more, the accession of "new" member states to the EU highly complicated the citizenship issue. In the autumn of 2005 48% of respondents perceived themselves as citizens both of their own country and Europe while 41% - only of their own country[37]. In 2012 the number of citizens with a negative image of the EU made up 29%, with a positive image - 30% and the majority of respondents held a neutral viewpoint[38]. According to the opinion poll conducted in 2014, the EU population indicated that the nations in the European Union are united rather by a eurozone and the commitment to the democratic values than by the common culture[39].

The rejected Draft Constitution served as a valuable lesson for all EU members whereas far-right parties positively welcomed this trend and later incorporated it into their party program using the resistance to the European integration and bureaucracy as the main instrument for combating all credible threats emerging in Europe.

Thus, Umberto Bossi, the leader of North League, strongly condemned "European technocrats" for nurturing moral degradation of Europeans and pursuing subversive immigration policy. Bossi's statements won full approval of other far-right leaders thereby displaying that nowadays the most explicit manifestation of euroscepticism in the whole political spectrum is demonstrated by the extreme-right sector. Nevertheless, in this regard Western European and Eastern European right-wing radicals point out some minor discrepancies.

The ultra-right parties of Western Europe oppose the transformation of the EU into a superstate crushing the national sovereignty of its members and direct their criticism towards free movement across the EU which can cause the immigration flow from Eastern Europe and third countries and the Western European ultra-right groups also argue against Brussels' pressure on national economies and subsidies for weak states.

---

[37] Public Opinion in the European Union, *Eurobarometer 64,* Report, 2006, pp. 43, 44, 46.

[38] Public Opinion in the European Union, *Eurobatometer 78/Autumn* 2012, p.15. Available at:
http://ec.europa.eu/public_opinion/archives/eb/eb78/eb78_first_en.pdf

[39] *Two years to go to the 2014 European elections*. Available at:
http://www.europarl.europa.eu/aboutparliament/en/00191b53ff/Eurobarometer.html?tab=2012_4

Of more significance for the Eastern European extreme-right parties have been the aspirations to return to the common Christian past but on this way they have faced the fact that Europe does not hold Christian values any longer and a high level of tolerance in the EU policy limits the opportunity to form and forward common European cultural traditions. In addition, the Eastern European countries encounter economic, political and legal challenges provoked by the EU requirements for the unification of the overall tax system, norms and laws. Therefore, activists of Jobbik, the Slovak People's Party, the League of Polish Families as well as their Western European allies have leveled at the European Union with fierce criticism thereby entering a dialogue with other political forces about the future of their states which again gives the extreme-right parties a chance to act on behalf of all people.

Conclusion

To sum up, politically far-right parties are already integrated into the existing party political system as over time they have won steady electorate's support underpinned by deeply ingrained conservative values and nationalistic feelings. Dealing with the most problematic for a modern European society issues, the extreme-right parties were the first to raise and clearly highlight them, pinpoint their sources and suggest optimal solutions. As a matter of fact, the extreme-right movements present one solution to all problems and propose the most efficient strategy to preserve the European culture and civilization – to protect the white population from the ethnic minority, for example, by introducing zero immigration policy or rigid border control. On the whole, the majority of political parties, as well as the general public in the European countries, do not regard extreme-right radicalism as a significant threat to the socio-political stability. However, imminently and eventually they will face or have already faced the fact that political forces which have long rested beyond the party political spectrum and aroused no grave concern, start participating in the political agenda, immediately reacting to the volatile conditions of the social and political environment. The extreme-right parties' political activity, wherever it is undertaken, inevitably sparks conflicts. Of particular concern in this regard are so-called "new" member states of the European Union (the countries of Central and Eastern Europe) since utopias and mass illusions are always used for wreaking destruction which in many respects explains the political potential of the extreme-right groups and their role in the public policy.

CHAPTER III

THE FAR-RIGHT IN EUROPE: TRAJECTORY OF POLITICAL SUCCESS

The far-right parties represent an increasingly large electoral segment of citizens who are discontent with the existing political practices and norms. Thus, the right-wing radicals are actively involved in public politics and their political potential can be determined by the results of election campaigns for winning seats in national parliaments, by the extent to which the far-right participate in the governmental activities and in elections to the European Parliament (if it is the case of parties from the member-sates of the European Union). Moreover, it is right-wing parties that regard themselves as indispensable actors in decision-making and the execution of these decisions. So this Chapter aims, by examining the involvement of the far-right in the political life (in the work of various governmental institutions) to find out what grounds the right-wing radicals have to influence political processes in countries of Europe and to what extent residents support them.

3.1. Far-right parties in the political life of the contemporary European states: the voting filter

To win a political victory far-right parties use the broadest possible range of instruments of political and party struggle. They participate in election campaigns, rub shoulders with common people and publish manifestoes, party public declarations, party newspapers and magazines. Moreover, many far-right groups and parties stage various street events that have far-reaching repercussions. This distinguishes far-right parties, which are not restricted in their actions and declarations, from other parties. During the election campaign, when political programmes of the main parties largely coincide and the main traditional parties are deep in political rivalry, far-right parties move to the fore of the political arena. The results of election campaigns to win seats in national parliaments, their success in local elections and in the European Parliament testify to it.

The election campaigns reflect a common European trend of “rightwardness”, and this takes place in various parts of Europe.

3.1.1. The far-right in North Europe

In North Europe the far-right have been gradually on the rise as an alternative political power for two decades now. The growth of these forces proved unexpected and unforeseen not only for traditional political actors but also for numerous experts. Yet, the public opinion polls had in a way warned against the making of such a distribution of political forces[1].

In Norway, the right-wing populist Progress Party, founded in 1973 by Aders Lange, since 2005 has firmly established itself in the Norwegian Parliament (the second largest faction)[2]. In October 2013 members of the party not only won seats in the Parliament but also were able to form the government. Far-right Progs took up 7 posts out of 28 in the Cabinet of Ministers. The party leader Erna Solberg became Prime Minister. And its members also filled the posts of the finance minister and the minister for Oil and Energy. Apart from this, they chaired the immigration policy and the policy of integrating immigrants into the Norwegian society. The Progress Party is perceived by the people as the only alternative to the existing political actors since nobody else invites the public to assess the burning issues as it does, it also proposes solutions to the problems[3]. This party does not cooperate with analogous forces of the European Union since Norway is not a member-state.

In Sweden, the right-wing radical tradition is rooted in the inter-war times. In 1924 the Swedish National Socialist Freedom Union was founded but it was not popular with the population and even was banned in 1946[4]. Right radicals reemerged only in the conditions of serious geopolitical changes and the collapse of the Soviet Union. In 1991 a party “New Democracy” was founded. In the election it won 24 seats in Rikstag with its tax and immigration programme which proposed to relieve the

---

[1] *Parliamentary Election 2010*. Available at: http://www.gmu-countries.ru/europa/swed/sweden-encl-vibory.html

[2] *Parliamentary Elections 2005*. Available at: http://www.dw.de/15272878

[3] *Vybory v Norvegii: Partia Andresa Breivika voshla v sostav pravitel'stvennoi koalitsii*. Available at: http://www.regnum.ru/news/polit/1706441.html. (*Election in Norway: the Party of Andres Breivik goes into the government coalition*). (in the original: *Выборы в Норвегии: партия Андреса Брейвика вошла в состав правительственной коалиции*).

[4] Wippermann, W. 1983. *Europäischer Faschismus in Vergleich 1992-1982*, Frankfurt am Main: Suhrkamp.

government of the bulk of social expenditure. But the Party was not Euro-skeptical, which reduced its electoral support, so in 2000 the Party broke up[5].

Another Swedish far-right party, the Swedish Democrats, was founded on the basis of neo-Nazi marginal groups by Leif Zeilon in 1988. Nevertheless, the Swedish democrats succeeded in making their image less radical and more attractive for the voters. In 2002 they excluded certain radical claims from their programme (for example, the claim to institute death penalty and to ban the adoption of non-Europeans). The Party itself declares that its attitude toward racism is negative. Yet the ideas of their nation's superiority and xenophobia remain central. In the Rikstag election the Swedish Democrats were persistently pushing for overcoming the election threshold, but in spite of the growing support of 2002 and 2006, they failed. It was only in 2010 that they won seats in the Rikstag[6].

The centre-right coalition won 172 seats out of 349 in the parliamentary election in September 2010. The Swedish Democrats won 20 seats in the Rikstag for the first time in its history. This event marks the crisis of tradition parties and a considerable success achieved by radical political actors, as well as the general rightwardness trend of Sweden[7].

The party consolidated its position during the crisis of political legitimacy of traditional actors under the conditions of growing nationalism. Yet, experts believe that the Party will not be able to considerably improve its position since their image is still marred by right-wing radicalism. Voters are still more concerned by issues of social and economic policies rather than that of immigration. Yet, voters favouring anti-immigration and anti-European policies constitute the bulk of the party's voter base, which amounts to 10% of all voters. The leader of the Party, Jimmy Åkesson, marked this result very high as the evidence of the people's growing trust in the Party[8].

In Denmark, the situation for the right-wing movement expansion is favorable. Superseding the Progress Party, the Danish People's Party

---

[5] Bolotnikova, E.G. 2008. Pravoradikal'nye partii Shvetsii, *Politex*, pp.49-57.Available at: http://www.politex.info/content/view/405/30/ (Bolotnikova, E.G. 2008. Right-wing radical parties of Sweden, *Politex,* pp.49-57). (in the original: Болотникова, Е.Г. 2008. Праворадикальные партии Швеции, *Политэкс*, с. 49-57).

[6] *The Swedish Democrats*. Available at:
http://www.right-world.net/countries/sweden/sd

[7] *Elections in Sweden.* Available at:
http://newsru.co.il/arch/world/20sep2010/sweden8001.html

[8] *Swedish democrats*. Available at: http://www.right-world.net/countries/sweden/sd

originated in 1996 under the leadership of Pia Kjærsgaard. In the Folketing election in March 1998 the Danish People's Party was a considerable success, having won 13 seats. In the election of November 2001 the party won 22 seats having allied with the conservative-liberal government. In February 2005 the Party won 24 seats, which had considerably strengthened its political positions. Now the Party is the third largest in the Folketing. It takes an active part in drafting bills and has enough political clout to influence the adoption of those ones which it finds agreeing with its political programme of action. In particular, this party consistently pushes for hardening the immigration policy[9].The Danish People's Party is gradually performing its own task to advance into power since its members have already secured seats in the parliament. Pressed by the Party, Denmark, contrary to the position adopted by the European Union, introduced custom examination at the borders with Germany and Sweden. Also, a law toughening the immigration and asylum rules was adopted. The Danish People's Party calling itself the party of all Danish established to protect national values. Owing to the flourishing idea that people of other cultures demolish the religious and cultural values of the Danish, this party receives the people's solid support.

In Finland, the far-right party "True Finns", founded in 2005, is also rather successful. Its current leader Timo Soini stood for presidential election in 2006 (he won the fifth place in the first round of elections) and became a member of the European Parliament in 2009. The Party polled 19% of votes in the general election in spring 2009, thus enlarging its faction fourfold. Many party members refer to themselves as racists and further the idea of "The Finns come first!" The party proposes to return to the 1950s and draws support from conservative elderly citizens[10].

In other Baltic countries, for example, Estonia and Latvia, discrimination of a considerable part of population, the so-called "non-citizens" is formalized in legislation, they are deprived of the right to hold posts in state institutions, work as lawyers, notary publics, engage in political activities, etc. At the state level the rights of the population are restricted by the criterion of ethnic origin. Thus, a negative discriminating

---

[9] Tulupov, D.S. 2008. Sovremennaya politika Datskoy narodnoy partii v otnoshenii immigrantov, *Politex*, pp. 58-67. Available at: http://www.politex.info/content/view/406/30/. (Tulupov, D.S. 2008. Contemporary policies pursued by the Danish People's Party toward immigrants, *Politex*, pp. 58-67). (in the original: Тулупов, Д.С. 2008. Современная политика «Датской народной партии» в отношении иммигрантов, *Политэкс*, с. 58-67.

[10] *The True Finns*. Available at: http://www.right-world.net/countries/%5Bcountry%5D/if

format has been established in the system of interaction between the state power and the sizable part of the population. These conditions account for the patent rightwardness of all political actors who are to act as guardians of the established order. And the far-right political forces feel very confident against this background. In Estonia in 2006 two parties, the ultra-national Isamaa and the neo-conservative Res Publica, merged to form the ultra-right party "Pro Patria and Res Publica Union" (IRL). Several dozens of municipal elders and members of local assemblies are members of this party. This is the only ultra-right party that holds seats in the Parliament and posts in the government: ministerial posts in defence, education, economy and communications, internal affairs, etc. The Reformist Party that calls itself liberal, always looking rightward, goes hand-in-hand with the IRL. It is in the tandem of the Reformist Party and the IRL that in 2007, in violation of the Geneva Convention, the remains of Soviet soldiers were unlawfully exhumed and the monument, best known as "The Bronze Soldier" was pulled down. The ensuing protests of the Russian population were ruthlessly subdued by the police and the paramilitary nationalist defence organization "Kaitseliit". The latter imposes the paragon of soldiers of the Estonian division of Waffen SS on its numerous members (about 22 thousand, which exceed the strength of the Estonian army)[11]. All these groups are very active advocating the "Estoniazation" of schools, support the discrimination of ethnic minorities and praise pro-national collaborationists. These parties are also mildly euro-skeptic, they prefer NATO. Since the ultra-nationalist views are held in such high esteem by the Estonian population, it is the very political regime, and not certain parties, that needs examining.

In Latvia discrimination of ethnic minorities is enshrined in legislation. It stems from the principle of national statehood that says that Latvia is the State of the Latvian nation. The laws on Citizenship and on the State Language legalize the ideology of radical nationalism. These forces are largely represented by the bloc of "National Alliance" that was founded in 2010. This bloc is part of the Saeima and the ruling coalition and champions the "Latvian Latvia". The leaders of the National Alliance always take part in marches in honour of veterans of the Waffen SS. National radicals are more popular in western parts of Latvia (supported by 16% to 18% of the population). They were the fourth in the parliamentary election of 2011, winning two posts in the government – that of the Minister of Justice and the Minister of Culture. This result was

[11] *Belaya kniga nazizma*. 2013, Moskva, p. 1079. (*The White Book of Nazism*. 2013, Moscow, p. 1079). (in the original: *Белая книга нацизма*. 2013, M., c. 1079).

made possible when other political forces refused to cooperate with the so-called "Russian" party "Harmony Centre"[12].

The problem of glorification of Nazi collaborationists is characteristic of Lithuania as well. This country is keen on ultra-nationalist fiction, films and music, and this tendency is upheld by the most important newspaper of the country "The Republic". Among radical nationalists are the "Young Lithuania", "The Union of National Unity", "National Solidarity" and others. In their marches they go with the slogan of "Lithuania for Lithuanians" and declare some of Belarus territories, Kaliningrad Oblast of Russia as belonging to Lithuania, they also demand that alien ideas should not be allowed in the country and that the genocide of Lithuanians during the Soviet rule should be recognized. By far the ultra-nationalists have failed to get into the parliament and to form a majority of representation in local government agencies. Yet, according to the public opinion polls, 13% of Lithuanians approve of the slogans of right-wing radicals, and 41% can not make up their minds whether they are good or bad. As a rule, this answer means to say that respondents like these slogans but are not ready to openly acknowledge it. Ultra-nationalist parties have their members in various government agencies holding various official posts – in municipal assemblies or as vice-mayors. So it is evident that the Latvian ultra-nationalists have a solid ground to erect their political edifice on[13].

In Great Britain the British National Party (BNP) is the largest ultra right-wing British party (the number of its members is over 14 thousand persons). The history of the party is linked with the activities of the British National Front propounding the racist ideals. After its split in 1982 the BNP became the leader of British far-right parties. Since 1999 it has been headed by Nick Griffin[14].

The electorate of the party consists of the middle class, workers and also the British in need of social assistance. And the electorate keeps on growing as do those who are sympathetic of the party, which may be accounted for by the fact of the changing attitude toward immigrants[15]. The important factor of the party's activities and enhanced influence is its urge to establish contacts with the analogous parties in Europe and the

[12] *Belaya kniga nazizma*. 2013, Moskva, pp.401-488.
[13] *Belaya kniga nazizma*. 2013, Moskva, pp. 489-546.
[14] *The British National Party*. Available at:
http://www.martinfrost.ws/htmlfiles/bnp1.html#History_ and_overview
[15] *The British National Party*, pp.14, 16. Available at:
http://www.northamptonshirerec.org.uk

USA. Thus, the BNP has established strong relations with the American National Alliance and the leaders of far-right parties in Germany[16].

In accordance with its ideological attitude, the BNP is classed among the right-wing party margin. Moreover, the party is constantly accused of racism and the incitement to racial and ethnic strife[17].

In 2001, following the riots in Oldham, the party declared itself the leader of a new immigration policy. In the election, Nick Griffin polled 16.4% of the vote in the House of Commons. In June 2005, exactly after the explosions in London, the party was again hit the headlines. Although it failed to win seats in the House of Commons, the British nationalists managed to improve the situation by winning in local elections. The party had 58 of its members holding seats in local councils in 2008[18]. This success can be attributed to the population's protest against the leading political parties of Great Britain that regard immigration as a sensitive issue and refrain from making any open speeches about it.

The support of the BNP in other constituencies had grown by over 5% since 1999. In 2005 it reached the 10% mark. It means that the party had consolidated its electoral base for future election campaigns[19]. In 2007 this tendency gained strength as 49 party members had been elected at local (municipal) elections[20]. On the whole, in 2007 the BNP polled about 300 thousand votes, which proved the nationalists' greatest achievement in the

---

[16] *The British National Party*, p. P.4. Available at: http://www.northamptonshirerec.org.uk

[17] *Leader of British Far-Right Party Acquitted of Race Hate Charges*. Available at: http://www.iht.com/articles/ap/2006/11/10/europe/EU_GEN_Britain_Far_Right_Party.php

[18] *Electoral Performance of the BNP*. Available at: http://www.parliament.uk/business/publications/research/briefing-papers/SN05064/electoral-performance-of-the-british-national-party-in-the-uk

[19] Eremina, N.V. 2008. Britanskaya natsional'naya partia: factory rosta I sderzhivania, *Politex*, pp. 36-48. Available at: http://www.politex.info/content/view/404/30/. (Eremina, N.V. 2008. The British National Party: Factor of Growth and Deterrence, *Politex,* pp. 36-48). (in the original: Еремина, Н.В. 2008. Британская национальная партия: факторы роста и сдерживания, *Политэкс*, с. 36-48); Kurnosov, D. 2008. Britanskaya natsional'naya partia: evolutsia I perspektivy, *Politex*, pp. 23-35. Available at: http://www.politex.info/content/view/403/30/. (Kurnosov, D. 2008. The British National Party: Evolution and Perspectives, *Politex*, pp.23-35). (in the original: Курносов, Д. 2008. Британская национальная партия: эволюция и перспективы, *Политэкс*, с. 23-35).

[20] *The British National Party Gains Strength*. 2007. Available at: http://www.thetimes.co.uk/tto/news/politics/article2023003.ece

history of the party. It is noteworthy that it is more popular in the north-west part of the country[21].

The Independence Party of the United Kingdom holds 12 seats in the European Parliament and positions itself, contrary to the BNP, as a conservative populist party. They reject the accusations of racism and claim to be proponents of civil nationalism. For a long time the party had been a very modest success in state elections, only in 2012 its popularity reached 5-6%, and in 2013 17%. The growth in popularity of the party chaired by Nigel Farage coincided with the decline in the popularity of the conservatives. It should be noted that its programme correlates with that of the BNP, but since the image of the Independence Party is somehow cleansed of Fascist reputation, it finds it easier to act on the political arena, hence its wider electoral base[22]. It is important that some of the Tories regard the idea of allying with the UK Independence Party during the election campaign as real.

3.1.2. Right-wing radicals in West Europe

The situation in West Europe during the last two or three decades has been favourable offering patent opportunities for a political success of far-right parties.

Belgium provides special conditions for right-wing radical political activities. Belgium, a country with a unique Constitution, consists of three communities – Flemish, French and German speaking populations. The Flemish constitute over a half of the whole population[23]. Yet the political power was concentrated in the hands of the French population for quite a long while. And only after the Second World War it was Flanders and not Wallonia that started to play a more important role, which put the Flemish-Wallonian dialogue on a different footing. After the war Karel Dillen founded the Flemish People's Union (Volksunie) noting that he was proud of having a chance to use the terms "racist" and "Fascist". In the second

---

[21] *Unite Against Fascism*. Available at: http://www.uaf.org.uk

[22] *V britanskuyu politiku vorvalas' partia grazhdanskih natsionalistov*. 2013. Available at: http://lenta.ru/articles/2013/03/21/ukip/. (*A party of civil nationalists has burst into the British politics*). (in the original: *В британскую политику ворвалась партия гражданских националистов*).

[23] Namazova, A. 2001. Konstitutsionnye reformy v Bel'gii v XIX – XX vekah, *Evropeyskyi al'manakh*, Moskva, p.201. (Namazova, A. 2001. Constitutional Reforms in Belgium in the 19th - 20th centuries, *European Almanac*, Moscow, p. 201). (in the original: Намазова, А. 2001. Конституционные реформы в Бельгии в XIX – XX веках, *Европейский альманах*, М., с. 201).

half of the 1980s the party split into two ones: the Flemish National and the Flemish People's parties. But in the 1978 election these parties stood together in the framework of the Flemish block. It is important that representatives of the Flemish National Union that collaborated with the Nazis during the occupation were part of this block. The Flemish National Union even had its own Flemish National Militia and the Flemish Military Order. This organization fixed its political ambition on resurrecting the territory of medieval Burgundy which included not only Belgium but also the Netherlands and other territories[24].

Such a partnership must have had an adverse effect on the Flemish block, for it could never win more than 2% of the vote in elections. Nevertheless, in the 1991 election the Flemish block polled 10% of the vote. In return for this, the Belgian government forbade other politicians to join coalitions and cooperate with the Flemish block, thereby setting the so-called sanitary cordon against nationalists. But the new leader of the Flemish block, Filip Dewinter, renounced the idea of anti-Semitism and concentrated on anti-immigration rhetoric in his new "70-point plan". In the 1998 election the Flemish right-wing radicals stood their ground. Following this, several amendments to the Belgium Constitution were adopted to prohibit persons giving air to racial views and making speeches to the same effect to engage in political activities. Under these conditions, F. Dewinter started openly cooperating with the Hasidic community in Antwerp protecting it from Muslim immigrants. This brought about positive results, and in the 2003 local election the party was the third in the country polling 19% of the vote[25].

On 9 November 2004, the Supreme Court of Belgium recognized the Flemish Block as a racist party, and it was dissolved. Yet, immediately after that, on 14 November, a new party emerged – the Flemish Interest. It excluded the notorious "70-Point Plan" from its policy papers since it had occasioned the recognition of the Flemish block as a racist party. The first

---

[24] *The Flemish National Union*. Available at: http://foriz.ru/flamandskij-nacionalnyj-sojuz

[25] Ivanova, E.V. 2011. Formirovanie kraine pravogo dvizhenia v Bel'gii na primere partii Flamandskyi Interes, *in Pravoradikal'nye politicheskie partii I dvizhenia sovremennoy Evropy*, Sankt-Peterburg, pp.215-231. (Ivanova, E.V. 2011. The making of the far-right movement in Belgium. Case-study: The Flemish Interest Party, *in Right-wing radical political parties and movements in contemporary Europe*, Saint-Petersburg, pp.215-231). (in the original: Иванова, Е.В. 2011. Формирование крайне правого движения в Бельгии на примере партии Фламандский интерес, *Праворадикальные политические партии и движения современной Европы*, СПб, с. 215-231).

general election when the new party fielded its candidates took place in June 2007, and it succeeded in polling a larger percentage than her predecessor. On the whole, about 10% of the population supports this party. The change of image had to do a lot with this success: party members speak about family values in good Dutch, which endears them to a larger group of people. Considering that the Flemish appreciate that a party should meet the interests of their community, such a party can rely on its unflagging support[26].

It is evident that in the Netherlands the far-right and all other right-wing parties are confident of achieving political victories. In May 2002 in the parliamentary election in the Netherlands a centre-right party of Christian Democrats won 43 seats out of 150. One of the most popular far-right parties during the election was the Pim Fortuyn List, whose programme centred on the task of protecting the identity of the Dutch from the 30% of non-Dutch population. Members of this party are well-known for their statements that Islam is a backwater religion and ideology. Although on the eve of the election Pim Fortuyn had been assassinated, the Pim Fortuyn List became the second largest having won 26 seats in the Parliament[27].

The far-right in the Netherlands maintain their political stability. Thus, another right-wing party – the Party for Freedom – founded by Geert Wilders in 2005 won 6% of the vote and 9 seats in its first 2006 election. In 2010 it achieved a greater success becoming the fourth largest party in the Parliament (15% of the vote and 24 seats)[28]. In 2010 the Muslim community called for legal action against Geert Wilders accusing him of inciting racial hate, but he was acquitted of the charge[29]. At present the leader of the Dutch Party for Freedom has become one of the key Dutch politicians. All those who fear the loss of the Dutch identity contribute to

---

[26] Ivanova, E.V. 2011. Formirovanie kraine pravogo dvizhenia v Bel'gii na primere partii Flamandskyi Interes, *in Pravoradikal'nye politicheskie partii I dvizhenia sovremennoy Evropy*, Sankt-Peterburg, pp.215-231.

[27] *Triumf pravykh I kraine pravykh*. Available at: http://www.pravda.ru/world/16-05-2002/807218-0/
(*Triumph of the right-wing and the far-right*). (in the original: *Триумф правых и крайне правых*).

[28] *Pozitsii kraine pravykh v Evrope krepnut*. Available at:
http://www.dw.de/15272878. (*The positions of the far-right gain strength in Europe*). (in the original: *Позиции крайне правых в Европе крепнут*).

[29] *Gollandia mezhdu shariatom I ul'trapravymi*. Available at:
http://www.forumn.kiev.ua/2012-02-117/117-15.html. (*Holland between the Shariath and the Ultra Right-wing*). (in the original: *Голландия между шариатом и ультраправыми*).

its success in elections; and since these fears are shared by people from different social strata, the party is gaining strong support of the whole country.

Yet the unconditional leader of the far-right is still the National Front.

The National Front, founded in 1972 by Jean-Marie Le Pen together with the group of collaborationists in the Second World War, is one of the major right-wing parties in Europe. So it naturally became the European leader of the right-wing parties acting in alliance with other ultra-right-wing parties. Its membership exceeds 70 thousand persons, which also accounts for its leadership. In the 1984 its party member was fielded and won a seat in the Parliament for the first time. In the mid 1990s, over 10% of voters supported the party, which allowed the party to win 11 seats in the Parliament[30].

Although the party has had its ups and downs, the far-right parties in France have become an inalienable part of the country's political establishment. And they are already representing an alternative political force capable of countering their political rivals. Thus, in the 2011 cantonal election, the National Front led by Marine Le Pen succeeded in further consolidating its position; according to the public opinion polls, Marine Le Pen could be regarded as a match for Nicolas Sarcozy in the presidential election[31].

The party is especially popular in the eastern part of the country, along the Mediterranean, in Alsace and Lorraine. It has a solid voter base. It is supported not only by those who fear losing traditional values, but also socially disadvantaged groups of population, especially young workers.

---

[30] Zolotova, M. Yu., Kurchanova, E.M. 2011. Evolutsia ideino-politicheskih pozitsii etnoradikalov v sovremennoy Frantsii v kontekste predstavleniya osnovnyh kontseptov ih politicheskogo diskursa, *in Pravoradikal'nye politicheskie partii I dvizhenia sovremennoy Evropy*, Sankt-Peterburg, pp. 324-355. (Zolotova, M. Yu., Kurchanova, E.M. 2011. The evolution of ideological and political positions of ethnic radicals in contemporary France in the context of the main concepts of their political discourse, *in Right-wing radical political parties and movements in contemporary Europe*, Saint-Petersburg, pp. 324-355). (in the original: Золотова, М.Ю., Курчанова, Е.М. 2011. Эволюция идейно-политических позиций этнорадикалов в современной Франции в контексте представления основных концептов их политического дискурса, *Праворадикальные политические партии и движения современной Европы*, СПб., с.324-353).

[31] Samuel, H. *Marine Le Pen Would Beat Nicolas Sarcozy in presidential election.* Available at:
http://www.telegraph.co.uk/news/worldnews/europe/france/8364812/Marine-Le-Pen-would-beat-Nicolas-Sarkozy-in-presidential-election.html

The 2006 opinion poll showed that 70% of respondents think that this party is justifiable on the political arena, 55% suppose that its members should hold office[32].

In Germany, in spite of its negative national socialistic experience, the number of neo-Nazi activists amounts to about 50 thousand persons belonging to various groups. And the tension in inter-ethnic relation keeps growing. In 2008, ultra-right-wing nationalists committed almost 20 thousand crimes, the majority of which are various manifestations of violence[33]. At the same time, the Germans think it important to have one party capable of protecting the German identity[34]. The ubiquitous criticism of the multicultural policy contributes to the growth in the popularity of the far-right parties.

Now in Germany there exist both legal far-right parties – for instance, National Democratic Party of Germany – and extremist organizations – Brigaden (Kameradschaften). The latter represent small groups of about 20 persons, largely, of aggressive youths. They constitute the main threat to immigrants, they are engaged in street activities, spread leaflets, etc[35].

At present the most powerful is the National Democratic Party of Germany (in 2011 the People's Union merged with it). Before the 2004 election they were strong enough to clear the 5% threshold in Saxony. The National Democratic Party won 9% of the vote; and in Brandenburg the People's Union won 6%. Members of the National Democratic Party,

---

[32] Zolotova, M. Yu., Kurchanova, E.M. 2011. Evolutsia ideino-politicheskih pozitsii etnoradikalov v sovremennoy Frantsii v kontekste predstavleniya osnovnyh kontseptov ih politicheskogo diskursa, *in Pravoradikal'nye politicheskie partii I dvizhenia sovremennoy Evropy*, Sankt-Peterburg, pp. 324-353.

[33] Krasinsky, V.V. 2011. Natsionalizm kaka element ideologii ul'trapravyh partii I ego ispol'zovanie na vyborah v Germanii, *in Rossiiskii Obschestvennyi Institut Izbiratel'nogo Prava (ROIIP)*, Available at: http://www.roiip.ru/publication/publication227.htm. (Krasinsky, V.V. 2011. Nationalism as an element of ideology of ultra-right-wing parties and its use in elections in Germany, *Russian Institute of Electoral Rights (RIER)*). (in the original: Красинский, В.В. 2011. Национализм как элемент идеологии ультраправых партий и его использование на выборах в Германии, *Российский общественный институт избирательного права (РОИИП)*).

[34] Sumlenny, S. 2010. Migranty otvetyat za vsyo, *Internet Proekt Expert Online*, Available at: http://expert.ru/expert/2010/42/migranty_otvetyt_za_vse/. (Sumlenny, S. 2010. Migrants will pay for everything, *Internet Project Expert Online*). (in the original: Сумленный, С. 2010. Мигранты ответят за всё, *Интернет-проект «Эксперт онлайн»*).

[35] Sumlenny, S. 2010. Migranty otvetyat za vsyo, *Internet Proekt Expert Online*, Available at: http://expert.ru/expert/2010/42/migranty_otvetyt_za_vse/.

which is regarded as a project to reanimate the Hitler National Socialist Party, achieved this success for the first time. It is important that, despite the counteraction of the government, the party was not banned by the Constitutional Court[36].

In 2013 another right-wing party came into being – the "Alternative for Germany" chaired by Bernd Lucke, and it is expected to enlist support of 5% of voters and win seats in the European Parliament[37].

3.1.3. Right-wing radical parties in South Europe

In South Europe right-wing radical parties and groups gained new opportunities from the deteriorated social and economic sphere.

In Italy, there are a number of Fascist parties. Among the far-right, Lega Nord (Northern League) maintains the lead; it holds more seats than its counterparts in Europe do. In the latest election it polled 10% of votes, which is twice as many as compared with result of the 2004 election. It is important that the Party is part of the parliamentary coalition. At the same time the party distances itself from Fascism. Yet, it is known for fascist speeches made by its members, for example, those by Giovanni (Gianni) Alemanno, whom the Party nominated for the mayor's post in Rome. Other fascist groups of Italy, such as Forza Nuova (New Force) and Movimento Sociale Fiamma Tricolore (Tricolour Flame), repeatedly lost the support of the population[38].

With the slackening pace of the degrading world market and the deterioration of the position of Italian enterprises, it was the Northern League that gathered momentum in politics. Umberto Bossi had always been good at mimicry and his statements made in various institutions and under different circumstances never gave one a chance to learn about the party's true views of the contour of things. Yet, the Northern League was the political force that formed a new political system in Italy in 1992. The Party can only rely on support of the voters in the northern and central

---

[36] Roze, A. 2012. Igra v Nazi, *Rossiiskaya Gazeta*, Available at: http://www.rg.ru/2012/01/23/germany.html. (Roze, A. 2012. A Nazi Game, *Russian Newspaper*). (in the original: Розэ, А.2012. Игра в nazi, *Российская Газета*).

[37] *V Germanii sozdana paria protivnikov evro*. Available at: http://lenta.ru/news/2013/03/11/antieuro/. (*A party to oppose the euro has been founded In Germany*). (in the original: *В Германии создана партия противников евро*).

[38] *The League of the North*. Available at: http://right-world.net/countries/italy/ls

parts of the country. It comes as no surprise that the Party relies heavily on the Italian entrepreneurs of northern Italy.

Quite unexpected was the growth of the far-right movement in Greece when the party Golden Dawn, founded in 1993, with its Ancient Greek symbols of solar ornaments came to the fore. The Party positions itself as nationalistic, but, according to the party's rhetoric, it professes to be called neo-Nazi. The leader of the Party, Nikolaos Michaloliakos, has been repeatedly arrested for his activities. At the present time, the Golden Dawn is part of the European National Front. The Party holds 18 seats in the parliament[39]. The influence and rapid growth of the far-right parties is quite evident since the ruling parties in Greece made changes in the immigration policy. In 2013 the far-right polled 11% of the vote, that is, 4 points more than in 2012. In 2013 it polled over 12%, according to the public opinion polls. The Party set a task to win seats in the European Parliament in 2014 to alter the attitude of the European Union to the problems of their concern[40].

3.1.4. Far-right parties and movements in Central and Eastern Europe

In Central and Eastern Europe the growth in the influence of far-right parties is getting increasingly alarming.

In Hungary, the Hungarian nationalists of different colours hold firm positions and are part of the government as they won two thirds of seats in the Parliament. Thus, V. Orban, the leader of the Independent Smallholders, Agrarian Workers and Civic Party (FKGP), is the Prime Minister. Such diplomatic landscape is very favourable for the Hungarian far-rightists whom the FKGP conservatives view as the key partner capable of introducing complex issues to the agenda and of solving them in a radical way. Predictably, radicals from the Movement for a Better Hungary (the Jobbik) are consolidating their position, which can be called neo-Nazi. Now it is the third powerful political party in the country. The Jobbik's main slogan is "Hungary for Hungarians", and party members blame Romanians and gypsies for all sorts of evils in the country. The

[39] Kostyuk, R. 2012. Nad Gretsiey zanimaertsya neofashistskii rassvet, *Novyi smysl,* Available at: http://www.sensusnovus.ru/analytics/2012/09/29/14591.html. (Kostyuk, R. 2012. The Neo-Nazi day is dawning in Greece, *New Sense*). (in the original: Костюк, Р. 2012. Над Грецией занимается неонацистский рассвет, *Новый смысл*).

[40] Kostyuk, R. 2012. Nad Gretsiey zanimaertsya neofashistskii rassvet, *Novyi smysl,* Available at: http://www.sensusnovus.ru/analytics/2012/09/29/14591.html.

leader of the Party Gábor Vona is also the leader of the people's company Hungarian Guard, which represents the armed wing of the Party. Members of the company, dressed in black uniforms decorated with symbols of pro-Nazi governments of the times of the Second World War, organize marches and street demonstration. The Guard was recognized illegal, for it had maltreated not only gypsies but also other groups of population, including those of different political views, for example, socialists. It is important to note that the Jobbik exerts powerful influence on the Independent Trade Union of Hungary whose leader Judith Sima called for starting the armed struggle against Jews and gypsies. The Jobbik has the support of the conservative sector, it cooperates actively with the FKGP, which does not regard the Jobbik party as racist and forms coalitions with representatives of the Jobbik at the local governmental level[41].

The Jobbik won seats in the Hungarian Parliament in 2010 having polled over 16% of the vote, and even during the slackening of the voters' concern 13% of the population come out in support of the party[42].

In Croatia the far-right movement is in the shadow of the conservative party the Croatian Democratic Union that positions itself as a party of a neo-conservative style. It outrivals all other parties, including the right-wing parties, since its party programme has absorbed the interpretation of many key issues of political and state development. It is the oldest party in the country and believes itself the successor of the 1861 party. The Croatian far-right movement stems from the movement of Ustashas active during the Second World War.

Of all active far-right parties in 2011 only the Croatian Party of Rights had its members in the Parliament. Apart from it, there are two more parties that are always in the limelight of the mass media: the Autochthonous Croatian Party of Rights and the Croatian Party of Freedom[43]. Also there are such small groups as the Croatian National Front and the National Resistance. For all these parties, the strong state is the necessary means for the survival of the Croatian nation. The majority of them openly declare their ideological continuity with the Ustashas movement.

---

41 *Belaya Kniga Nazizma*. 2013, Moskva, pp. 159-220. (*White Book of Nazism*. 2013, Moscow, pp. 159-220). (in the original: *Белая книга нацизма*. 2013, M., c. 159-220).

42 *Belaya Kniga Nazizma*. 2013, Moskva, pp.159-220.

43 Obucina, Vedran. 2011. Radical Right-Wing *Parties* in Former Communist Countries: Challenges to Liberal Democracy or a Social Economic Protest?, *Anals*, N 8. p.2.

At present the most significant party of all the far-right is the Croatian Party of Rights. Its founders Ante Starčevič and Eugen Kvaternik, believing that the Croatian nation is unique and ethnically unrelated to any other nations, made it a paragon and resolved to protect it[44]. Their voter base consists of conservative and traditionalist citizens from various social groups who fear the influence of other ethnic minorities on the Croatian nation and oppose globalization and European integration[45]. Yet, this support is not strong enough for the party to gain a solid footing in the country.

In Romania the far-right party Great Romania was founded in1991 by Eugen Barbu and Vadim Tudor. The latter became its leader following the death of his partner. The Party developed as a force countering the Democratic Union of Romanian Hungarians. The ideas of nationalism and extremism played a great role in its making. The year 2000 was the most successful for the Party when it won seats in the Parliament (21% in the Senate, 19% in the House of Representatives)[46]. In the consecutive years their political heft dwindled.

In Poland in 2013 ultra conservative nationalist forces united to form a conservative people's movement (RN) and were ready to field candidates in the 2014 European Parliament election. This electoral block unites ultra-Catholics, euro-skeptics and nationalists into a single force. The block relies on cooperation with other European far-right parties to jointly oppose the sole rule and dictate of Brussels[47]. The block holds demonstrations and marches that frequently devolve into clashes with the police and anti-Fascist forces of Poland. It sets a task to protect the Polish "national identity" founded on Christian values. On the whole, the Polish ultra-nationalism opposes all other ethnicities of the country.

Experts note that representatives of neo-Nazi groups with little political clout are active in Poland, such as the Blood and Honour, the Combat 18 and the so-called Polish fascists. At the same time they strive to distance themselves from the Nazism of the German style. Among them

---

[44] Obucina, Vedran. 2011. Radical Right-Wing *Parties* in Former Communist Countries: Challenges to Liberal Democracy or a Social Economic Protest?, *Anals*, N 8. p.2.

[45] Obucina, Vedran. 2011. Radical Right-Wing *Parties* in Former Communist Countries: Challenges to Liberal Democracy or a Social Economic Protest?, *Anals*, N 8. p.2.

[46] *Belaya Kniga Nazizma*. 2013, Moskva, pp. 721-768.

[47] *Poland's fledging far-right party RN to run in European Parliament election.* Available at: http://www.rawstory.com/rs/2014/01/08/polands-fledgling-far-right-party-rn-to-run-for-eu-parliament-election/

are the National Radical Camp Falanga and the National Revival of Poland. The latter has launched into a full-scale activities and established contacts with numerous analogous parties in Europe. For example, the National Movement of Poland is part of the European National Front along with the Greek Golden Dawn and the Italian New Force; also it develops cooperation with the British National Party. Although representatives of this movement propagate the ideas of syndicalism, it is not popular with workers[48].

The Polish Youth and the Radical National Camp are the major organizations in the nationalistic movement. These movements model upon fascist units of the National Army fighting against communists. The Polish Youth organization was revived in the 1990s and became part of the youth League of Polish Families. Having no independent political support, they side with their ally – the National Conservative Party of Poland. Thus, a representative of the Polish Youth held office in the government and the post of Minister of Education from 2005 to 2007. In general, the nationalist far-right movement has strong ties with the National Conservative Party of Poland, one of the political leaders of the country[49].

The leader of the Polish Youth movement, R. Vinnicki, deciding to improve the image of the party, assumed a more respectable attitude. So now Przemyslaw Holoher, head of the Radical National Camp, who makes open anti-Semite declarations is the acknowledged key figure of the right radicalism in Poland. Representatives of these far-right movements hold marches and use Nazi symbols. In many matters the far-right and the right-wing collude and support one another. For example, Polish conservatives backed the independence marches; they model themselves upon the Hungarian example and the path the Jobbik follows[50].

Nevertheless, these movements cannot clear the election threshold in the parliamentary struggle. For example, the National Revival of Poland, which in order to be eligible for running for the Parliament in the 2001 election had allied with other far-right parties, after the defeat left the bloc and started acting on its own polling less than 1% at different elections.

---

[48] *Poland's fledging far-right party RN to run in European Parliament election.* Available at: http://www.rawstory.com/rs/2014/01/08/polands-fledgling-far-right-party-rn-to-run-for-eu-parliament-election/

[49] *49 Poland's fledging far-right party RN to run in European Parliament election.* Available at: http://www.rawstory.com/rs/2014/01/08/polands-fledgling-far-right-party-rn-to-run-for-eu-parliament-election/

[50] *Novye pravye v Pol'she.* Available at: http://voprosik.net/novye-pravye-v-polshe/. (*The New Right-wing in Poland*). (in the original: *Новые правые в Польше*).

Party members have made themselves notorious for radical statements and Mein Kampf citations[51]. On the whole, the ultra-right-wing Polish movement remains divided into various groupings active in different parts of the country; they are not keen to form a single far-right party so stand no chance to play an independent political game and realize their political ambitions.

Different opportunities for political activities have been offered to the far-right in Slovakia. The Slovak National Party, founded in 1989, relies on the international support from other far-right parties, in particular, it has been developing relations with the Freedom Party of Austria. The core of the Slovakian National Party is made up of the followers of its leader, Jan Slota, who believes that all the troubles and evils in the country stem from the large communities of gypsies and Hungarians. The party also campaigns against homosexualism and Europeanism. Yet, the party is not unanimous, for example, its part headed by Andrei Danko holds a less radical position. In 2002 the party managed to clear the 5% threshold and won several seats in the Slovak National Council. Till 2010 the right-wing parties had held 9 to 18 seats in the Council. But they polled none in the 2010 election[52].

Gradually, another far-right party "Our Slovakia" joined the political struggle, the party upholds the conceptions of the Jozef Tico pro-fascist regime established in 1939. The victory won by M. Kotleba when he was elected Governor proved very significant for this movement. At the 2013 regional election, Our Slovakia declares its intention to preserve the national identity as the major value of the Slovaks. So the principal slogan in the election was to fight against the enemies of the Slovak people, first and foremost, gypsies[53].

In Bulgaria several right-wing radical groups have become more active in the recent years, among which the largest is the Attack. In 2009 and 2013 its members won parliamentary seats polling 9.2% and 7.2% of the vote respectively, thus representing the fourth largest faction in the Parliament. The Attack is against cultural pluralism in the state and champions the Bulgarisation of trade, industries and banking. At present, right-wing radicals are strong only in rural areas, but on the whole they

---

[51] *The National Revival of Poland*. Available at: http://www.right-world.net/countries/poland/nop

[52] *The Slovak National Party*. Available at: http://optoshka.ru/styhrmnyhriovteof/

[53] Plyasunov, S. 2013. Slovakia: Neozhidannaya pobeda, *Vsya Evropa*, Available at: http://www.alleuropa.mgimo.ru/slovakiya-neozhidannaya-pobeda. (Plyasunov, S. 2013. Slovakia: Unexpected Victory, *All Europe*). (in the original: Плясунов, С. 2013. Словакия: неожиданная победа, *Вся Европа*).

have won support from 10% of the population, which correlates with the European indicators. The Attack became known for its protest meetings, street marches and extremist slogans. And the Attack frequently joins other ultra-nationalist groups of Bulgaria in their activities, for example, the Bulgarian national Movement and the National Front for Salvation of Bulgaria[54].

The most headline-making have been the political events involving the far-right of Ukraine. After gaining independence in 1991, several neo-Nazi groups emerged and have been rather successful in this country. Thus, the O. Tyahnybok's All-Ukrainian Svoboda Association at its first go for the election was supported by 10% of the population[55].

This party was founded in 1991. Its initial name, The Social National Party of Ukraine, was changed to the Svoboda Party in 2004. Until 2009 this party had not enjoy firm backing from the population. At the 2006 and 2007 parliamentary elections it polled 0.3% and 0.76% of the vote. It was in the regional election in Ternopil oblast in 2009 that the Svoboda Party won polling 34.69% of the vote. After that the party consolidated its position winning seats in 7 regional councils in the western and central parts of the country; and three regional councils are now headed by members of Svoboda[56].

The victory of this party is an outgrowth of the keen struggle between Yulia Timoshenko's Block and Our Ukraine Movement since Svoboda was then an alternative force outside the political strife and bickering. As a result Svoboda as the main critic of the then political power reaped the laurels. And soon became widely acknowledged. Many political actors started to regard it as a political partner in spite of ultra-nationalist declarations of its members. In particular, it was invited to the Committee set up to investigate Yulia Timoshenko's activities. This party is the only one that has been actively involved in organizing protest marches and street fights. Since the end of 2011 one third of all protest rallies in Ukraine have been staged by Svoboda. It has become the main political force, the political alternative to all other parties for the liberal youth, the main force equipped with a unique political programme. Thus, it was largely because of the people who had been fed up with the existing

---

[54] *Belaya Kniga Nazizma*. 2013, Moskva, pp. 51-94.

[55] Shekhovtsov, A. *Ukraine: the far-right in parliament for the first time*. Available at: http://www.opendemocracy.net/od-russia/anton-shekhovtsov/ukraine-far-right-in-parliament-for-first-time

[56] Shekhovtsov, A. *Ukraine: the far-right in parliament for the first time*. Available at: http://www.opendemocracy.net/od-russia/anton-shekhovtsov/ukraine-far-right-in-parliament-for-first-time

political turmoil that Svoboda got its chance to move to the fore of the political life of the country by orchestrating protest rallies in the Kiev Maidan.

In Russia the situation with the far-right has been rather peculiar. The Russian Federation has solid legislation on the ban of all kinds of activities aimed at ethnic discrimination and incitement of national and religious discord. The Russian society has been multinational for ages, which prevents national radicals from exerting strong influence on the political culture and the political consciousness of the population. Nevertheless, under the conditions of social, economic and political instability when national republics were making a parade of sovereignty and factions were struggling for power in the 1990s, ultra-nationalist movements were formed which placed the Russian national question on the agenda. These political forces and their main support base are found in large cities.

One of the largest is the Russians movement. It was founded by leaders of marginal right-wing radical movements. Their common aim is to stop the genocide of the Russian people and to restore its status of a state forming nation. This movement gave rise to the Party of Nationalists that claimed that the Russian population had taken more abuse from the Bolshevism than other nationalities. The New Force echoes it and proposes to reconsider the outcome of the privatization, to stop disbursing tranches to Caucasus and to protect the interests of Russian speaking citizens. All national democrats demand that the rights of Russian regions be equated with those of national regions (where non-Russian nationalities constitute a titular majority) in the framework of federalism and a "Russian state" be created, as well as tougher immigration policy be conducted[57].

In 2012 the nationalist movement started actively collaborating with the liberal oppositions and as a result it was demarginalized. In particular, A. Navalny is known to have said that it was necessary to found in Russia a party in the style of the Front National. Owing to joint protest acts, nationalists got a job to do. In return for this, other political forces started fiddling with the agenda and making free with xenophobic speeches. Traditionally, closest to national radicals has been the Liberal Democratic Party of Russia, whose leader V. Zhirinovsky frequently refers to the so-called Russian question. And although national radicals do not stand up in elections in Russia and cannot exert direct influence on decision-making, they grasp at every possible opportunity to have a say in politics. We

---

[57] *Belaya Kniga Nazizma*. 2013, Moskva, pp. 629-720. (*White Book of Nazism*. 2013, Moscow, pp. 629-720). (in the original: *Белая книга нацизма*. 2013. М., pp. 629-720).

cannot help noticing that alongside with the Russian nationalism other nationalisms keep coming into being, for example, in Tatarstan and Chuvashia. It is important that in Russia and Ukraine, contrary to other European countries, the growth of far-right parties owes much to liberal ideas, to be more precise, to liberal surroundings that open the floor for right-wing radicals on the public and political arena[58].

Thus, there are a lot of varieties of European right-wing forces – those having much in common and those that are different. It is of great interest that certain parties, such as the British National Party, the Hungarian Jobbik and the Greek Golden Dawn now are trying to position themselves as xenophobic and racist. But such parties as the French Front National or Austrian Party for Freedom, vice versa, are trying to avoid association with xenophobia and racism. The political success is determined by the way a society interprets their political stand, for the far-right in different European countries have had a different start and have to grow under different circumstances. Yet one cannot miss some common grounds for the development and consolidation of the whole European far-right movement. They consist of the right-wing and conservative traditions in the European states and of the mix of liberal and right-wing conservative ideas in Russia and Ukraine. Considering that liberalism has become in a sense the basis of the conservative tradition, it still can be regarded as part of right-wing party and political sector. Support of the right-wing flank of the political spectrum proves very important for the ultra-right-wing. In certain cases, right-wing parties do not venture to perform serious tasks, which emboldens the far-right (in Germany, for instance). In other cases, conservative parties form coalitions and act jointly with the far-right (for example, in Poland and Hungary).

One cannot help but note that certain objective European tendencies have already been formed – citizens are losing their trust in the Institutions of the European Union (in the EU member-states) and they do not place unquestioning trust in national leaders any more. It is now that, first and foremost owing to these tendencies, that right-wing parties are becoming more confident of their political clout[59]. Far-right leaders in Europe form alliances and keep restoring their positions in the cases if they have lost them recently. During the crisis started in 2008, the ultra-right-wing consolidated their positions practically everywhere.

---

[58] *Belaya Kniga Nazizma*. 2013, Moskva, pp. 629-720.

[59] *How Europe's far-right will and won't flourish in 2014*. Available at: http://www.newstatesman.com/politics/2014/01/how-europes-far-right-will-and-wont-flourish-2014

3.2. Far-right parties in the international dimension in Europe: European Parliament election campaigns

All types and kinds of right-wing parties, despite their skepticism, long to win seats in the European Parliament. At the 2009 election the Dutch Party for Freedom rated heaviest polling 17% of the vote. The ideological "mix" of its leader Geert Wilders had secured a political advantage over other political actors. At the 2009 parliamentary election members of this party enlisted support from the population and won 4 seats. Experts differed in their classifying the party and Wilder's rhetoric as ranging between populism and fascism. At the next election in 2014 of all other far-right the French Front National took the lead. The Front National holds a firm ground in elections to the European Parliament, which annoys its rivals, socialists, who speak of changes in the functioning of the European Union. Since the far-right can block many communitarian initiatives if they hold office in the European Parliament, this could bring about, from their standpoint, the destruction of the European project[60]. Although in 2009 the Front National won only three seats in the European Parliament, it manifested its political capacities. The rest far-right parties in Europe had also tried to keep up with the Front National.

On the whole, as the results of the 2009 election reveal, the far-right were able to increase the number of their representatives in the European Parliament. At that time the European Parliament had formed a parliamentary group (such is the name given to a faction on the official site of the European Parliament) of nationalist euroskeptics – "Europe of Freedom and Democracy" chaired by Nigel Farage, leader of the Independence Party of the United Kingdom.

Thus, in the 2009 election the far-right of many European states succeeded in winning seats.

The Danish People's Party succeeded at the 2009 election in winning two seats. The True Finns, the third most important party in the country, won two seats in the 2009 election. The success of the British National Party in the election proved demonstrative. In the 2009 election they managed to win two seats for the first time. The Flemish Interest also won two seats in the 2009 election. Moreover, the League of the North holds 9 offices in the European Parliament. The Hungarian Jobbik is always capable of balancing its losses at the national election with its successes in

---

[60] *European Socialists fret about far-right victory at EU election.* Available at: http://www.euractiv.com/eu-elections-2014/european-socialists-warn-far-rig-news-533048

the European Parliament. Thus, it won three seats in 2009. After the 2009 election the Jobbik formed an international association of ultra-right-wing parties outside the European Parliament – The Alliance of European National Movements that also encompassed the French Front National, the British National Party, the Belgian National Front and the Italian party Tricolour Flame. The Greater Romania party feels confident only at the elections to the European Parliament. In 2009 it polled 8% of the vote. The Slovak National Party won one seat in 2009. The Bulgarian Attack usually holds 2-3 seats, for example, according to the results of the 2009 election its members won 2 seats out of 17 seats set for Bulgaria in the European Parliament.

Against the background of these successes there were periods of slight weakening of the parliamentary positions of insignificant number of far-right parties in various regions of Europe.

For example, members of the Swedish Democrats Party had not held office in the European Parliament until 2014, but they voiced their wish to take part in common European politics in alliance with other far-right parties (Front National, Party for Freedom, etc.). In the elections to the European Parliament the Latvian ultra-nationalists are not successful. The Lithuanian far-right parties cannot unite to stand up in elections to the European Parliament, which so far has been closed for them, but they compensate for this misfortune by achieving successes in Lithuania. The Croatian Party of Rights has also been unsuccessful at the European Parliament level, it holds no seats there.

In December 2013 many European politicians were disturbed by the urge with which the far-right had tried to consolidate their ranks before the 2014 elections to the European Parliament. We have already seen that their positions were being consolidated and at the same time the number of seats in national parliaments was getting larger, which surely increases opportunities for the far-right to win more seats in the election to the European Parliament. Yet, their presence in the European Parliament remains insignificant, so the attempts made by the far-right to unite are justifiable. In May 2014, prior to the European election, in Strasbourg, the leaders of the French Front National, the Austrian Party for Freedom and the Flemish Interest in Belgium announced their intention to form an alliance of the far-right forces[61].

---

[61] *"Zavoevat' Frantsiyu, a zatem unichtozhit' Evropu": Marine Le Pen I proryv kraine pravyh na evrovyborah.* Available at: http://www.regnum.ru/news/polit/1808594.html *("To conquer France and liquidate Europe": Marine Le Pen and far-right victory).* (in the original:

On 18 November, representative of the far-right parties – the Front National, the League of the North, the Flemish Interest, the Dutch Party for Freedom, the Slovak National Party and the Austrian Party for Freedom convened in Vienna to discuss the opportunities for such a coalition. These forces constituted the core of the new alliance.

The European Alliance for Freedom advanced by these parties in the European Parliament may expand if it encompasses more members. Yet, right before the election several far-right parties in European countries had distanced themselves from the Alliance, for one, the Independence Party in Great Britain. And the Alliance itself refused to cooperate with the British National Party and the Jobbik, outright branding those parties fascists. The European Alliance for Freedom stated that it advocates the interests of the indigenous population whose rights are encroached on, and counts on the support of the middle class that is regarded as the guardian of national interests[62].

The far-right proved worthy of the established trend in May 2014. The first elections held after the financial crisis revealed that the EU status as a stable largest economy in the world had been undermined. Also, the turnover was only a little over 40% never changing after the precious election in 2009. After appraising the state of affairs, representatives of numerous political forces drew a right conclusion that they would have to take account of the demands of the voters, who were aware of the threats to the society and the state, which would result in the reconsideration of the interaction between the founding states and the communitarian bodies of power.

In the course of the elections the poll registered for the first time a considerable growth in the number of euro-skeptic parties, right-wing and far-right, which had made central the anti-immigration and anti-Islam policies, and also it revealed the urge of member-states to conduct independent state financial and economic policies.

In the 2009 Parliament the far-right sector was represented by the faction Europe of Freedom and Democracy (in 2014 Europe of Freedom and Direct Democracy) consisting of members of the far-right Independence Party of the United Kingdom, the League of the North and others. After the 2014 election there was an attempt to form yet another

---

"Завоевать Францию, а затем уничтожить Европу": Марин Ле Пен и прорыв крайне правых на выборах).

[62] Dzhozvyak, R. *Vybory dayuschie Moskve bol'shoy stopor v Evroparlamente*. Available at: http://ru.krymr.com/content/25383492.html. (Dzhozvyak, R. *Elections allowing Moscow to lock the European Parliament*). (in the original: Джозвяк, Р. *Выборы, дающие Москве большой стопор в Европарламенте*).

far-right group the European Alliance for Freedom, the key participants of which are the Front National chaired by Marine Le Pen and the Dutch Party for Freedom chaired by Geert Wilders. The faction invited far-right representative of at least seven countries (38 members) to form the group. Thus, we can state the intent of the far-right to create a powerful group to be able to draw the agenda, for to create a faction in the European Parliament at least 25 members of 7 member-states (that is, a quarter of the total number of EU member-states) are needed. Yet the project to create this faction fell utterly flat[63].

The victory of particular far-right parties in the 2014 election to the European Parliament was especially significant. For example, for the first time the French Front National won a stunning victory (25% and 24 seats) having outrun the Socialist Party. A resounding victory was scored by the UK Independence Party (29.7% and 4 seats). The Danish People's Party became the unconditional leader (over 23% of the vote and 4 seats). In Hungary the Jobbik won the second place with 14.7% and 3 seats in the European Parliament. In Greece, quite unexpectedly, the radical ultra-nationalist party the Golden Dawn finished third (over 9% of the vote and 3 seats). The Austrian Party for Freedom improved its stand, as compared with the result of 2009, wining the third place and polling 19.5% of the vote (that is, instead of two members the Party had 4 seats in the European parliament)[64]. It came as a big surprise that in Poland the radical euroskeptic party the New Right-wing polled 7% and 4 seats. In Germany the Alternative for Germany was a great success (7% of the vote and 7 seats). The Swedish Democrats Party also improved its results by 6% in comparison with those in 2009, polling 13% of the vote (2 seats in the European Parliament). The Estonian far-right party Pro Patria and Res Publica polled 20.3% of the vote (1 seat in the European Parliament). The Greater Romania won 3 seats. The rest far-right maintained their positions. The True Finns won 2 seats. The Dutch Party for Freedom preserved its 4 seats. The Italian League of the North polled 6% of the vote in the

---

[63] *Evroparlament*. Available at: http://ria.ru/cj_analytics/20140627/1013817404.html (*European Parliament*) (in the original: *Европейский парламент*).

[64] *Pervye itogi vyborov v Evroparlament demonstriruyut usilenie pozitsii radikalov I polulistov*. Available: http://itar-tass.com/mezhdunarodnaya-panorama/1215406 (*First results of Euro parliament elections demonstrate strong positions of radicals and populists*) (in the original: *Первые итоги выборов в Европарламент демонстрируют усиление позиций радикалов и популистов*).

election. Thus, if in 2009 the far-right parties won 56 seats, in 2014 there were 140 euro-skeptics holding office in the European Parliament[65].

The new landscape of political parties will influence the discussion of key issues of internal and external policies of the European Union, which can also transform its nature. In this case, the rightward turn means that the Europeans fear lest they should lose their national identity, and this poses lots of questions about the European Union as a representative of interests of its member-states.

Nevertheless, far-right parties find it easy to form a coalition but difficult to preserve it. This can be accounted for by several reasons. First of all, since these parties focus in their rhetoric on national interests, they cannot reach complete agreement about all matters. The far-right are euro-skeptic, but they cannot fathom what to offer the European nations instead of a European Union. Apart from that, these parties pursue a policy of economic national protectionism, which questions the existence of the common market in the framework of the European Union. And, to a great extent, voting for radicals in parliamentary elections is a kind of protest and does not reflect the actual support from the population.

Conclusion

The rise of the far-right, no matter how significant or minimal it might be, demands attention and clear understanding not only on the level of the state but also on the level of the European Union and regional security structures. The far-right raise a complex of questions, they become leaders in the forming of the agenda, while the growing trend towards xenophobia and aggressive nationalism causes additional tension. Political successes of the far-right and parties of the right-wing are patent. And this alignment of forces leads to a gradual consolidation of positions of the far-right parties that differ from other parties in their rhetoric about tough methods of countering contemporary threats and speak about the preservation of national identity. With national constitutional law frequently favouring public disintegration by encouraging nationalism in its constitutional form, the far-right do not look "alien" on the European political arena, which is the subject of the next chapter. So the burning question before us is how to detect from among the big number of far-right parties, movements and

[65] *Kraine pravye v Evroparlamente*. Available at: http://www.russian.rfi.fr/evropa/20140526-kraine-pravye-v-evroparlamente-ili-u-strakha-glaza-veliki (*Far-right in the European Parliament*) (in the original: *Крайне правые в Европарламенте*).

groups those that have already taken the path of ultra-nationalism, that is, who profess Nazism in its contemporary form.

CHAPTER IV

FAR-RIGHT POLITICAL PARTIES IN PUBLIC POLICY OF THE CONTEMPORARY EUROPEAN STATES: CONSTITUTIONAL DIMENSION

Public policy is, primarily, a set of principles of political and legal interaction between different institutions and groups of populations, based on the constitutional and political culture. The norms of political and legal interaction of various political actors are flexible and can undergo changes in a particular historical period of time, and the rule of law is superior to political norms. It is still more important when it is a question of discussion and decision-making in topical issues of the contemporary society, the process that involves numerous political and public actors, including far-right movements.

Far-right parties are capable of influencing the public policy and the public and political life in European states, since they propose most radical ways of solving problems on the basis of ultra-nationalism, which distinguishes them from other actors of the political process. Although researchers and experts frequently place these organizations outside the traditional party and political struggle, there are grounds for ideologists of right-wing radicalism to be successful in their political activities. For example, strange as it may seem, but the existing constitutional norms in different European states form a solid basis for growth and development of the ideology of right-wing radicalism and even ultra-nationalism – an inalienable component of Nazism. And these norms, which testify to the existence of the problem of constitutional nationalism in this or that state, have not been properly examined by experts. The aim of this Chapter is to determine the grounds for right-wing radicalism to influence public policy in the countries of Europe by examining the extent to which nationalism has been consolidated in constitutional texts.

4.1. Constitutional ways allowing right-wing radicalism and ultra-nationalism (Nazism) to penetrate into the political life

4.1.1. Nationalism, constitutional nationalism and Nazism: preliminary remarks

The analysis of constitutions of many European states has revealed certain problems of constitutional nationalism, which planted a time bomb in the state development of many European states and created favourable conditions for right-wing radicals and ultra-nationalists. But this problem has not received undivided attention in the academic science, though there are at least two reasons for studying this matter.

First, since constitutions differ in describing constitutional nationalism, there is a strong need for creating a catalogue of ways for nationalism to penetrate into the constitutional texts of different countries of contemporary Europe. Second, the constitutional grounds for the development of nationalism require elaborate examination since they were instrumental in forming ultra-nationalism, which is a constituent part of the contemporary right-wing radicalism, yet it remains an element of Nazism. This is the reason why this part of Chapter IV focuses on the analysis of the interconnection of notions of "constitutional nationalism" and "Nazism". With this aim in view, we must define the essence of constitutional nationalism and study by way of comparative analysis the problem of nationalism and national (ethnic) and racial discrimination in international law and the corresponding laws of separate states signatory to international instruments.

Constitutional nationalism in many ways is a peculiar bridge from civil nationalism to ethnic and aggressive nationalism since it grants special privileges to a certain ethno-national group. This means discrimination on the ground of national origin and testifies to the persisting threat of the growing influence of Fascist and Nazi parties (far-right political forces) in contemporary Europe, which proved most consistent in developing the ideas of nationalism. A number of points require special attention.

First, everything that relates to the notion of 'nationalism', 'ultra-nationalism' and even more so "Nazism' defies concretization and remains gibberish. For many scholars, it is easier to come up with a "new" nationalism than to classify this nationalism in accordance with the existing patterns. This derives from the fact that nationalism is inseparable from a certain mystique and faith that disguises nationalist aspirations; it is sufficient that the "initiated" understand it, while 'outsiders" are not supposed to. So when reading any work on nationalism, one needs to understand the context.

Second, "nationalism" in this Chapter features in its narrow sense – as a discriminative criterion, the criterion of unequal treatment. If the constitution awards privileges for one (or more) nationality irrespective of how this nationality is defined, then it is a matter of our concern.

Third, "discriminative (aggressive) nationalism" as such is the main marker of 'Nazism"; other markers are introduced to identify the threat of ultra-nationalism proper (Nazism) in a separate country. The study relies exclusively on constitutional acts of European countries.

Fourth, the majority of researchers agree that nationalism is, first and foremost, an ideology. So the reference in constitutional texts to "national state" together with a statement that "there is no state ideology" is regarded as a special marker.

The contemporary mishmash of notions of "nationality" and "national" hinders our struggle against ultra-nationalism and Nazism. The situation, strange as it may be, is further exacerbated by the fact that various international organizations use different languages (consequently, international documents are also written in different languages) and many terms defy adequate translations. Characteristic examples: the use of the English word "nationality" meaning "citizenship" or the phrase "national legislation" standing for "legislation of a particular country", also "national procedures" meaning "procedures stipulated by the legislation of a particular country".

To recognize the threat of ultra-nationalism and Nazis, we need to distinguish the "good" nationalism from the "bad", aggressive, nationalism. What is "good" nationalism, what is its practical use? It is quite possible that it is a special form of social capital; for example, an Estonian has a more perfect confidence in another Estonian than in an "alien" person. Common language and culture, common ideas of national spirituality are of secondary importance here. An Estonian has a better and deeper understanding of another Estonian compared with any other alien. The outcome is a considerable reduction in transactional expenses and increased effectiveness of social actions.

"Bad" nationalism stems, banal as it may sound, from discrimination, that is, from the violation of formal equality between nationalities and the resort to unequal treatment. Nobody denies the actual inequality – there are large and small nations, developed cultures and cultures that are in decline. The sustenance of formal equality is never-ending work since actual inequality is forever evolving.

Formal inequality between nationalities usually takes a form of superiority enshrined in legislation and it aims at the redistribution of both social benefits and risks. Can an “inferior” nationality willingly recognize the superiority of another one? Theoretically, it is possible, and there are examples to prove this: the Russian nobility, for one, found it easy to adopt the French language during the Napoleonic times. Many pages in Leo Tolstoy’s War and Peace are written in French. Yet such examples are scarce, and as often as not, people are up in arms the moment formal equality is at stake. Sometimes, in the literal sense.

In case the “inferior” refuses to recognize the superiority of the aggressive nationality and to accept formal inequality, the aggressive side has to resort to violence. In most cases, the aggressor tries to take legal coercive measures, hence the attempts to introduce the idea of superiority into positive law, first of all, into constitutions as acts taking precedence over all other laws (the use of “aggressor” is justified by the entry of “aggressive nationalism” in the UN dictionary). How it can be achieved is shown below. Meanwhile, we should note that ultra-nationalism, as a rule, is linked with violence.

4.1.2. The United Nations and constitutional nationalism

On 20 December 2014 the General Assembly of the United Nations adopted the 67/154 Resolution entitled “Glorification of Nazism: inadmissibility of certain practices that contribute to fuelling contemporary forms of racism, racial discrimination, xenophobia and related intolerance”. This Resolution contains Item 30 in which the General Assembly “recalls that any legislative or constitutional measures adopted with a view to countering extremist political parties, movements and groups, including neo-Nazis and skinhead groups, and similar extremist ideological movements should be in conformity with the relevant international human rights norms”[1].

It is for the first time that the General Assembly pays attention to the issues of constitutional regulation, which had always been regarded as “sovereign”, and uses the imperative meaning of the modal verb “must”. The difficulty here lies in the traditional hierarchy of legal acts according

[1] *67/154 Resolution of the General Assembly of the United Nations “Glorification of Nazism: inadmissibility of certain practices that contribute to fuelling contemporary forms of racism, racial discrimination, xenophobia and related intolerance”*. Available at:
http://www.un.org/en/ga/search/view_doc.asp?symbol=A/RES/67/154.

to which constitutions always have had precedence and in the fact that international instruments shall not contradict them.

"Sovereignty" was questioned for the first time in the Document of the Moscow Meeting of the Conference on Human Dimension of the CSCE (signed in Moscow on 3 October 1991), which says the following: "The Participating States emphasize that issues relating to human rights, fundamental freedoms, democracy and the rule of law are of international concern, as respect for these rights and freedoms constitutes one of the foundations of the international order. They categorically and irrevocably declare that the commitments undertaken in the field of the human dimension of the CSCE are matters of direct and legitimate concern to all participating States and do not belong exclusively to the internal affairs of the State concerned"[2].

Thus, the States are obliged to watch over the enforcement of human rights and not allow any manifestation of hate on the national grounds; they must protect the society against the escalation of conflicts, aggressive nationalism and the development of the Fascist ideology. Nevertheless, ultra-nationalism has already long existed in constitutions of many European countries. Let us consider the examples of how ultra-nationalism may penetrate into constitutions.

4.1.3. Nationalism and constitutional regulation

The analysis of constitutions allowed us to single out several forms that ultra-nationalism takes to penetrate into them.

Form 1. Substitution of notions: from the right of people to self-determination to "the right of nations and nationalities".

Article 1.2 in Chapter I of the UN Charter clearly distinguishes peoples and nations: "To develop friendly relations among nations based on respect for the principle of equal rights and self-determination of peoples, and to take other appropriate measures to strengthen universal peace"[3]. The above-mentioned problem of translation, however, arises in the Russian language[4], but the English version states that it is *peoples* who have the right to self-determination. Thus, it speaks of "peoples", which is

---

[2] *Document of the Moscow Meeting of the Conference on Human Dimension of the CSCE*. Available at: http://www.osce.org/odihr/elections/14310?download=true

[3] *Charter of the United Nations*. Available at: http://www.un.org/en/documents/charter/

[4] *UN Charter*. Available at: http://www.un.org/ru/documents/charter/chapter1.shtml

the plural of *people*, and not of *nationalities*, which, as it is, is even father from nationalism and the "right of nations to self-determination".

Indeed, the analysis of the corresponding UN documents allows us to draw a conclusion that the subject of law enjoying the right to self-determination is "people inhabiting the territory", that is, people of all nationalities. Nevertheless, constitutions of many states frequently say that the right to self-determination has been exercised by this or that nationality. To illustrate this we shall provide some excerpts from several constitutions.

For example, the Preamble to the Constitution of Slovakia says, "We, the Slovak nation..., recognizing the natural right of nations to self-determination, together with members of national minorities and ethnic groups living on the territory of the Slovak Republic...[5]"

It is interesting that the more questionable the right to "national self-determination" is, the more "flowery" it is. For example, the Constitution of Croatia in the chapter "Historical Foundations" specifies, "Setting forth from these historical facts and the universally accepted principles governing the contemporary world and the inalienable and indivisible, non-transferable and perpetual right of the Croatian nation to self-determination and state sovereignty, including the inviolable right to secession and association as the fundamental conditions for peace and stability of the international order, the Republic of Croatia is hereby established as the nation state of the Croatian nation and the state of the members of its national minorities: Serbs, Czechs, Slovaks, Italians, Hungarians, Jews, Germans, Austrians, Ukrainians, Rusyns, Bosniaks, Slovenians, Montenegrins, Macedonians, Russians, Bulgarians, Poles, Roma, Romanians, Turks, Vlachs, Albanians and others who are its citizens and who are guaranteed equality with citizens of Croatian nationality and the exercise of their national rights in compliance with the democratic norms of the United Nations and the countries of the free world[6]". As is evident from the adduced excerpt, "the people" is understood as a "nationality".

The draft of the Preamble to the Constitution of Latvia says, "The State of Latvia, proclaimed on 18 November 1918, has been established by uniting historical Latvian lands and on the basis of the unwavering will of the Latvian nation to have its own State and its inalienable right of self-determination in order to guarantee the existence and development of the Latvian nation, its language and culture throughout the centuries, to ensure

---

[5] *Constitution of Slovakia*. Available at: http://www.slovak-republic.org/constitution/

[6] *Constitution of Croatia*. Available at: http://www.sabor.hr/Default.aspx?art=2406

freedom and promote welfare of the people of Latvia and each individual"[7].

Quite often the text is deliberately indistinct with obscured phrases like "the right of a nationality to self-determination". Such is, for example, the preamble to the Constitution of Ukraine: "…based on the centuries-old history of Ukrainian state-building and on the right of self-determination realized by the Ukrainian nation, all the Ukrainian people …." The use of comma separated "nation" and "people" must not delude anyone – Article 11 clearly shows that "the Ukrainian nation" means the Ukrainian nationality: "The State promotes the consolidation and development of the Ukrainian nation, of its historical consciousness, traditions and culture, and also the development of the ethnic, cultural, linguistic and religious identity of all indigenous peoples and national minorities of Ukraine"[8].

Form 2. The establishment of the "national state" in constitutions

"National state" has two meanings – the "positive" and the "negative". The "positive": a nation-state (political nation) is a constitutional and legal type of state meaning that the state represents a form of statehood and a form of government that a certain nation chooses within a certain sovereign territory while expressing the will of this nation. The "negative": a state in which a certain nationality is legally dominating. Such is the Estonian term "rahvusriik", where "rahvus" means exclusively "nationality". Yet the Estonian Constitution does not contain this notion though the Constitutional Assembly did debate this issue. The debate boiled down to the understanding that it is the Estonians that have the priority right (!), with human rights in tow (!). This wording gives us another important key to understanding "negative" nationalism: the rights of a particular nationality have a priority over human rights. Hence, the development of ultra-nationalism is a direct threat to human rights, and, more broadly, to humanism. By the way, the Estonian Constitution does not contain such phrases as "a human being" or "human rights"[9]. Yet another example of such a threat is found in Part 1 Article 1 of the 1991

---

[7] Seredenko, S. *Analiz preambuly Latviiskoy konstitutsii*. Available at: http://www.baltexpert.com/2013/12/05/sseredenko_analiz_preambula/ (Seredenko, S. *Analysis of the Preamble to the Constitution of Latvia*). (in the original: Середенко, С. *Анализ преамбулы Латвийской конституции*).

[8] *Constitution of Ukraine*. Available at: http://www.legislationline.org/documents/section/constitutions/country/52

[9] *Constitution of Estonia*. Available at: http://www.president.ee/en/republic-of-estonia/the-constitution/

Constitution of Romania, "Romania is a sovereign, independent, unitary and indivisible National State"[10].

The Preamble to the Constitution of Latvia ventured to define a national state in a very peculiar way. It suggested that the Latvians should be declared the "sovereign nation"[11].

But one should not think that internationalism, and to be more accurate, humanism is irrevocably ceding ground. The Constitution of Azerbaijan provides an alternative example; Article 5 says, "The Azerbaijan people shall be united. The Azerbaijan people's unity shall set up the foundation of the Azerbaijan state. The Azerbaijan Republic shall be wholly and indivisibly Homeland for all the citizens of the Azerbaijan Republic". Article 6 specifies: "No part of the Azerbaijan people, either an individual, or a social group or an organization shall have the right to usurp the authority of the Azerbaijan people to exercise the power. Power usurpation shall be the most serious crime directed against the people"[12]. Here we should mention that constitutions rarely contain references to crimes. It is all the more valuable that power usurpation by a (any) nationality is deemed, according to the Constitution of Azerbaijan, a crime, and the most serious at that, so all attempts to incorporate nationalism as an ideology in constitutional texts should be considered with this point in view. Here it is appropriate to compare excerpts from the Constitution of Azerbaijan with the Preamble to the National Constitution of Ukraine proposed by a Nazi party Svoboda, "Capital punishment shall be instituted for crimes against the Ukrainian nation, the Ukrainian state"[13].

The problem of the abusive practice of interpreting the term "national state" by politicians urged UNESCO to respond at its official site with an exhaustive explanation. Thus, from the viewpoint of this international organization, "the nation-state is one where the great majority are

---

[10] *Constitution of Romania*. Available at: http://www.cdep.ro/pls/dic/site.page?den=act2_2&par1=1

[11] Seredenko, S. *Analiz preambuly Latviiskoy konstitutsii*. Available at: http://www.baltexpert.com/2013/12/05/sseredenko_analiz_preambula/

[12] *Constitution of Azerbaijan*. Available at: http://confinder.richmond.edu/admin/docs/local_azerbaijan.pdf

[13] *Proekt Natsional'noy konstitutsii Ukrainy, prinyatoy s'ezdom nazistskoy partii "Svoboda"*. Available at: http://www.svoboda.org.ua/pro_partiyu/prohrama/konstytutsiya/. (*Draft of the National Constitution of Ukraine proposed by the Congress of the Nazi party Svoboda*). (*Проект Национальной конституции Украины, принятой съездом нацистской партии «Свобода»*).

conscious of a common identity and share the same culture". It is the state "where the cultural boundaries match up with the political boundaries". Acknowledging the sheer magnitude of this term, UNESCO notes that in the contemporary world such states have practically ceased to exist, so it has become rather a hypothetical ideal than an actual phenomenon[14].

Form 3. Declaration of one's own nationality to be the supreme value

In some European constitutions, the nationality (in fact, ethnos) is becoming the most important value for the state. For example, instead of "state nationality" the Estonians chose a different path and declared themselve the supreme value. The Preamble to the Constitution of Estonia words it like this: the people of Estonia "with unwavering faith and a steadfast will to strengthen and develop the state (…) which shall guarantee the preservation of the Estonian nation and culture through the ages…" In 2007, the Estonian language was added to this list[15].

Drawing upon this idea, Egils Levits, the principal author of the draft of the Preamble to the Lettish Constitution (it is difficult to call it Latvian) came up with an ingenious wording, "With a view of ensuring the existence of the Latvian nation for centuries to come, the preservation and development of the Latvian language…."

Article 16 of the Ukrainian Constitution contains an interesting attempt: "… to preserve the gene pool of the Ukrainian people, is the duty of the State"[16]. What this gene pool can possibly mean when describing the Ukrainian People (capital letter) remains obscure.

Form 4. "Brothers of one blood"

A special type of ultra-nationalism finding its way into constitutions is the concern about consanguineous expatriates. This concern, external decorum aside, is nothing but redistribution of common state resources in favour of one, ususally titular, nationality, that is, it is a patent example of unequal treatment. Examples are plentiful.

Article 108 of the Constitution of Greece: "The State must take care for emigrant Greeks and for the maintenance of their ties with the

---

[14] *Nation-State*. Available at: http://www.unesco.org/new/en/social-and-human-sciences/themes/international-migration/glossary/nation-state/

[15] *Constitution of Estonia*. Available at: http://www.president.ee/en/republic-of-estonia/the-constitution/

[16] *Constitution of Ukraine*. Available at: http://en.wikisource.org/wiki/Constitution_of_Ukraine

Fatherland. The State shall also attend to the education, the social and professional advancement of Greeks working outside the State"[17].

Article 12 of the Constitution of Ukraine: "Ukraine provides for the satisfaction of national and cultural, and linguistic needs of Ukrainians residing beyond the borders of the State"[18].

Article D of the Constitution of Hungary: "Bearing in mind that there is one single Hungarian nation that belongs together, Hungary shall bear responsibility for the fate of Hungarians living beyond its borders, shall facilitate the survival and development of their communities, shall support their efforts to preserve their Hungarian identity, the effective use of their individual and collective rights, the establishment of their community self-governments, and their prosperity in their native lands, and shall promote their cooperation with each other and with Hungary"[19].

The same goes for the Constitution of Albania, Article 8 (1) of which says: "The Republic of Albania protects the national rights of the Albanian people who live outside its borders"[20].

Form 5. The presence of special national rights

Special national rights are a rare occurrence, but each time they do occur their discriminational character is clamant. Thus, for example, Article 122 of the Constitution of Portugal describing the requirement for candidates for presidency says, "Citizens of Portuguese origin who are registered to vote and have attained the age of thirty-five shall be eligible for election"[21].

Or Part 3 of Article 36 of the Constitution of Estonia: "Every Estonian has the right to settle in Estonia"[22]. Considering that at the time of the adoption of the Constitution the notion of "Estonian citizen" was practically equal to "an Estonian", the actual list of these rights is much longer. Some of these special rights were discussed at the Assembly of the

---

[17] *Constitution of Greece*. Available at: http://www.hri.org/docs/syntagma/artcl120.html

[18] *Constitution of Ukraine*. Available at: http://en.wikisource.org/wiki/Constitution_of_Ukraine,_2010

[19] *Constitution of Hungary*. Available at: http://www.kormany.hu/download/e/02/00000/The%20New%20Fundamental%20Law%20of%20Hungary.pdf

[20] *Constitution of Albania*. Available at: http://www.osce.org/albania/41888?download=true

[21] *Constitution of Portugal*. Available at: http://www.wipo.int/wipolex/en/text.jsp?file_id=179405

[22] *Constitution of Estonia*. Available at: http://www.president.ee/en/republic-of-estonia/the-constitution/

Constitution though they never got incorporated into the Constitution. Here is, for example, an account of the discussion of the institute of president by the working group responsible for drafting the Preamble: "They discuss whether the head of state (state elder) must be Estonian by origin. They cannot determine whether both his parents must be Estonians, etc. They decide to end the discussion here. On Runnel's suggestion, Salum, chairman of the group, promises to table at the Assembly meeting that issue and also the issue of the height of this state elder: 1.75 m for men, 1.62 m for women"[23].

Form 6. Breach of the privilege of determining nationality (ethnicity)

Here it is important to examine how the right to nationality self-determination is treated in different constitutions. For example, Article 49 of the Constitution of Estonia reads that "Everyone has the right to preserve his or her national identity"[24]. The "right to preserve" always looks "crooked"; it should have been worded as "a privilege of a person to determine his or her nationality (ethnicity)". Here we do not set a task of establishing any reasonable borders of such self-determination and we rely on the common sense of the reader (an obvious breach of borders of such self-determination occurred, for example, when people defined themselve as elves or goblins, as was the case during the census in Russia).

Yet, the subsitutions to be considered below do provide a good illustration of the difference between a "nation-state" and a "national state". They are manifested in different ways: Estonians, for example, threaten to make Russians "Estonians of Russian origin".

One of the examples of this type is the "equating" of citizens of a country to persons of the titular nationality. Here is a good example from the Constitution of Greece. Article 4: "1. All Greeks are equal before the law. 2. Greek men and women have equal rights and equal obligations. 3. All persons possessing the qualifications for citizenship as specified by law are Greek citizens. Withdrawal of Greek citizenship shall be permitted only in case of voluntary acquisition of another citizenship or of undertaking service contrary to national interests in a foreign country, under the conditions and procedures more specifically provided by law. 4. Only Greek citizens shall be eligible for public service, except as otherwise provided by special laws. 5. Greek citizens contribute without distinction to public charges in proportion to their means. 6. Every Greek

---

[23] Riigiarhiiv. *State Archives of Estonia, Repository No. R2324*, name No. 1, shelving unit 14, p. 10.

[24] *Constitution of Estonia*. Available at: http://www.president.ee/en/republic-of-estonia/the-constitution/

capable of bearing arms is obliged to contribute to the defence of the Fatherland as provided by law"[25]. This example shows that "Greek citizens", irrespective of their ethnic origin (and, respectively, national self-determination), are persistently treated as "Greeks".

Another pervasive example is a play with nouns and adjectives denoting a country and a nationality. For instance, in the Estonian language this borders on absurdity since "Eesti" means both Estonia (capital letter) and Estonian (lower case letter in Estonian), so each time an Estonian says "Eesti" it is sheer guesswork and one never can be sure whether he meant "the people of Estonia" or "the Estonian people". Same occurs in the Preamble to the Constitution of Bulgaria: "We, the National Representatives of the Seventh Grand National Assembly, aspiring to express the will of the Bulgarian people, … aware of our irrevocable duty to safeguard the national and state unity of Bulgaria …"[26].

Form 7. Corruption of national sovereignty is a threat to democracy

The United Nations and the Organization for Security and Cooperation in Europe urge the states to uphold and foster democracy, but it is ultra-nationalism that directly threatens people's sovereignty, hence, democracy.

Sovereignty, as is well-known, has two dimensions: the "external" (state sovereignty) and the "internal", most frequently assuming the form of "people's sovereignty" (popular sovereignty). The classical definition of popular sovereignty has not been formulated yet, but attempts have been made a dozen of times – "power comes from the people", "power is vested in the people", the people are the power holders" and so forth. In all these formulations the people are a single and indivisible subject.

Nationalistic formulations break people's sovereignty into two parts – the dominant nationality and "all the rest", "members of national minorities". As a result, we have a queer (dual?) power that undermines the very notion of "internal sovereignty". It is clear that without an elaborately delineated "partition of sovereignty", the power in such diarchy belongs to the ruling and, as a rule, aggressive nationality.

The Preamble to the Constitution of Slovenia declares the will of "the Slovene nation" and "Slovenes"[27]. Attempts have been made to introduce

---

[25] *Constitution of Greece.* Available at: http://www.hri.org/docs/syntagma/artcl25.html#A4

[26] *Constitution of Bulgaria.* Available at: http://www.vks.bg/english/vksen_p04_01.htm

[27] *Constitution of the Republic of Slovenia.* Available at: http://www.wipo.int/wipolex/en/text.jsp?file_id=180804

the notion of "national sovereignty"; for example, Article 2 of the Constitution of Romania runs, "Sovereignty. (1) The National sovereignty shall reside within the Romanian people."[28]

In this context we need to question the term "ethnic democracy" used by some researchers in respect of, in particular, the Baltic regimes. The adduced examples show that "ethnos" and "demos" do not go together well: "ethnos" either declares itself "demos" or reduces it to the category of "all the rest". Of course, with all the due respect. As has already been shown, without the formal partition of power between "ethnos" and "demos", the dual power in question is fictitious. Strange as it may seem, there are, however, examples of "contractual", "delimiting" constitutions characterized by the juxtaposition of one aggressive "ethnos" with the other, less aggressive.

Form 8. International agreements – peace treaties

The protracted armed international conflict between Turkish Cypriots and Greek Cypriots in the confined space of the island of Cyprus resulted in a totally exotic peace treaty – the Constitution of the Republic of Cyprus. Its first three Articles seem to summarize the above-listed ways for nationalism to get into constitutional texts:

"Article 1. The State of Cyprus is an independent and sovereign Republic with a presidential regime, the President being Greek and the Vice-President being Turk elected by the Greek and the Turkish Communities of Cyprus respectively as hereinafter in this Constitution provided.

Article 2. For the purposes of this Constitution:

1. The Greek Community comprises all citizens of the Republic who are of Greek origin and whose mother tongue is Greek or who share the Greek cultural traditions or who are members of the Greek-Orthodox Church;
2. The Turkish Community comprises all citizens of the Republic who are of Turkish origin and whose mother tongue is Turkish or who share the Turkish cultural traditions or who are Moslems;
3. Citizens of the Republic who do not come within the provisions of paragraph (1) or (2) of this Article shall, within three months of the date of the coming into operation of this Constitution, opt to belong to either the Greek or the Turkish Community as individuals, but, if

[28] *Constitution of Romania*. Available at: http://www.cdep.ro/pls/dic/site.page?den=act2_2&par1=1#t1c0s0a2

> they belong to a religious group, shall so opt as a religious group and upon such option they shall be deemed to be members of such Community...[29]".

A (bi-)national state, as we may see, holds the "rest" in low esteem, in the same way as, for example, does an "ordinary" national state in the Baltic understanding. But the constitutional division into two communities makes these communities not only the key political subjects and legal authorities but also destroys the civil society as such. So how and about what parties, about what ideological pluralism can one speak as long as there are communities? One can form any party in the Turkish community, but the president will be a Greek all the same. The Constitution of Cyprus clearly demonstrates that nationalism is an ideology.

An analogous "peace treaty" now between three nationalities was concluded by the adoption of the Constitution of Bosnia and Herzegovina: "... Bosniacs, Croats, and Serbs, as constituent peoples (along with Others), and citizens of Bosnia and Herzegovina hereby determine that the Constitution of Bosnia and Herzegovina ...". As is evident, here it is the same attitude to "others", the same actual juxtaposition of the three nationalities and the civil society – "citizens of Bosnia and Herzegovina"[30].

Form 9. The official language

In the contemporary world almost all constitutions make provision for the official language; they use three terms – the state language, the official language and even the national language (for example, in Malta[31]). Such countries as Bosnia and Herzegovina, Sweden, Greece, Denmark, Iceland, Italy, the Netherlands and San Marino do without any reference to any language as the official one.

The state language in the domestic context differs from the official language only by its supplementary symbolic meaning, which is indirectly substantiated by the provisions establishing the state language always being bracketed with the provisions specifying the state symbols (in

---

[29] *Constitution of the Republic of Cyprus*. Available at: http://www.presidency.gov.cy/presidency/presidency.nsf/all/1003AEDD83EED9C7C225756F0023C6AD/$file/CY_Constitution.pdf

[30] *Constitution of Bosnia and Herzegovina*. Available at: http://www.ccbh.ba/public/down/USTAV_BOSNE_I_HERCEGOVINE_engl.pdf

[31] *Constitution of Malta*. Available at: http://justiceservices.gov.mt/DownloadDocument.aspx?app=lom&itemid=8566

Estonia, by the way, the state flag is also the national flag, according to the law).

The establishment of the language of one, usually titular, nationality as the language of clerical correspondence and court proceedings is sheer discrimination, partly justified by the fact that officials cannot master all the languages, especially in regions of "ethnic cauldrons". Problems with the state language begin when it starts breaking out of the boundaries of the state apparatus to the private sphere, including the sphere of entrepreneurship. For instance, the Baltic States use their languages as a bludgeon against national minorities establishing special controlling – in fact, punitive – bodies.

The topic of the state language as a marker of the penetration of nationalistic ideology into constitutional texts should have been considered earlier, but the temptation was very strong to draw a parallel with the preceding point and to show that, apart from multinational constitutions – "peace treaties", multi-language analogues are also possible. Such is, for one, the Constitution of Belgium. "Article 2. Belgium comprises three Communities: the Flemish Community, the French Community and the German-speaking Community. Article 3. Belgium comprises three Regions: the Flemish Region, the Walloon Region and the Brussels Region. Article 4. Belgium comprises four linguistic regions: the Dutch-speaking region, the French- speaking region, the bilingual region of Brussels-Capital and the German-speaking region. Each municipality of the Kingdom forms part of one of these linguistic regions. The boundaries of the four linguistic regions can only be changed or corrected by a law passed by a majority of the votes cast in each linguistic group in each House, on condition that a majority of the members of each group is present and provided that the total number of votes in favour that are cast in the two linguistic groups is equal to at least two thirds of the votes cast"[32].

Not everyone is aware of the discriminating effect produced by elevating the language of titular nationality to the status of the state language; it was even more surprising to find in the textbook on the theory of state and law edited by Prof. M.N. Marchenko and published in 1998 the following, "The notion of the "state language" has got established in the political and legal consciousness. It is the language of international agreements and conventions. Some sovereign countries regard the knowledge of the "state language' as a prerequisite to naturalization. That

[32] *Constitution of Belgium*. Available at: www.legislationline.org/documents/id/9045

the law on citizenship establishes political, social and economic restrictions for those who do not have a command of the language is sheer discrimination violating Article 2 of the Universal Declaration of Human Rights which says, "Everyone is entitled to all the rights and freedoms set forth in this Declaration, without distinction of any kind, such as race, colour, sex, language, religion, political or other opinion, national or social origin, property, birth or other status. Furthermore, no distinction shall be made on the basis of the political, jurisdictional or international status of the country or territory to which a person belongs, whether it be independent, trust, non-self-governing or under any other limitation of sovereignty"[33].

It is evident that the main reason for the adoption of laws on languages in the independent states that had emerged in the territory of the former Soviet Union is related to the idea of national revival. The adepts of the "state language" proceed from the fact that language is the most important condition for the survival and preservation of a nation; that for the sake of a national identity and the future of the autochthonous nation members of other nations can be "mistreated". It is appropriate to remember that the Soviet Union did not have a state language at all.

Draft Constitutions

Drafts of Constitutions also deserve close scrutiny, first of all, because they are, as a rule, not burdened with the compromises that invariably follow from their public discussions. The draft of the Ukrainian Constitution, approved by the Council of the All-Ukrainian Union Svoboda in 2007, has been already mentioned; but this draft is blatantly Nazi and it should be considered in the next part of the Chapter.

4.2. Markers of Nazism

The term "Nazism" causes as many problems as that of nationalism, if not more. In this case "Nazism" will be considered not as a discrimination criterion and not as an ideology, which it undoubtedly is, but as a socially dangerous phenomenon, criminal in its essence, described by Roger Griffin as a "populist palingenetic ultra-nationalism"[34]. And the

---

[33] *Teoriya gosudarstva I prava*. 1998, ed. by Marchenko M.N., Moskva, p.448. (*Theory of State and Law*. 1998, ed. by Marchenko M.N., Moscow, p.448). (in the original: *Теория государства и права*. 1998, под ред. проф. М.Н.Марченко. М. с.448).

[34] Griffin, R. 1991. *The Nature of Fascism*, London.

phenomena of Nazism and Fascism will be equated, though, of course, it does not mean that they are identical in every aspect.

"Fascism", and even more so "Nazism", is a rare occurrence in constitutions expressis verbis. Yet, it is found in the constitutions of Poland, Italy, Portugal, Croatia and San Marino.

The problem of defining "Nazism" is further complicated by the fact that, contrary to "nationalism", the formulation of such a definition is a very demanding task, for few are the states that will keep quiet after being branded as a Nazi. Irrespective of the fact if they are Nazi or not. (The Baltic States, for example, commonly make use of exclusion for those scientists whom they do not like). But the problem of early diagnostics of the Nazi threat is an entirely practical matter, since Nazism that has risen to power cannot be cured by democratic methods. The palingenesis criterion allows for a conclusion that Nazi states are not successors to the pre-Nazi regimes, that a Nazi state is a totally different state.

We should note that Nazism proper has no need for constitutions, for under Nazism instead of "supremacy of law" and "supremacy of the constitution" there is the dictatorship of the leader and the ruling (sole) Nazi party.

Below we shall consider the markers of Nazism in constitutions.

4.2.1. "Palingenesis" and the "Golden Age"

In a simplified form, "palingenesis" as applied to Nazism can be understood as a renaissance of the "golden age" of a nation in return for its recent historical, actual or putative, humiliation. At the mythic level, "renaissance" must be understood literally as the resurgence from the dead (national humiliation). The Third Reich had "revived" itself in the Holy Roman Empire of the German nation. Accordingly, at the constitutional level, palingenesis is a return to history with a detailed discriotion of the "golden age" and the state that is to be "revived".

We shall confirm this idea by an innocent example from Article 4 of the Constitution of Abkhazia, "The Republic of Abkhazia consists of the historical provinces of Sadz, Bzyp, Guma, Dal-Tsabal, Abzhywa, Samyrzakan...[35]". What was the word "historical" to emphasize in this case? In the context of the conflict with Georgia, as it seems, it was to emphasize the special right of the Abkazian to these lands.

In the same innocent vein the Constitution of Lithuania speaks in its Preamble of the Lithuanian nation (not the people of Lithuania!) that

---

[35] *Constitution of Abkhazia*. Available at: http://apsnypress.info/en/constitution

"created the State of Lithuania many centuries ago" and based its legal foundations on the Lithuanian Statutes and the Constitutions of the Republic of Lithuania"[36].

Much more aggressive looks the Preamble to the Constitution of Macedonia: "Proceeding from the historical, cultural, spiritual and statehood heritage of the Macedonian people and their centuries-long struggle for national and social liberty and the creation of their own state, and particularly from the statehood and legal traditions of the Kruševo Republic and the historic decisions of the Anti-Fascist Assembly of the People's Liberation of Macedonia, from the constitutional and legal continuity of the Macedonian state as a sovereign republic within Federal Yugoslavia, from the freely expressed will of the citizens of the Republic of Macedonia in the referendum of September 8th, 1991, as well as from the historical fact that Macedonia is established as a national state of the Macedonian people, in which full equality as citizens and permanent coexistence with the Macedonian people is provided for Albanians, Turks, Vlachs, Roma and other nationalities living in the Republic of Macedonia…[37]"

The indicated markers ("the statehood and legal traditions of the Kruševo Republic", "the historic decisions of the Anti-Fascist Assembly of the People's Liberation of Macedonia", "the historical fact that Macedonia is established as a national state of the Macedonian people") are meant not only to signify the fact of Macedonia's secession from the Yugoslav Federation, but also to determine the format of Macedonia's statehood, different from "the right of nations to self-determination". In this case, these "peculiarities" consolidate the priority of the Macedonian nationality and "historically" substantiate it.

The "Slovak nation" in this sense is "clean"; it proceeds from the "natural right of nations to self-determination, together with members of national minorities and ethnic groups living in the Slovak Republic", only mindful of "the spiritual bequest of Cyril and Methodius, and the historical legacy of Great Moravia"[38]. In this case, the Preamble to the Constitution of Slovakia unequivocally points to the "golden age" – "Great Moravia".

---

[36] *Constitution of the republic of Lithuania*. Available at: http://www3.lrs.lt/home/Konstitucija/Constitution.htm

[37] *Constitution of the Republic of Macedonia*. Available at: http://eudo-citizenship.eu/NationalDB/docs/MAC%20Constitution%20%28amended%20by%20XXX%29%20eng.pdf

[38] *Constitution of the Slovak Republic*. Available at: http://www.slovak-republic.org/constitution/

An extreme example of this genre is not a preamble but the whole Chapter "Historical Foundations" preceding the Constitution of Croatia[39].

4.2.2. A new reading of palingenesis – continuity

Palingenesis got a new reading with the "reconstruction of independence" of the Baltic States, which made it clear that they were not successors to the Lithuanian Socialist Republic, Latvian Socialist Republic and Estonian Socialist Republic but to Lithuanian, Latvian and Estonia Republics, respectively, existing till the summer of 1940. How it correlates with the theory of law, and if it corresponds to it at all, is a separate matter, but in the case of the Baltic States it led to a new understanding of palingenesis. From the point of view of "legal continuity" and the theory of "occupation", the "golden age" was the time before 1940, while being part of the Soviet Union ("occupation") was a period of national humiliation. Yet the pre-war republics never "died" (see the "rising from death") but stayed in a political lethargic slumber, they existed de jure. The legal consequences of putting into effect these theories proved different for all the three Baltic States; Latvia, for one, "resurrected", as a visible symbol of continuity, the 1922 Constitution under which it was absolutely impossible to get by at the end of the 20th century, so its importance as a legal act is negligible. Actually, the role of the Constitution in Latvia is played by the Constitutional Court.

It is characteristic that neither the Constitution of Estonia nor that of Latvia specifies the concepts of "occupation" and "legal continuity", but the idea of this peculiar "continuity" had been sought after and it is embodied in the Draft of the National Constitution of Ukraine, while the active Constitution of Ukraine runs, "We, citizens of Ukraine, aware that the Ukrainian nation is a successor to the rich spiritual and material culture of Tripillians, Scythians and hundreds of succeeding generations of Ukrainians, that the present Ukrainian State stands in direct continuity with the Kievan Rus, the Principality of Galicia-Volhynia, the Cossack Hetmanate, Ukrainina People's Republic, Carpathian Ukraine and the Ukrainian Power restored by Act of 30 June 1941, that Independent Ukraine emerged as a result of over 300 years' struggle for national liberation"[40].

---

[39] *Constitution of the Republic of Croatia*. Available at: http://www.constitution.org/cons/croatia.htm

[40] *Proekt Natsional'noy konstitutsii Ukrainy, prinyatoy s'ezdom nazistskoy partii "Svoboda"*. Available at:

The draft of the Preamble to the Constitution of Latvia formulates the same ideas in the following way, "Aware that the nation had recovered its state in the struggle for freedom, that it never acknowledged the occupational authorities, resisted them and regained its freedom by restoring the state independence by virtue of statehood continuity"[41].

4.2.3. National humiliation, tragedy

It is clear that from the viewpoint of Nazism the "golden age" can end in nothing but a tragedy, since it is to be interrupted by an outside force. Otherwise, the nation itself will have to bear responsibility for the termination of the "golden age", and no nation welcomes it. Estonian President Toomas Hendrk Ilves came up with the best irresponsibility formula, "We are not to blame for being free!" The less gold in the "golden age", the more shattering the tragedy will be. Lamenting over past misfortunes ("occupation", "genocide", accident at the atomic power station, etc.) takes form of "how wonderful our life would be but for…".

Accordingly, national grievances are catalogued in the constitutional texts as tragedies – real and putative. It is noteworthy that the records of any "grievances" in the latest constitutional texts of post-Soviet countries should be deemed as a very alarming signal, since not one of the first post-Soviet constitutions ever referred to "occupation" and suchlike acts, let alone the USSR. On the constitutional level, the super power had vanished into thin air.

Contrary to the USSR, the Socialist Federal Republic of Yugoslavia (SFRY) is mentioned, for example, in the Constitution of Slovenia in the following context: "considering that the SFRY does not function as a legal state…"[42].

The draft of the National Constitution of Ukraine proposed by Party Svoboda represents the tragedy in absolute terms: "We are aware that the Ukrainian Nation had been under the 300-year-old yoke of colonialism;

---

http://www.svoboda.org.ua/pro_partiyu/prohrama/konstytutsiya/. (*Draft of the National Constitution of Ukraine proposed by the Congress of the Nazi party Svoboda*). (*Проект Национальной конституции Украины, принятой съездом нацистской партии «Свобода»*).

41 Seredenko, S. *Analiz preambuly Latviiskoy konstitutsii.* Available at: http://www.baltexpert.com/2013/12/05/sseredenko_analiz_preambula/.
(Seredenko, S. *Analysis of the Preamble to the Constitution of Latvia*). (in the original: Середенко, С. *Анализ преамбулы Латвийской конституции*).

42 *Constitution of Slovenia*. Available at:
http://www.wipo.int/wipolex/en/text.jsp?file_id=180804

that it had passed through the genocide during the Golodomor, the famine that brought about drastic demographic losses; that throughout hundreds of years its language and culture were being demolished, that it was subjected to cruel communist repressions”[43].

It is impossible to imagine what this “golden age” was like if such an overwhelming catastrophe was required to put an end to it!

4.2.4. Lebensraum – territorial claims

Territorial claims, irrespective of how well they are substantiated, can be either explicit or implicit in the constitutions. For example, the wording of Article 122 of the Constitution of Estonia, “The land boundary of Estonia is determined by the Tartu Peace Treaty of 2 February 1920”[44], is a disguised claim for Pechora Region of Pskov Oblast and Zanarovje Region in Leningrad Oblast.

The notorious “territorial integrity” of Georgia is embodied in the Constitution in three stages: “Article 1. 1. Georgia shall be an independent, unified and indivisible state, as confirmed by the Referendum of 31 March 1991, held throughout the territory of the country, including the Autonomous Soviet Socialist Republic of Abkhazia and the Former Autonomous Region of South Ossetia and by the Act of Restoration of the State Independence of Georgia of 9 April 1991(…). Article 2. 1. The territory of the state of Georgia shall be determined as of 21 December 1991. The territorial integrity of Georgia and the inviolability of the state frontiers, being recognised by the world community of nations and international organizations (…). 3. The territorial state structure of Georgia shall be determined by a Constitutional Law on the basis of the principle of circumscription of authorisation after the complete restoration of the jurisdiction of Georgia over the whole territory of the country”[45].

In the same way, in three stages, Ireland formulates and lists its territorial claims. At first, the Preamble speaks about the urge to “restore

---

[43] *Proekt Natsional'noy konstitutsii Ukrainy, prinyatoy s'ezdom nazistskoy partii “Svoboda”*. Available at: http://www.svoboda.org.ua/pro_partiyu/prohrama/konstytutsiya/ (*Draft of the National Constitution of Ukraine proposed by the Congress of the Nazi party Svoboda*). (*Проект Национальной конституции Украины, принятой съездом нацистской партии «Свобода»*).

[44] *Constitution of Estonia*. Available at: http://www.president.ee/en/republic-of-estonia/the-constitution/

[45] *Constitution of Georgia*. Available at: http://www.wipo.int/wipolex/en/text.jsp?file_id=194552

the unity of our country". Then Article 2 states that "It is the entitlement and birthright of every person born in the island of Ireland, which includes its islands and seas, to be part of the Irish Nation". And finally, Article 3 reads, "Until then [the time a united Ireland has been brought about], the laws enacted by the Parliament established by this Constitution shall have the like area and extent of application as the laws enacted by the Parliament that existed immediately before the coming into operation of this Constitution"[46].

Conclusion

The markers of nationalism and Nazism defined in the paper correlate with the matters the researchers single out when studying the problems of national and socio-political stability of any state.

Additional markers, such as, for example, leaderism and populism, also may be examined, but in the context of this work it should be noted that "constitutional Nazism" as such is hardly like to happen, since Nazism does not need constitutional justification. What Nazism needs is Mein Kampf.

That is why the nationalist markers in this work are separated from the Nazi markers, for nationalism does rely on the power of state coercion. Since constitutions by nature are the toughest legal acts resisting changes and since their power is far-reaching and overbearing, the afore-cited markers can hardly serve as the only determinant of corresponding regimes. All the more so that in identifying a regime as a Nazi we need all the key markers in place. The aim of this Chapter is much more modest – to compile a catalogue of markers that should be taken into consideration when implementing the 67/154 Resolution of the General Assembly of the United Nations of 20.12.2013. At the same time we needed to outline the real constitutional grounds for the development and consolidation of the ideology of right-wing radicalism, the ideology that proves, in this sense, integrated into the political and state life. It is important that frequently it is constitutions that divide the public and this division impedes public and state integration, spawning a host of problems. The embodiment of nationalism in constitutions is an outgrowth of certain political consciousness of the law-maker and the voter; and this factor testifies to the scope of influence exerted by the political actors whose performance demonstrates the principles of ultra-nationalism, constitutional nationalism

---

[46] *Constitution of Ireland.* Available at: http://www.irishstatutebook.ie/en/constitution/

and who aim to disintegrate the society in its present format. They canvass and work for various social and political institutions, which testifies to their involvement in the party and political struggle.

CHAPTER V

FROM THE RIGHT TO NAZIS: INTERNATIONAL INSTRUMENTS ESTABLISHING THE BOUNDARIES OF WHAT IS PROHIBITED AND WHAT IS PERMISSIBLE

The criterion for delimitation of right-wing, far-right and Nazi parties should be 'the permissible' as opposed to 'the criminal', only then, we believe, shall we be able to draw a formal demarcation line between them. Political scientists, proposing various classifications of parties, are very keen on defining this very line between right-wing, far-right and Nazi parties, yet they seem to ignore the fundamental criterion – the obvious social danger of the lattermost ones. Nazi parties are parties that cannot possibly be allowed to exercise power, and their very formation must be banned. The Nazi parties that already exist must be liquidated.

Establishment of this boundary line can be done both theoretically and "empirically" – in accordance with legal acts and judicial precedents.

The "empirical" establishment of the above-mentioned formal borderline (the fact of the very existence of which is beyond questioning) should begin with the delineation of the range of sources. It would be logical to proceed from international acts through national constitutions to regular national laws and subordinate legislation. The universality of the latter, however, is highly questionable. Of inestimable value in establishing this borderline would be court decisions on compulsory liquidation of parties acknowledged as Nazi, or at least indictments and/or claims and complaints. We should also consider judgments passed by international tribunals in cases related to genocide and crimes against humanity, but the obvious political bias of the International Court Tribunal for Former Yugoslavia (ICTY) casts doubt on their universality.

Since as a rule Nazi parties are parties of one leader, a special source can be found in acts on prosecution of leaders and activists of such parties – ranging from disciplinary (a member of Parliament can be denied the right to speak from the floor for racial speeches, for one) to criminal.

Here it should be noted that there is neither an International Convention to Combat Nazism, nor is there a clear-cut international ban on Nazi parties. The Nuremberg Judgment has so far been the only principal anti-Nazi international act[1]. Criminal responsibility for public denial, approval or justification of Nazi crimes during the Second World War and denial of crimes against humanity established by the Nuremberg Judgment had been long introduced in Austria, Germany, Belgium and France, for example, and at the beginning of 2014 the discussion started in Russia.

Prohibition on Nazi parties and, more broadly, extremist parties would come logical in the International Covenant on Civil and Political Rights, but it is not there. Moreover, the Covenant speaks not of parties, but of associations and trade unions, as a special case of associations. The Covenant, however, contains Article 20 that restricts freedom of speech in the context of our concern: "1. Any propaganda for war shall be prohibited by law. 2. Any advocacy of national, racial or religious hatred that constitutes incitement to discrimination, hostility or violence shall be prohibited by law"[2].

The closest to the issue under study are the UN Declaration on the Elimination of All Forms of Racial Discrimination (hereinafter referred to as the Declaration)[3] adopted by the 1904 UN Resolution (XVIII) of 20th November 1963, the International Convention on the Elimination of All Forms of Racial Discrimination (hereinafter referred to as the Convention)[4] adopted by the General Assembly Resolution 2106 (XX) of 21st December 1965, the Durban Declaration on the Elimination of All Forms of Racial Discrimination[5] and the Programme of Action on implementation of the Declaration on the Elimination of All Forms of Racial Discrimination (hereinafter referred to as The Programme of

---

[1] *Judgment of the International Military Tribunal*. Available at: http://avalon.law.yale.edu/subject_menus/judcont.asp

[2] *International Covenant on civil and political rights*. 1966. Available at: http://www.unhcr-centraleurope.org/pdf/resources/legal-documents/international-refugee-law/international-covenant-on-civil-and-political-rights-1966

[3] *United Nations Declaration on the Elimination of all forms of Racial Discrimination*. 1964. Available at: http://www.un-documents.net/a18r1904.htm

[4] *International Convention on the Elimination of All Forms of Racial Discrimination*. 1966. Available at: http://www.refworld.org/docid/3ae6b3940.html

[5] *Report of the World Conference against Racism, Racial Discrimination, Xenophobia and Related Intolerance. (Durban Declaration and Programme of Action)*. 2001. Available at: http://www.derechos.org/nizkor/ley/doc/durban.html

Action)[6] adopted at the World Conference for combating racism, racial discrimination, xenophobia and related intolerance in Durban, South Africa, 31st August – 7th September 2001.

The conception embodied in these documents develops along the two related 'lines' of annual Resolutions of the General Assembly of the United Nations (UNGAR), either of the two bearing its own name, identical for all resolutions. The first 'topic' is entitled "Global efforts aimed at total elimination of racism, racial discrimination, xenophobia and related intolerance and at comprehensive measures to be taken to implement the Durban Declaration and the Programme of Action", the second one – "the inadmissibility of certain kinds of practices that encourage the escalation of modern forms of racism, racial discrimination, xenophobia and related intolerance".

Apart from the above-mentioned UN acts, of great importance for this study is the adopted in accordance with Article 13 of the European Union Treaty the three-part strategy on combating discrimination contained in the two Council Directives – 2000/43/EC "implementing the principle of equal treatment between persons irrespective of racial or ethnic origin (the so-called 'racial directive')[7], 2000/78/EC establishing a general framework for equal treatment in employment and occupation (the so-called occupation directive)[8] and the Programme of Action of the European Community to combat discrimination according to all provisions listed in Article 13 (Council Decision 2000/750/EC)[9].

Also of great importance are the instruments adopted by the OSCE (CSCE), namely, the Final Act concluded by the Conference on Security and Cooperation in Europe (hereinafter referred to as the Helsinki Final Act)[10] and the Document of the Moscow Meeting of the Conference on the

---

[6] *Durban Declaration*. 2001. Available at: http://www.un-documents.net/durban-d.htm

[7] Council Directive 2000/43/EC of 29 June 2000 implementing the principle of equal treatment between persons irrespective of racial or ethnic origin, *Official Journal L 180*, 19/07/2000 P. 0022 – 0026. Available at: http://eur-lex.europa.eu/LexUriServ/LexUriServ.do?uri=CELEX:32000L0043:en:HTML

[8] Council Directive 2000/78/EC of 27 November 2000 establishing a general framework for equal treatment in employment and occupation, *Official Journal L 303*, 02/12/2000 P. 0016 - 0022. Available at: http://eur-lex.europa .eu/LexUriServ/LexUriServ.do?uri=CELEX:32000L0078:en:HTML

[9] *2000/750/EC: Council Decision of 27 November 2000 establishing a Community action programme to combat discrimination (2001 to 2006).* Available at: http://eur-lex.europa.eu/legal-content/EN/TXT/?uri=CELEX:32000D0750

[10] *Conference on Security and co-operation in Europe, Final Act 1975*. Available at: http://www.osce.org/mc/39501?download=true

Human Dimension of the CSCE (hereinafter referred to as the Moscow Document)[11].

Special attention deserves the Convention on the Prevention and Punishment of the Crimes of Genocide[12].

The study and the ways of establishing this boundary should be conducted along two lines: defining what is permissible (recommended) and what is prohibited (criminal). Here we must specify that the notion of "criminal" is used in this work in a loose sense since international public law, likewise constitutional law, is not binding for the national courts passing judgments in particular criminal cases. Of the overriding priority in this sphere is national criminal law, which is the universal principle in criminal law: a crime is not deemed a crime if at the moment of its perpetration it was not provided for in the corresponding national criminal law. As an example of such a priority, the Programme of Action contains Item 88 in which the Conference "calls upon States to criminalize all forms of trafficking in persons, in particular women and children, and to condemn and penalize traffickers and intermediaries, while ensuring protection and assistance to the victims of trafficking, with full respect for their human rights", without proposing any precise wording, yet defining trafficking in people as a "crime'.

So, what can we find in the cited documents that can be of use in our search for the boundary line?

5.1. Definition of Racial Discrimination

First of all, there is the definition of the term 'racial discrimination' given in Part 1, Article 1 of the Convention: "In this Convention the term 'racial discrimination' shall mean any distinction, exclusions, restriction or preference based on race, colour, descent, or national or ethnic origin which has the purpose or effect of nullifying or impairing the recognition, enjoyment or exercise, on an equal footing, of human rights and fundamental freedoms in the political, economic, social, cultural or any other field of public life".

Although this definition is of long standing, the mess in "racial discrimination" encompassing generic, national, and ethnic discrimination still persists, especially in post-Soviet States. This standard has not

[11] *Document of the Moscow Meeting of the Conference on Human Dimension of the CSCE.* Available at:
http://www.osce.org/odihr/elections/14310?download=true

[12] *Convention on the Prevention and Punishment of the Crime of Genocide.* 1948. Available at: http://www.un-documents.net/cppcg.htm

become universal, either, it is sufficient to note the title of the corresponding EU Directive, which uses both terms – "racial or ethnic origin". Now we can state that the attempt to define "racial discrimination' as a specific perpetration and ethnic (national) as generic has been made, but it has not become an unconditional success. In the context of our concern, this wording is sooner a drawback because "racial discrimination" "encompassing discrimination on the grounds of race, colour, generic, national, or ethnic origin is an unfortunate "transition adapter" to Nazism where ultra-nationalism is an obligatory constituent part. That this "transition adapter" is bad follows from the fact that there is no phrase "racist parties" to go along with "Nazi parties". Yet the logic of Acts of International Law proceeds from combating racism to combating Nazism.

Running ahead, we can note that the term "ultra-nationalism" borrowed from scientific papers is not used in the Acts of International Law. They use the term "aggressive nationalism"; proceeding from the context where it occurs we can come to a tentative conclusion that it means one and the same thing.

We can also state that discrimination proper is not understood in the initial UN documents as "unequal treatment", but as purposeful ("sounding"), that is, intended activity, or as unintended activity ("implied"). The distinction between direct and indirect discrimination does not exists yet.

The European Union, as was stated above, has significantly developed the anti-discrimination law within the concept of discrimination embodied in the Council Directive 2000/43/EC implementing the principle of equal treatment between persons irrespective of racial or ethnic origin. It is expedient to cite the first two articles:

"Article 1. Purpose.

The purpose of this Directive is to lay down a framework for combating discrimination on the grounds of racial or ethnic origin, with a view to putting into effect in the Member States the principle of equal treatment.

Article 2. Concept of discrimination.

1. For the purposes of this Directive, the principle of equal treatment shall mean that there shall be no direct or indirect discrimination based on racial or ethnic origin.

2. For the purposes of paragraph 1:

(a) direct discrimination shall be taken to occur where one person is treated less favourably than another is, has been or would be treated in a comparable situation on grounds of racial or ethnic origin;

(b) indirect discrimination shall be taken to occur where an apparently neutral provision, criterion or practice would put persons of a racial or ethnic origin at a particular disadvantage compared with other persons, unless that provision, criterion or practice is objectively justified by a legitimate aim and the means of achieving that aim are appropriate and necessary.

3. Harassment shall be deemed to be discrimination within the meaning of paragraph 1, when an unwanted conduct related to racial or ethnic origin takes place with the purpose or effect of violating the dignity of a person and of creating an intimidating, hostile, degrading, humiliating or offensive environment. In this context, the concept of harassment may be defined in accordance with the national laws and practice of the Member States.

4. An instruction to discriminate against persons on grounds of racial or ethnic origin shall be deemed to be discrimination within the meaning of paragraph 1".

Nonetheless, the General Assembly of the United Nations, almost half a century later, still insists on this definition and Item 33 of the 68/150 Resolution that "encourages States to adopt the legislation necessary to combat racism while ensuring that the definition of racial discrimination set out therein complies with article 1 of the Convention".

The understanding of racial (in the loose sense proposed by the United Nation) discrimination is of crucial importance for establishing the desired boundary, for the encouragement of unequal treatment or, which is the same, the acknowledgment of racial exclusivity is, as the authors believe, common with far-right parties, part of extremists and all Nazi parties, which distinguishes them from 'ordinary' right-wing parties.

5.2. The causes of racism

Sources, causes, forms and contemporary manifestations of racism, racial discrimination, xenophobia and related intolerance are described in the Durban Declaration Chapter of the same name. How much science and how many political assessments this Chapter contains is a separate matter, but the Chapter is long and it provides us with opinions politicians have of the issue of our concern. The Chapter contains Articles 13-30. The content can be summed up as follows:

- slavery and slave trade, including the transatlantic slave trade, are crimes against humanity and must always be regarded as such, they also are among the major sources and manifestations of racism, racial discrimination, xenophobia and related intolerance;
- colonialism has resulted in racism, racial discrimination, xenophobia, and related intolerance;
- in terms of international law, apartheid and genocide constitute crimes against humanity and the major sources and manifestations of racism, racial discrimination, xenophobia, and related intolerance;
- xenophobia against non-nationals, particularly migrants, refugees and asylum-seekers, constitutes one of the main sources of contemporary racism and that human rights violations against members of such groups occur widely in the context of discriminatory, xenophobic and racist practices;
- youth and other vulnerable groups may be expose to new manifestations of racism, racial discrimination, xenophobia, and related intolerance;
- poverty, underdevelopment, marginalization, social exclusion and economic disparities are closely associated with racism, racial discrimination, xenophobia and related intolerance, and contribute to the persistence of racist attitudes and practices which in turn generate more poverty;
- racism, racial discrimination, xenophobia, and related intolerance attach negative economic, social, and cultural conditions, which, in turn, determine the underdevelopment of developing countries, in particular, of Africa;
- racism, racial discrimination, xenophobia, and related intolerance are among the root causes of armed conflict and very often one of its consequences;
- nondiscrimination is a fundamental principle of the international humanitarian law, and all sides of armed conflicts must unfailingly follow this principle.
- widespread internal conflicts which are due, among other causes, to gross violations of human rights, including those arising from racism, racial discrimination, xenophobia and related intolerance, and from lack of democratic, inclusive and participatory governance, which is hampering socio-economic development;
- in some States political and legal structures or institutions, some of which were inherited and persist today, do not correspond to the multi-ethnic, pluricultural and plurilingual characteristics of the

population and, in many cases, constitute an important factor of discrimination in the exclusion of indigenous peoples;

- racism, racial discrimination, xenophobia and related intolerance may persist in some States in the functioning of the penal systems and in the application of the law, as well as in the actions and attitudes of institutions and individuals responsible for law enforcement, especially where this has contributed to certain groups being over-represented among persons under detention or imprisoned;
- slavery and slavery-like practices still exist today in various parts of the world, which constitutes flagrant violations of human rights;
- victims of trafficking are particularly exposed to racism, racial discrimination, xenophobia and related intolerance.

This catalogue is of great significance, first of all, as an attempt to sort out the causes of the racial discrimination phenomenon. Such attempts are rare, their scientific value, we repeat, is dubious, and what is most unfortunate is that this attempt has not been further developed. We regret to acknowledge that politics and social studies go their separate ways when researching into right-extremist, ultra-right and Nazi parties.

5.3. Pseudoscientific character of the racial theory in international law

The Preambles to the Declaration and the Convention demonstrate their strong attitude to "scientific" substantiations of the idea of racial superiority: "any doctrine of racial differentiation or superiority is scientifically false, morally condemnable, socially unjust and dangerous, and that there is no justification for racial discrimination either in theory or in practice".

This idea is further developed in the Preamble to the 66/144 Resolution adopted by the General Assembly on 19 December 2011[13]: "any doctrine of racial superiority is scientifically false, morally condemnable, socially unjust and dangerous and must be rejected, together with theories that attempt to determine the existence of separate human races". In this case,

---

[13] *Global efforts for the total elimination of racism, racial discrimination, xenophobia and related intolerance and the comprehensive implementation of and follow-up to the Durban Declaration and Programme of Action.* Available at: Available at:
http://www.un.org/en/ga/search/view_doc.asp?symbol=%20A/RES/66/144

of great importance are both the political assessment the corresponding "scientific" research and the direct indication of their danger.

This UN statement is echoed by the European Council in Item 6 of the Preamble to the "Racial Directive": "The European Union rejects theories which attempt to determine the existence of separate human races. The use of the term "racial origin" in this Directive does not imply an acceptance of such theories". This research by no means attempts to judge to what extent such a political interference can be justified, though, of course, this rejection of race theory can puzzle not only anthropologists but ethnographers as well.

Of political importance is the statement in the Durban Declaration that "racism, racial discrimination, xenophobia and related intolerance constitute a negation of the purposes and principles of the Charter of the United Nations".

The same idea is further developed in Item 9 of the European Council "Racial Directive": "Discrimination based on racial or ethnic origin may undermine the achievement of the objectives of the EC Treaty, in particular the attainment of a high level of employment and of social protection, the raising of the standard of living and quality of life, economic and social cohesion and solidarity. It may also undermine the objective of developing the European Union as an area of freedom, security and justice".

The provision of pseudoscientific character of race theories is of crucial importance in analyzing the party documents (first of all, programs and bills), as the ideas and the rationale of race superiority automatically 'shifts' the party beyond the border of the permissible, and primarily not in the legal but in the scientific sense.

5.4. The theme of Nazism in International Law

Neither the Declaration nor the Convention mentions fascism (Nazism) or nationalism; they focus their attention on apartheid and segregation. In particular, the Convention speaks of "manifestations of racial discrimination still in evidence in some areas of the world and by governmental policies based on racial superiority or hatred, such as policies of apartheid, segregation or separation".

"Nazism" is first mentioned in Item 84 of the Durban Declaration, "We condemn the persistence and resurgence of neo-Nazism, neo-Fascism and violent nationalist ideologies based on racial or national prejudice, and state that these phenomena can never be justified in any instance or in any circumstances."

Item 86 of the Programme of Action also "transgresses" the set thematic format of deliberations on racism as a generic phenomenon, and the Conference "Calls upon States to promote measures to deter the emergence of and to counter neo-fascist, violent nationalist ideologies which promote racial hatred and racial discrimination, as well as racist and xenophobic sentiments, including measures to combat the negative influence of such ideologies especially on young people through formal and non-formal education, the media and sport", pointing expressis verbis to the "Neo-Fascist ideology". Yet, this ideology is assigned a "modest" role of an "encourager" of racial discrimination.

The topic of Nazism is developed in a series of the UN General Assembly Resolutions entitled "Inadmissibility of certain practices that contribute to fuelling contemporary forms of racism, racial discrimination, xenophobia and related intolerance". This series started on 16.12.2005 with the Resolution 60/143 and contains the Resolutions 61/147 of 19.12.2006, 62/142 of 18.12.2007, 63/162 of 18.12.2008, 64/147 of 18.12.2009, 65/199 of 21.10.2010 and 66/143 of 19.12.2011.

Since these resolutions are more diverse in content than those of the "first series", we shall consider them diachronically. The first thing that attracts attention is their anti-Nazi "bias" toward general combating Nazism, though the very word 'Nazism" and its derivatives are still missing from the title of the Resolution.

The Preamble to the 60/143 Resolution of 16.12.2005, starting from the reference to the Charter of the United Nations, the Universal Declaration of Human Rights, the International Covenant on Civil and Political Rights, the International Convention on the Elimination of All Forms of Racial Discrimination and other relevant human rights instruments, first and foremost the relevant provisions of the Durban Declaration and Programme of Action, finds it appropriate to refer to the "Charter of the Nuremberg Tribunal and the Judgment of the Tribunal, which recognized the Waffen SS organization and all its integral parts as criminal and declared it responsible for many war crimes and crimes against humanity".

This reference is obviously reactive and stems from the ongoing glorification of Nazism, first of all, units of the Waffen SS, in East Europe, in the Baltic States. It is clear that it was not the Waffen SS that was the major generator and disseminator of the Nazi ideas, but the fate of the NSDAP (The National Socialist German Workers' Party) is missing from the Resolutions. From the reactive point of view it is clear – there is no visible glorification of the NSDAP in the world, but the main source and conductor of the Nazi ideology was the party and not the army.

This Resolution of the General Assembly of the United Nations refers to the topic of Nazism several times. The first time it occurs in the Preamble when the General Assembly expresses its concern about "the spread in many parts of the world of various extremist political parties, movements and groups, including neo-Nazis and skinhead groups" and such-like extremist ideological movements. The same is reiterated in Item 6 which states that "such practices" contribute to "the spread and multiplication" of the indicated groups.

For the second time, in Item 1, the General Assembly "reaffirms the provision of the Durban Declaration in which States condemned the persistence and resurgence of neo-Nazism, neo-Fascism and violent nationalist prejudice and stated that those phenomena could never be justified in any instance or in any circumstances".

In the context of our concern it is important and, from the viewpoint of method, true that "Nazism" is regarded as both an ideology and a phenomenon.

Item 7 of the 60/143 Resolution of the General Assembly "emphasizes the need to take the necessary measures to put an end to the practices described above, and calls upon States to take more effective measures to combat those phenomena and the extremist movements, which pose a real threat to democratic values".

Item 8 of this Resolution is totally devoted to the obligations of the States, defined rather broadly. Thus, the General Assembly "reaffirms that, according to article 4 of the International Convention on the Elimination of All Forms of Racial Discrimination, States parties to that instrument are, inter alia, under the obligation:

a) to condemn all propaganda and all organizations that are based on ideas of racial superiority or that attempt to justify or promote racial hatred and discrimination in any form;
b) to undertake to adopt immediate and positive measures designed to eradicate all incitement to, or acts of, such discrimination with due regard to the principles embodied in the Universal Declaration of Human Rights and the rights expressly set forth in article 5 of the Convention;
c) to declare as an offence punishable by law all dissemination of ideas based on racial superiority or hatred, incitement to racial discrimination, as well as all acts of violence or incitement to such acts against any race or group of persons of another colour or ethnic origin, and also the provision of any assistance to racist activities, including the financing thereof;

d) to declare illegal and prohibit organizations and organized and all other propaganda activities that promote and incite racial discrimination and to recognize participation in such organizations or activities as an offence punishable by law;
e) to prohibit public authorities or public institutions, national or local, from promoting or inciting racial discrimination".

Item 3 of the 62/142 Resolution was the result of the immediate response of the General Assembly to the events of the "Bronze Night" in Tallinn in April 2007, it goes as follows: the General Assembly "expresses concern at recurring attempts to desecrate or demolish monuments erected in remembrance of those who fought against Nazism during the Second World War, as well as to unlawfully exhume or remove the remains of such persons, and urges States in this regard to fully comply with their relevant obligations, inter alia, under article 34 of Additional Protocol I to the Geneva Conventions of 1949".

The theme of the "glorification of the Nazi movement" was further developed in the 63/162 Resolution where the General Assembly "expresses deep concern about the glorification of the Nazi movement and former members of the Waffen SS organization, including by erecting monuments and memorials and holding public demonstrations in the name of the glorification of the Nazi past, the Nazi movement and neo-Nazism, as well as by declaring or attempting to declare such members and those who fought against the anti-Hitler coalition and collaborated with the Nazi movement as participants in national liberation movements" (Item 2).

Item 13 of the 66/143 Resolution "emphasizes the recommendation of the Special Rapporteur regarding the importance of history classes in teaching the dramatic events and human suffering that resulted from the ideologies of Nazism and Fascism".

The 67/154 Resolution of 20.12.2012, while developing the analyzed "series", changes its title by introducing "Nazism" into the topic: "Glorification of Nazism: inadmissibility of certain practices that contribute to fuelling contemporary forms of racism, racial discrimination, xenophobia and related intolerance". The name seems far from perfect: it implies that there is no such danger as Nazism, only its glorification constitutes a menace. Nor is there the realization that Nazism is a qualitatively different phenomenon from those listed in the title of the Resolution to which the above-mentioned "glorification" only contributes.

Item 10 of the Resolution reiterates that "such practices fuel contemporary forms of racism, racial discrimination, xenophobia and related intolerance and contribute to the spread and multiplication of various extremist political parties, movements and groups, including neo-Nazis and skinhead groups, and in this regard calls for increased vigilance".

Item 18 "calls upon States to continue to invest in education, inter alia, in order to transform attitudes and correct ideas of racial hierarchies and superiority promoted by extremist political parties, movements and groups and counter their negative influence".

The General Assembly in Item 27 "stresses the importance of cooperating closely with civil society and international and regional human rights mechanisms in order to counter effectively all manifestations of racism, racial discrimination, xenophobia and related intolerance, as well as extremist political parties, movements and groups, including neo-Nazis and skinhead groups, and other similar extremist ideological movements that incite racism, racial discrimination, xenophobia and related intolerance".

In Item 30, the General Assembly, as was already spelled out in the previous chapter, "recalls that any legislative or constitutional measures adopted with a view to countering extremist political parties, movements and groups, including neo-Nazis and skinhead groups, and similar extremist ideological movements should be in conformity with the relevant international human rights norms".

Item 5 in the latest 68/150 Resolution of 18.12.2013 "emphasizes the recommendation of the Special Rapporteur that "any commemorative celebration of the Nazi Waffen SS organization and its crimes against humanity, whether official or non-official, should be prohibited by States".

If reflection, rather than reaction, should be considered as characteristic of the General Assembly, it should be noted that the General Assembly responds promptly: the Resolution adopted in December responds to the topical events of the year. Thus, the General Assembly provided a timely response to the "Bronze Night" events in Tallinn in 2007. Item 9 of the Resolution is devoted to the corresponding scandal in Estonia – it "expresses deep concern at attempts at commercial advertising aimed at exploiting the sufferings of the victims of war crimes and crimes against humanity committed during the Second World War by the Nazi regime".

Remember that the Resolutions were considered over time, and the specifics of the 'topics' of the Resolutions of the General Assembly is that the points, once they occur there, they never disappear, they are reiterated year in and year out, each time gaining in force. Preambles to the Resolutions reflect the whole history of the matter with references to corresponding previous Resolutions. In the case of our concern, references are made for both "topics".

The above-mentioned passages allow us to note the fact the United Nations is very vague about parties that are beyond the prohibited, and, in general, avoiding using the phrase "Nazi party", it labels parties as "extremist". Such an approach is understandable – why should one describe what must not exist by definition? Even more so that the United Nations traditionally avoids naming the countries in which incidents that it condemns have occurred. By no means can this facilitate the task of diagnosing "organizations and organized and all other propaganda efforts that promote and incite racial discrimination". But of great value are certain activities described by the United Nations, involvement into which can help diagnose a party as a Nazi party.

5.5. Danger and Security Ideas

After putting forward a hypothesis that the parties in question constitute a danger to the society, we shall examine the conceptions of danger and security contained in the documents of international public law. Here, in the framework of this research, "security" will be examined exclusively from the point of view of the danger that "socially-dangerous" parties, ideologies and phenomena in the far-right side of the political spectrum create. Military, ecological, energy and other types of danger will not be considered. Yet, Part III of the Document on confidence-building measures and certain aspects of security and disarmament in the Helsinki Final Act specifies "the complementary nature of the political and military aspects of security".

Here we shall examine national constitutional restrictions for parties, and when they are missing – for associations where such restrictions are imposed "for reasons of security". Apart from this, ideologies and practices also declared as dangerous will be considered. Simultaneous analysis of "danger" and "security" will, from the authors' point of view, help to come to a better understanding of the desired "boundary line". Let us resort to the documents in question.

Article I of the Declaration says, "Discrimination between human beings on the ground of race, colour or ethnic origin is an offence to human dignity and shall be condemned as a denial of the principles of the Charter of the United Nations, as a violation of the human rights and fundamental freedoms proclaimed in the Universal Declaration of Human Rights, as an obstacle to friendly and peaceful relations among nations and as a fact capable of disturbing peace and security among peoples".

The cited passage shows that racial discrimination, as such, is regarded as a potential ("capable of disturbing") menace to "peace and security among peoples".

Article 103 of the Durban Declaration reports, "We recognize the consequences of past and contemporary forms of racism, racial discrimination, xenophobia and related intolerance as serious challenges to global peace and security, human dignity and the realization of human rights and fundamental freedoms of many people in the world, in particular Africans, people of African descent, people of Asian descent and indigenous peoples". Here we must say that it is typical of acts of international law to frequently specify "groups of risk", this will occur many a time in the course of our research.

Unfortunately, the principal security act – The Final Act of the Conference on Security and Cooperation in Europe, 1975 (Helsinki Declaration) – contains only few conceptual statements related to the topic of our concern. The part entitled "Questions relating to Security in Europe" is devoted, on the whole, to matters of détente, but it also recognizes "the indivisibility of security in Europe", and as a remedy proposes to search "for possibilities of joining their efforts with a view to overcoming distrust and increasing confidence, solving the problems that separate them and cooperating in the interest of mankind". "The indivisibility of security" is further developed in "Questions relating to Security and Co-operation in the Mediterranean", that holds a strong belief that "security in Europe is to be considered in the broader context of world security and is closely linked with security in the Mediterranean area as a whole, and that accordingly the process of improving security should not be confined to Europe but should extend to other parts of the world, and in particular to the Mediterranean area.

The Preamble to the Charter of Paris for a New Europe, 1990, the document stemming from the Helsinki Final Act, also speaks about "equal security for all our countries". The same document expresses the following undisguised optimism, "With the ending of the division of Europe, we will strive for a new quality in our security relations while fully respecting each other's freedom of choice in that respect. Security is indivisible and the security of every participating State is inseparably linked to that of all the others".

As the most broad-scale and multifaceted document of all those examined in this work, the Helsinki Final Act implicitly puts a question of what ideology or what worldview should be matched against the ideologies that have been proven dangerous. The vocabulary for the Helsinki Final Act contains the terms "solidarity", "cooperation", "mutual understanding", "common interests", etc., which, sooner, bespeaks of the lack of such an ideology, since the emphasis is definitely made on the pragmatism of relations. Humanistic notes occur only in Item 1 "Human Contacts" in the part "Co-operation in Humanitarian and Other Fields", for example, when the participating States "affirm, in relation to their present effort to improve conditions in this area, the importance they attach to humanitarian considerations". The contemporary state of humanism, however, should be characterized as uncertain, as "professional humanists, first of all, those from the American Association of Humanists, define humanism neither as a science nor as an ideology. The ideologically dangerous ideologist L.D. Trotsky wrote that humanism could not possibly be a scientific method, "I understood even then that the humanitarian, the moral, point of view of the historical process was the most sterile"[14]. V.A. Lyashchenko calls humanism "an elegant trend in philosophy"[15].

Article 28 of the Durban Declaration returns us to the topic of humanism, it says that "persecution against any identifiable group, collectivity or community on racial, national, ethnic or other grounds that are universally recognized as impermissible under international law, as well as the crime of apartheid, constitute serious violations of human rights and, in some cases, qualify as crimes against humanity". The use of the two accordant terms ("violation of human rights" and "crime against humanity") applied to one object is noted by many authors; for example, thc Statute of the International Criminal Tribunal for Rwanda, adopted by the UN Security Council Resolution on 8 November 1994, also calls this group of crimes "crimes against humanity".

To understand the aspects of security under international law one cannot help but note the idea of danger, its scale and victims.

The first sources of norms for responsibility for these crimes were the Judgments of the International Military Tribunal in Nuremberg and Tokyo, established for the trials of major war (German and Japanese) criminals guilty of unleashing and waging the Second World War. They specified the grounds of criminal responsibility for crimes against peace and humanity and war crimes and also the particular content of the indicated three types of penal prohibitions (Article 6 Charter of the Nuremberg Tribunal). Following the Nuremberg and the Tokyo Trials, the UN

---

[14] Trotsky, L.D. 1930. *My Life*. (-my-life-trotsky.epub), Chapter XVII, p. 184. Available at: https://www.marxists.org/archive/trotsky/1930/mylife/1930-lif.pdf

[15] Lyashchenko, V.A. 2003. Biologicheskie aspekty gumanizma, *Zdravyi smysl*, N 4. (Lyashchenko, V.A. 2003. Biological Aspects of Humanism, *Common sense*, N 4). (in the original: Ляшенко, В.А. 2003. Биологические аспекты гуманизма, *Здравый смысл*, N 4).

continued to elaborate the normative framework necessary to combat crimes against peace and mankind. With this view, as long ago as 1947, the 177 Resolution of the General Assembly of the United Nations directed the International Law Commission of the United Nations to frame the principles of international law recognized in the Charter of the Nuremberg Military Tribunal (and also in the Judgment), and draft a Code of crimes against peace and humanity. The General Assembly has repeatedly turned back to this issue. In 1991 at the XLIII session, the International Law Commission tentatively adopted the draft of the Code in the first reading. Yet, considering the discussion of this draft and the work the Commission is still to do, the adoption will take a long time. Major crimes against peace and human safety (including war crimes, genocide and crimes against humanity) fell within the jurisdiction of the International Tribunal established by the Resolution of the Security Council of the United Nations on 22 February 1993 for legal prosecution of persons responsible for serious violations of the international humanitarian law committed in the territory of former Yugoslavia and also within the jurisdiction of the International Tribunal for Rwanda[16] established by the Resolution of the Security Council of the United Nations on 8 November 1994 for legal prosecution of persons responsible for genocide and other serious violations of international law committed in the territory of Rwanda and Rwandan citizens responsible for such crimes committed in the territory of the neighbouring states. Moreover, on 17 July 1998, the United Nations Rome Diplomatic Conference on the establishment of an International Criminal Court adopted the Statute of the International Criminal Court as a permanent court of justice meant to mete out justice for such crimes against peace and human safety as genocide, crimes against humanity, war crimes, and crimes of aggression[17].

These comments reveal a formal approach to such crimes: they disregard the political aspect of crimes for which people are "condemned",

---

[16] *Statute of the International Criminal Tribunal for the Prosecution of Persons Responsible for Genocide and Other Serious Violations of International Humanitarian Law Committed in the Territory of Rwanda and Rwandan Citizens Responsible for Genocide and Other Such Violations Committed in the Territory of Neighbouring States*, between 1 January 1994 and 31 December 1994. Available at:
http://www.ohchr.org/EN/ProfessionalInterest/Pages/StatuteInternationalCriminalTribunalForRwanda.aspx

[17] *Kommentarii k Ugolovnomu kodeksu Rossiiskoy Federatsii*. Available at: http://novoart7.narod.ru/simple.html. (*Comments to the Criminal Code of the Russian Federation*). (in the original: *Комментарии к УК РФ*).

but speak of criminal offenses for which people are "tried". We emphasize that the point in question is international crimes.

Noteworthy is the passage in which the General Assembly "expresses deep concern about the inadequate response to the new and resurgent forms of racism, racial discrimination, xenophobia and related intolerance and urges States to take measures to combat this evil with a view to ending this practice". In this case, it is important to use irrational "evil" as a metaphysical marker of the desired boundary line between the good and the evil.

The Preamble to the 68/150 resolution establishes a direct link between "all recent manifestations of violence and terrorism" and "violence associated with nationalism, racism, xenophobia and related intolerance", which allows us to conclude that these phenomena may well constitute the source of terrorist danger.

Noteworthy is the imperative "never", which first occurred in the Durban Declaration and then was reiterated, for example, in Item 1 of the 68/150 Resolution of General Assembly in the wording "those phenomena (preservation and resurgence of neo-Nazism, neo-Fascism and aggressive nationalist ideologies – authors' note) could never be justified in any instance or in any circumstances". The authors believe that the use of "never" by the General Assembly is far more justified than the use of a similar pledge in national constitutions. From the legal point of view, "never" used by the people in a constitution is nothing but a compromise, and a void one at that, for the violation of the given pledge does not result in any legal effects. Article 9 "Renouncement of War" of the Japanese Constitution is a living illustration of the violation of such a pledge that brought about no effect. Although the Article states that "land, sea, and air forces, as well as other war potential, will never be maintained", Japan, in violation of its own Constitution, now has very powerful defence forces. "Never" with the General Assembly, contrary to national performance, carries weight because it puts a State under control of other States.

In spite of the gradual, though slow, expansion of the framework of international law in respect of the subject under study, the very problem of racial discrimination, and subsequently of Nazism, is getting far more acute. Awareness of the scale of the problem is necessary both for the mustering up of the notorious "political will" and in more pragmatic matters of sentencing decisions, as well as in determining the measure of complexity or simplicity of the process of sentencing. Although the notion of "global emergency" does not exit, executors of law, when imposing sanctions, should bear in mind the general situation in the world so that, first, they could correlate its tension with the state of a particular country and, second, they could administer proper punishment aimed at general prevention.

Such conduct is encouraged by the declared "indivisibility of security". Yet, in our time, the attitude to security as a resource is viewed differently, thus, according to M.A. Kolerov, "it is clear for everyone that after Kosovo there is not enough security to go round"[18].

The dynamics of tension, according to the documents of international law, keeps slackening. The Preamble to the 1963 Declaration noted "manifestations of racial discrimination still in evidence in some parts of the world", "although international action and efforts in a number of countries have made it possible to achieve progress in that field", that is, we can assume that the United Nations regarded racial discrimination as aftereffects of colonialism and Nazism of the Second World War.

The Preamble to the 66/144 Resolution reflects the idea the General Assembly had of the contemporary scale and inclusivity of the phenomenon: the General Assembly is "alarmed at the increase in racist violence and xenophobic ideas in many parts of the world, in political circles, in the sphere of public opinion and in society at large as a result, inter alia, of the resurgent activities of associations established on the basis of racist and xenophobic platforms and charters, and the persistent use of those platforms and charters to promote or incite racist ideologies"[19].

Failure to resolve these and other problems related to the dissemination of the far-right and primarily ultranationalist ideologies was reflected in "grave concern that universal ratification of the Convention has not yet been reached, despite commitments under the Durban Declaration and Programme of Action". Moreover, Item 6 of the Resolution "expresses deep concern at inadequate responses to emerging and resurgent forms of racism, racial discrimination, xenophobia and related intolerance, and urges States to adopt measures to address those scourges vigorously with a view to preventing their practice". Item 44 speaks of the need for "mobilizing political will at the national, regional and international levels", considering this to be a compulsory constituent in "the strives against evil".

---

[18] Kolerov, M.A. 2009. *Voyna: vneshnyaa politika Rossii I politicheskaya bor'ba, 1999-2009*. Moskva, p. 16. (Kolerov, M.A. 2009. *War: External Politics of Russia and Political Struggle, 1999-2009*. Moscow, p.16).
(in the original: Колеров, М.А. 2009. *Война: внешняя политика России и политическая борьба, 1999-2009*. М., с. 16).

[19] *Resolutions adopted by the General Assembly at its 66 Session*. Available at: http://www.un.org/depts/dhl/resguide/r66_en.shtml

Item 7 of the 68/150 Resolution of the General assembly "notes with concern the increase in the number of racist incidents worldwide, including the rise of skinhead groups, which have been responsible for many of these incidents, as well as the resurgence of racist and xenophobic violence targeting, inter alia, persons belonging to national, ethnic, religious or linguistic minorities"[20]. In this case of great importance is not only the scale ("worldwide") and intensity ("the resurgence of violence") but also the delineation of the circle of victims belonging to the appropriate minorities.

Item 11 of the 65/199 Resolution goes further and "recalls the recommendation of the Special Rapporteur, made in his latest report to the General Assembly, to introduce into domestic criminal law a provision according to which committing an offence with racist or xenophobic motivations or aims constitutes an aggravating circumstance allowing for enhanced penalties, and encourages those States whose legislation does not contain such provisions to consider that recommendation"[21].

One of the problems we are going to deal with later is the problem of making an expert examination of Nazism, racism, xenophobia, segregation, apartheid, etc. For a Judge passing a judgment in a particular criminal case it is of crucial importance to classify the type of extremism in legal language (the law is still to be adopted), otherwise the dispute whether the nose of the aggrieved was damaged out of Nazi feelings or merely of "xenophobic" sentiments may result in the remission of the sentence with a particular aggravating circumstance, if such is fixed by law. But can there be precise wordings at all? In Item 1 of the 66/144 Resolution the General Assembly "Recognizes and affirms that a global fight against racism, racial discrimination, xenophobia and related intolerance and all their abhorrent and evolving forms and manifestations is a matter of priority for the international community", which allows for drawing a tentative conclusion that of vital importance is a thorough scientific – first of all, theoretic, conceptual – study of Nazism, racism, xenophobia, etc., that will consider the "changing", as well as "new and resurgent forms" (the Preamble to the Durban Declaration speaks of " more subtle and contemporary forms") of the latter impeding their actual diagnostics. Law enforcement officials, and first of all, judges, must be equipped not only with delineations but also with a theory permitting them to detect different types of extremism in their "changing" forms. Item 9 of

---

[20] *Resolutions adopted by the General Assembly at its 68 Session.* Available at: http://www.un.org/depts/dhl/resguide/r68_en.shtml

[21] *Resolutions adopted by the General Assembly at its 65 Session.* Available at: http://www.un.org/depts/dhl/resguide/r65_en.shtml

the Resolution indirectly urges States to "implement and enforce appropriate and effective legislative, judicial, regulatory and administrative measures to prevent and protect against acts of racism, racial discrimination, xenophobia and related intolerance".

Item 2 of the Resolution draws a desired clear-cut boundary line: the General Assembly "acknowledges that no derogation from the prohibition of racial discrimination, genocide, the crime of apartheid or slavery is permitted, as defined in the obligations under the relevant human rights instruments". First, it establishes an express prohibition, and second, "apartheid" is treated as a "crime", which, contrary to "genocide", is scarce in criminal law on national levels.

Item 11 also calls for criminalization: "any advocacy of national, racial or religious hatred that constitutes incitement to discrimination, hostility or violence shall be prohibited by law, and also reaffirms that the dissemination of ideas based on racial superiority or hatred, or incitement to racial discrimination, as well as all acts of violence or incitement to such acts, shall be declared offences punishable by law, in accordance with the international obligations of States, and that those prohibitions are consistent with freedom of opinion and expression".

This resolution ends with the General Assembly's decision "to remain seized of this important matter at its sixty-seventh session under the item entitled "Elimination of racism, racial discrimination, xenophobia and related intolerance". Here we should note the consistency and continuity of the policy for the "elimination" of racism, racial discrimination, xenophobia and related intolerance, which originated in the corresponding 1963 Declaration. The sufficiency of this policy will be examined below.

When summing up the concepts, as stipulated in international public law, of security and security threats arising from the ideologies and phenomena under study, we should, first, note the changing character of these concepts – from the attitude to the very same racial discrimination as an outgrowth of colonialism to the acknowledgment of its growing threat as threat to peace.

The second thing demanding attention is, on the one hand, the increasing pace of this threat and, on the other hand, the slackening response to it on the national levels. It feels as if international organizations are far better at monitoring the situation that participating states are. This is the effect of the phenomenon of sarcastic definition of international law: international law is something that others violate.

Third, the perception of threat is stronger than the wish to detect and neutralize it. Certain helplessness of political vocabulary (for example, it is difficult to take the term "skinheads" seriously) coupled with the lack of actual links among politics, social sciences and law-enforcement contributes to this phenomenon.

On the whole, we can state that acts of international public law are quite adequate in their description of "what is good and what is bad", which, as it is, is of great value for our search of the desired boundary line. "Groups of risk" or victims of the phenomena under consideration are not consolidated in one document and occur in texts ad hoc. We shall note in passing that although skinheads are singled out as a group constituting a source of danger, no text speaks, for example, of governmental action against anti-Fascists, characteristic of the Baltic States. Xenophobia is treated both as a general phenomenon and as a particular case, for example, in a number of EU programmes for elimination of xenophobia in relation to gypsies. The term "Russophobia" is altogether missing in spite of the fact that this phenomenon is well developed, especially in some countries of post-Soviet political space.

The survey shows that the threats under consideration are complex; they have different causes and manifestations, which makes the task of judicial diagnostics difficult, or even next to impossible. Nevertheless, it is dangerous organizations (parties) that require regulatory enforcement.

5.6. Prohibited organizations (parties)

Three Articles of the Durban Declaration have a direct bearing on the topic of parties "beyond goodness", though they do not speak of parties as such, "Article 85: We condemn political platforms and organizations based on racism, xenophobia or doctrines of racial superiority and related discrimination, as well as legislation and practices based on racism, racial discrimination, xenophobia and related intolerance, as incompatible with democracy and transparent and accountable governance. We reaffirm that racism, racial discrimination, xenophobia and related intolerance condoned by governmental policies violate human rights and may endanger friendly relations among peoples, cooperation among nations and international peace and security.

Article 86: We recall that the dissemination of all ideas based upon racial superiority or hatred shall be declared an offence punishable by law with due regard to the principles embodied in the Universal Declaration of Human Rights and the rights expressly set forth in article 5 of the International Convention on the Elimination of All Forms of Racial Discrimination.

Article 87. We note that article 4, paragraph b, of the International Convention on the Elimination of All Forms of Racial Discrimination places an obligation upon States to be vigilant and to proceed against organizations that disseminate ideas based on racial superiority or hatred, acts of violence or incitement to such acts. These organizations shall be condemned and discouraged".

Certain untouchability of political parties and their tangential occurrence in acts of international law have, in our opinion, quite reasonable causes.

First, being undoubtedly "organizations" and "associations", thereby enjoying the freedom of associations, parties, however, tend to rely not on freedom of associations embodied in all major international documents on human rights but on national party legislation, which can hardly be called unified. There is no international convention for political parties, so party legislation remains an internal affair of the state. This point has never been questioned yet.

Second, parties in the national context, are characterized by strictly competitive relations, first and foremost, during elections, which is uncharacteristic of associations, the assortment of which in a country today frequently (and, as should be noted, erroneously) understood as a "civil society". Parties, being political subjects, are, as a rule, excluded from the "civil society". Competition between parties makes the very statement of the question of prohibition of a party very difficult, since a party that is incriminated in exceeding the limits will immediately respond saying that its political competitors, who always have an objective interest in it, have been scheming.

Third, the practical matters of party liquidation, which will be examined below, do not have case-law. The actual task of liquidation, say, of a parliamentary party entails a number of questions that do not have contemporary answers. If the judgment of liquidation of a party enters into force, this will be a violation of the right to elect of those voters who voted for it. There arises a question of validity of the laws the party to be liquidated took part in passing. There arises another question of early termination of powers for those members of the parliament who were elected from the party to be liquidated.

Fourth, involvement of parties in power, and parties in coalitional governments in parliamentary republics constitute power, which opens for them, on the one hand, opportunities to legitimize their actions, and on the other hand, to exert pressure on the court. It refers primarily to parties of long standing, the critical attitude toward whose acts and statements is hard to bring to a court of law, since these parties are "the pillars of society" on which the political system of the State rests.

Considering the foresaid, the topic of prohibitory injunction and party liquidation is at best characterized as "delicate" and "sensitive", owing to which international public law prefers referring to it in passing.

5.7. Politics, parties and politicians

As was shown above, the questions of party liquidation in general and Nazi parties in particular are usually sidestepped in international public law. Nevertheless, it offers certain recommendations in respect of parties and political figures.

Thus, Item 115 of the Programme of Action of the Durban Declaration contains provisions emphasizing the role of politicians and political parties – the provisions whose very existence makes them very important for our study. The recommendations proper can hardly be called decisive. The Programme of Action only "underlines the key role that politicians and political parties can play in combating racism, racial discrimination, xenophobia and related intolerance and encourages political parties to take concrete steps to promote equality, solidarity and non-discrimination in society, inter alia by developing voluntary codes of conduct which include internal disciplinary measures for violations thereof, so their members refrain from public statements and actions that encourage or incite racism, racial discrimination, xenophobia and related intolerance".

Item 27 of the Durban Declaration also is cautious in stating, "We express our concern that, beyond the fact that racism is gaining ground, contemporary forms and manifestations of racism and xenophobia are striving to regain political, moral and even legal recognition in many ways, including through the platforms of some political parties and organizations and the dissemination through modern communication technologies of ideas based on the notion of racial superiority".

In turn, the General Assembly in Item 3 of the 67/154 Resolution "expresses its appreciation to the United Nations High Commissioner for Human Rights for her commitment to maintaining the fight against racism, racial discrimination, xenophobia and related intolerance as one of the priority activities of her Office"[22]. And Item 12 of the 68/150 Resolution says that the General Assembly "Expresses concern at the human rights and democratic challenges posed by all extremist political parties, movements and groups". Apart from the "concern" and a direct reference to "extremist political parties", the next Item contains a specific demand

---

[22] *Resolutions adopted by the General Assembly at its 67 Session.* Available at: http://www.un.org/depts/dhl/resguide/r67_en.shtml

"to take the measures necessary to put an end to the practices described above, and calls upon States to take more effective measures in accordance with international human rights law to combat those phenomena and the extremist movements, which pose a real threat to democratic values".

The analysis of the vocabulary of the General Assembly reaffirms the previous viewpoint: it is "concern" for "extremist political parties", and "to put an end" for "extremist movements".

Item 14 of the 68/150 says that the General Assembly "encourages States to adopt further measures to provide training to the police and other law enforcement bodies on the ideologies of extremist political parties, movements and groups whose advocacy constitutes incitement to racist and xenophobic violence, to strengthen their capacity to address racist and xenophobic crimes, to fulfil their responsibility of bringing to justice the perpetrators of such crimes and to combat impunity".

Item 17 of the same Resolution again speaks about parties and about young people: the General Assembly "underlines that the roots of extremism are multifaceted and must be addressed through adequate measures such as education, awareness-raising and the promotion of dialogue, and in this regard recommends the increase of measures to raise awareness among young people of the dangers of the ideologies and activities of extremist political parties, movements and groups".

The Programme of Action encompasses not only politicians and parties but politics proper on the whole: Item 97 "recommends that further studies be conducted on how racism, racial discrimination, xenophobia and related intolerance may be reflected in laws, policies, institutions and practices". Item 91 also draws attention to political and legal systems: the Conference Urges States to work to ensure that their political and legal systems reflect the multicultural diversity within their societies and, where necessary, to improve democratic institutions so that they are more fully participatory and avoid marginalization, exclusion and discrimination against specific sectors of society".

The mass media play a special role in the interaction between the radical parties and the population.

5.8. The Role of the Mass Media

A separate question that can arise when diagnosing ultra-right and Nazi parties and movements is a question of relations between parties and their own or affiliated mass media. Such mass media are individual juridical personalities in good legal standing and bearing, accordingly, their own responsibility. In conflict situations, when a party faces liquidation at a court of law for disseminating prohibited statements through such mass media, the latter may play an unsavory, yet saving, role of ballast and bear the brunt meant for the party.

The role of the mass media is treated in detail in the Durban Declaration. Item 88 spells out, "We recognize that the media should represent the diversity of a multicultural society and play a role in fighting racism, racial discrimination, xenophobia and related intolerance. In this regard we draw attention to the power of advertising". Item 89: "We note with regret that certain media, by promoting false images and negative stereotypes of vulnerable individuals or groups of individuals, particularly of migrants and refugees, have contributed to the spread of xenophobic and racist sentiments among the public and in some cases have encouraged violence by racist individuals and groups". Item 90: "We recognize the positive contribution that the exercise of the right to freedom of expression, particularly by the media and new technologies, including the Internet, and full respect for the freedom to seek, receive and impart information can make to the fight against racism, racial discrimination, xenophobia and related intolerance; we reiterate the need to respect the editorial independence and autonomy of the media in this regard". Item 91: "We express deep concern about the use of new information technologies, such as the Internet, for purposes contrary to respect for human values, equality, non-discrimination, respect for others and tolerance, including to propagate racism, racial hatred, xenophobia, racial discrimination and related intolerance, and that, in particular, children and youth having access to this material could be negatively influenced by it". Item 92: "We also recognize the need to promote the use of new information and communication technologies, including the Internet, to contribute to the fight against racism, racial discrimination, xenophobia and related intolerance; new technologies can assist the promotion of tolerance and respect for human dignity, and the principles of equality and non-discrimination". Item 93: "We affirm that all States should recognize the importance of community media that give a voice to victims of racism, racial discrimination, xenophobia and related intolerance".

Without doubt, mass media have become the most important instrument of influencing the public opinion and they do have an impact of behaviour and choice of every individual.

Conclusion

Summing up the analysis of very diverse and voluminous provisions of international law for establishing the borderline between "the prohibited" and "the permissible", we can draw the following conclusions. First of all, "the border of the prohibited" in fact is not a borderline but a zone, and a complex zone at that, including terrorism, racial discrimination, slavery, apartheid, etc.; few of the terms used in this field have a clear-cut interpretation, but practically all are emotionally charged; apart from that, scientific and political dictionaries differ greatly from each other, as often as not it is not clear whether it denotes one and the same phenomenon, related phenomena (as in the case of "aggressive nationalism" and "ultra-nationalism", for example) or different phenomena; moreover, the General Assembly of the United Nations takes heed not to mention "Nazi (neo-Nazi) parties", and it uses the term "extremist" in relation to socially-dangerous parties; the General Assembly of the United Nations registers the weakness of national legislation in the part countering extremist political parties, movements and groups, and points out areas in need for the corresponding legislations and its methodological orientation – "should be in conformity with the relevant international human rights norms".

In many respects and senses, national law when drawing the line between "the prohibited" and "the permissible" cannot rely on international law, and it actually resolves many problems proceeding from its own political and legal practice and historical and social realities.

This Chapter dealing with the study and the analysis of sources of international public law was meant to provide a general overview of legal delineation of dividing line between "ordinary" right-wing and dangerous (Nazi) parties, and also to establish criteria that can help declare parties socially dangerous. It is obvious that the practice of liquidation of criminal parties is underdeveloped – this is proven by a multitude of different wordings related to the end of party activities. But this is the topic of the next chapter.

CHAPTER VI

REGULATION OF PARTY ACTIVITIES IN NATIONAL LAW: PRACTICE OF PROHIBITION

The study of national regulation of prohibitions for parties is conducted in the framework of this work with several aims in mind.

First, to determine if the prohibition against Nazi parties is universal.

Second, to examine how well the spirit and the letter of international public law in the sphere of our concern are transposed into national constitutional law. We have already touched upon the "intrusion" of international law into constitutional law in connection with the "constitutional measures" laid down in Item 30 of the 67/154 Resolution of the General Assembly of the United Nation, which "should be in conformity with the relevant international human rights norms".

Third, the Constitution chapters devoted to fundamental human rights and freedoms (many Constitutions add "the citizen" here), as a rule, are a national rendering of the Universal Declaration of Human Rights and other humanitarian acts of international public law. And this "rendering" is always creative, inevitably containing "scribal errors" – new wordings, new interpretations, etc. This "scribal error" is always valuable since it can spur new ideas – the same as in the medieval ages "scribal errors" sometimes gave rise to a heresy.

The sampling of Constitution texts to be analyzed was conducted largely within the European region, and it was of no importance if a Constitution at that moment was working or not, the important thing was that certain prohibitions had been embodied in national constitutional law.

6.1. Constitutional References to Nazism (Fascism)

As was mentioned above, such references are few, yet they do occur. The farthest of them from the issue under study is the reference to the

Territorial Antifascist Council of the National Liberation of Croatia in the Chapter "Historical Foundations".[1]

The Preamble to the Declaration of Citizens' Rights and of the Fundamental Principles of San Marinese Legal Order also mentions fascism, "The Great and General Council, conscious of the Republic's glorious traditions of freedom and democracy, having the firm intention of rejecting fascism and any totalitarian concept of the State, and with the aim of guaranteeing further civil, social and political progress for the people of San Marino…"[2].

Of immediate relevance to the topic of prohibited parties is Article 13 of the Constitution of Poland: "Political parties and other organizations whose programmes are based upon totalitarian methods and the modes of activity of Nazism, fascism and communism, as well as those whose programmes or activities sanction racial or national hatred, the application of violence for the purpose of obtaining power or to influence the State policy, or provide for the secrecy of their own structure or membership, shall be prohibited"[3].

Article XII of the Transitory and Final Provisions of the Constitution of Italy spells out that "It shall be forbidden to reorganize, under any form whatever, the dissolved fascist party. Notwithstanding Article 48, the law has established, for not more than five years from the implementation of the Constitution, temporary limitations to the right to vote and eligibility for the leaders responsible for the fascist regime"[4].

The Constitution of Portugal refers to fascism twice. The first reference occurs in the Preamble: "On the 25th of April 1974 the Armed Forces Movement crowned the long years of resistance and reflected the deepest feelings of the Portuguese people by overthrowing the fascist regime. Freeing Portugal from dictatorship, oppression and colonialism was a revolutionary change and the beginning of an historic turning point for Portuguese society"[5].

---

[1] *Constitution of Croatia*. Available at: http://www.sabor.hr/Default.aspx?art=2406

[2] *Constitution of San Marino*. Available at: http://unpan1.un.org/intradoc/groups/public/documents/un-dpadm/unpan040713~1.pdf

[3] *Constitution of Poland.* Available at: http://www.sejm.gov.pl/prawo/konst/angielski/kon1.htm

[4] *Constitution of Italy*. Available at: http://legislationline.org/download/action/download/id/1613/file/b4371e43dc8cf675b67904284951.htm/preview

[5] *Constitution of Portugal*. Available at: http://www.wipo.int/wipolex/en/text.jsp?file_id=206670

The second reference in Part 4 Article 46 Freedom of association fully corresponds to the topic under study: “Armed associations, military, militarised or paramilitary-type associations and organisations that are racist or display a fascist ideology shall not be permitted”[6].

As follows from the cited provisions, the constitutional prohibition on Nazi parties is far from being universal, which accounts for the concern expressed by the General Assembly of the United Nations that speaks about “constitutional measures” taken by the States. The scantiness of the material makes it difficult to draw any general conclusions, we will pay attention to the fact that, when speaking about the prohibition on Nazi parties (organizations) in one case it is “fascist ideologies” (Portugal), in the other “totalitarian methods and the modes of activity of Nazism” (Poland), which is not one and the same thing – these totalitarian methods and modes of activity may be adopted by other parties, it is not for nothing that Poland mentions “communism” along with Nazism and fascism.

6.2. Types and Forms of Constitutional Prohibitions for Parties

This part will show that the “scribal error” assumption was true, and there exist more variations in the topic of constitutional prohibitions for parties than one could imagine.

Yet we shall begin with stating that the constitutions of such countries as, for example, Slovenia, Bosnia and Herzegovina, Cyprus, Sweden, Austria, Belgium, Denmark, Luxembourg, Malta, Ireland, Iceland, the Netherlands and Finland never mention parties at all.

The constitutions of such countries as, for example, Hungary, Latvia, Romania, Andorra, Italy, Spain, Norway and San Marino contain clauses related to parties, but nothing is said about prohibitions.

Here we should make two technical observations related to constitutional law.

Constitutions vary greatly in their forms (though there is a certain tendency of unification), and party activities are subject (if at all) to provisions of the chapter related to fundamental human rights and not to the chapters regulating the principal state institutions, first of all, parliaments. Constitutions traditionally treat parties as a particular case of freedom of associations and not as an element of the political system of a state. This study does not undertake the task of deciding to what extent

---

[6] *Constitution of Portugal*. Available at:
http://www.wipo.int/wipolex/en/text.jsp?file_id=206670#LinkTarget_567

such an approach is justifiable at present when political parties can be found practically everywhere. The technical significance of this observation is that we shall examine the corresponding prohibitions on the exercise of freedom of association for both cases – for constitutions with no mention of parties and for constitutions with no prohibitions for parties. (Of great interest is the example of Belgium: Article 27 of the Constitution denies the possibility of prohibitions for associations – "Belgians have the right to enter into association; this right cannot be subjected to any preventative measures").

The second observation relates to the correlation of constitutions and laws, to be more precise, to the delegating norms (reservation clauses) thereof. As a particular case of associations, parties are subject to special laws. Yet the study shows that, on the whole, the constitutional regulation of prohibition for parties (associations) does not use the delegating approach when the only thing said of parties is that their formation and their activities "are regulated by the law on parties" or by a "corresponding law". Nevertheless, such reservation clauses are not infrequent.

As an example, the clause of part 2 of Article 26 of the Constitution of Georgia defines parties as a special case of associations: "Citizens of Georgia shall have the right to form a political party or other political association and participate in its activity in accordance with the Organic Law"[7].

Another example related to associations occurs in Article 40 of the Constitution of Ireland, "6.1. The State guarantees liberty for the exercise of the following rights, subject to public order and morality: (…). iii) The right of the citizens to form associations and unions. Laws, however, may be enacted for the regulation and control in the public interest of the exercise of the foregoing right. 2. Laws regulating the manner in which the right of forming associations and unions and the right of free assembly may be exercised shall contain no political, religious or class discrimination"[8].

This example does not contain a "pure" delegating norm, and the Constitution stipulates both restrictions on associations – "… liberty for the exercise of the flowing rights" is "subject to public order and morality", and on the laws regulating them – they "shall contain no political, religious or class discrimination".

[7] *Constitution of Georgia*. Available at:
http://www.wipo.int/wipolex/en/text.jsp?file_id=194553#LinkTarget_1155
[8] *Constitution of Ireland*. Available at:
http://www.irishstatutebook.ie/en/constitution/index.html#part13

A delegating norm proper can be found in Article 42 of the Constitution of Slovenia where the framework of restriction is also set by the Constitution:

"The right of peaceful assembly and public meeting shall be guaranteed. Everyone has the right to freedom of association with others. Legal restrictions of these rights shall be permissible where so required for national security or public safety and for protection against the spread of infectious diseases"[9].

Yet, the principal prohibitions on activities of parties and associations are provided for in the constitutional texts, in support of which we adduce the following evidence.

6.2.1. Prohibition on the forcible overthrow of the constitutional regime

Used wordings: "forcible change", "destruction", "undermining of state security", "application of violence for the purpose of obtaining power" (Bulgaria, Poland, Albania), "application of violence to influence the State policy" (Poland), "infringement upon the independence and territorial integrity of the country", "infringement of sovereignty", "constitutional system (regime, order)" "by violent means" (in the majority of State Constitutions). This most frequently used prohibition is typical of such states as, for example, Serbia, Georgia, Macedonia, Slovakia, Croatia, the Czech Republic, Estonia, Germany, Abkhazia, Ukraine, Bulgaria, Poland, and Albania.

The above-studied ideas of security are best matched to this prohibition, as this prohibition is meant to ensure security of a State as such and the existing state regime. Whereas parties may cause only "internal" damage, this prohibition, nonetheless, reveals a clear "external" motive – such as a threat to the territorial integrity, which makes us think of a prohibition against foreign influence on parties. Such prohibition usually is formulated in two forms: prohibition on foreign parties' activities within a particular state, and a prohibition on foreign financing of parties. However, as a rule, these prohibitions are not spelled out by constitutions; they are provided for in the corresponding laws on parties. Yet, the prohibition on "propagandizing war" ("military aggression") (Georgia, Macedonia, Ukraine) is embodied in the constitutions, which

---

[9] *Constitution of Slovenia*. Available at: http://www.us-rs.si/en/about-the-court/legal-basis/

ensues that the general prohibition on violence is complex. The prohibition for parties to have paramilitary forces (Abkhazia, Ukraine) props up this thesis, since such forces can be used for forcible overthrow of the constitutional regime and for external aggression. Formulations come in two types: parties are forbidden to have military (paramilitary, quasi-military) forces, and military formations, as associations, are prohibited.

Yet the prohibition on military formations is not universal: Article 48 of the Constitution of the Republic Estonia speaks of "The establishment of organisations and unions which possess weapons, are militarily organised or perform military exercises requires prior permission, for which the conditions and procedure of issuance shall be provided by law"[10].

The prohibition on forcible overthrow of the constitutional regime, as will be shown below, has a direct bearing on Nazism, since Nazis always, in accordance with the nature of this phenomenon, strive to a different regime. Article 18 of the Constitution of Abkhazia is a good illustration of this: "Prohibited shall be the formation and activities of non-governmental associations, parties and movements whose aims and operations include the forceful transformation of the constitutional system, the undermining of state security, the creation of armed groups, the incitement of social, racial, ethnic and religious discord"[11].

Article 37 of the Constitution of Ukraine is devoted to the topic of prohibition on party activities and the matter of party dissolution, "The establishment and activity of political parties and public association are prohibited if their programme goals or actions are aimed at the liquidation of the independence of Ukraine, the change of the constitutional order by violent means, the violation of the sovereignty and territorial indivisibility of the State, the undermining of its security, the unlawful seizure of power, the propaganda of war and violence, the incitement of inter-ethnic, racial and religious enmity, and the encroachment on human rights and freedoms and the health of the population. The prohibition of the activity of associations of citizens is exercised only through judicial procedure. The creation and activity of organizational structures of political parties shall not be permitted within bodies of executive and judicial power and executive bodies of local self-government, in military formations, and also in state enterprises, educational establishments and other state institutions and organizations."[12]

---

[10] *Constitution of the Republic of Estonia*. Available at: http://www.president.ee/en/republic-of-estonia/the-constitution/

[11] *Constitution of Abkhazia*. Available at: http://apsnypress.info/en/constitution

[12] *Constitution of Ukraine*. Available at:

Here we should note that it is characteristic of constitutions to list prohibitions one by one. Such linear constructions facilitate the tracing of frequency of certain prohibitions.

Part 1 of Article 117 of the Constitution of Malta, entitled "Prohibition of certain associations" contains a very elaborate wording, "It shall be unlawful to establish, maintain or belong to any association of persons who are organised and trained or organised and equipped for the purpose of enabling them to be employed for the use or display of physical force in promoting any political object"[13].

6.2.2. Prohibition on infringement of democracy

When enacting into law the prohibition on infringement of democracy the following wordings are used, "destruction of undermining of the constitutional order", "contrary to the constitutional order" (Cyprus), "provided that the aims and activities (of societies, political parties and associations) are not contrary to the Constitution and laws" (Lithuania), "for ends which are not forbidden to individuals by criminal law" (Italy).

This prohibition takes an inverse form in a number of constitutions. For instance, Article 26 of the Constitution of the Principality of Andorra formulates this prohibition as a requirement, "Andorrans have the right freely to create political parties. Their functioning and organization must be democratic and their activities lawful"[14]. The Constitutions of Spain and the Federal Republic of Germany formulate this in an analogous way[15]. In Denmark and Iceland parties can be formed "for any lawful

---

http://www.legislationline.org/documents/section/constitutions/country/52

[13] *Constitution of Malta*. Available at: http://www.constitution.org/cons/malta/chapt0.pdf

[14] *Constitution of Andorra*. Available at: http://www.wipo.int/wipolex/en/text.jsp?file_id=187171

[15] *Constitution of Spain*. Available at: http://www.lamoncloa.gob.es/lang/en/espana/leyfundamental/Paginas/index.aspx, *Basic Law for the Federal Republic of Germany*. Available at: https://www.btg-bestellservice.de/pdf/80201000.pdf

purposes"[16]. In Monaco "Freedom of association is guaranteed, subject to regulation of law"[17].

Part 2 of Article 10 of the Constitution of Portugal provides an interesting formulation, "The political parties contribute to the organization and expression of the will of the people and respect the principles of national independence and political democracy"[18].

A more universal limitation related to all the fundamental rights and freedoms is more frequent. In Article 20, Division Two, of the Charter of Fundamental Rights and Freedoms of the Czech Republic it is most pronounced, (2) Citizens also have the right to form political parties and political movements and to associate therein. (3) The exercise of these rights may be limited only in cases specified by law, if it involves measures that are necessary in a democratic society for the security of the state, the protection of public security and public order, the prevention of crime, or the protection of the rights and freedoms of others"[19].

6.2.3. Prohibition on totalitarian parties

Prohibition on totalitarian parties is rare in constitutions. It occurs only in Constitutions of Albania, Poland and San-Marino.

For instance, part 2 of Article 9 of the Constitution of Albania says, "Political parties and other organizations, the programs and activity of which are based on totalitarian methods, which incite and support racial, religious, regional or ethnic hatred, which use violence to take power or influence state policies, as well as those with a secret character, are prohibited pursuant to the law"[20].

---

[16] *Constitutional Act of Denmark*. Available at: http://www.ilo.org/wcmsp5/groups/public/---ed_protect/---protrav/---ilo_aids/documents/legaldocument/wcms_127469.pdf; *Constitution of the Republic of Iceland*. Available at: http://www.concourt.am/armenian/legal_resources/world_constitutions/constit/iceland/icelnd-e.htm

[17] *Constitution of the Principality of Monaco*. Available at: http://www.venice.coe.int/webforms/documents/default.aspx?pdffile=CDL-REF%282013%29021-e

[18] *Constitution of Portugal*. Available at: http://www.servat.unibe.ch/icl/po00000_.html

[19] *Charter of Fundamental Rights and Freedoms of the Czech Republic*. Available at: http://www.usoud.cz/en/charter-of-fundamental-rights-and-freedoms/

[20] *Constitution of Albania*. Available at: http://unpan1.un.org/intradoc/groups/public/documents/untc/unpan013810.pdf

6.2.4. Prohibition on the direct exercise of state power and monopoly of power

Such prohibition is laid down, for example, in the Constitutions of Serbia, Hungary, Bulgaria, Slovakia, the Czech Republic. Thus, Article 5 of the Constitution of Serbia contains the formulation, "Political parties may not exercise power directly or submit it to their control"[21].

The Constitution of Bulgaria has such a prohibition twice worded in a more elaborate form. Part 3 of Article 1 says, "No part of the people, political party or any other organization, institution of state, or individual may usurp the exercise of the people's sovereignty." and Part 2 of Article 11 spells out, "Not a single political party or ideology may be proclaimed or asserted as state-sponsored"[22].

Quite in a different way treats the matter Part 4 of Article 29 of the Constitution of Slovakia, "Political parties and political movements, as well as unions, societies or other associations shall be separate from the State"[23].

6.2.5. Constitutional limitations on party membership

The topic of "the separation of parties and State" is treated in provisions related to the prohibition for certain categories of public officers to join a party. These prohibitions vary greatly from country to country. Thus, the following categories cannot belong to a party: the military and policemen (Slovenia, Georgia, Cyprus and Italy), national security officials, prosecutors and judges (Georgia), diplomats (Italy).

More broadly this prohibition is spelled out in Part 3 of Article 29 of the Constitution of Greece, which speaks not of membership but of partisanship of the party. "Manifestations of any nature whatsoever in favour of political parties by judicial functionaries, the military in general, members of the security corps and public servants, as well as the active support in favour of a party by employees of public law legal persons,

---

[21] *Constitution of Serbia*. Available at: http://en.wikisource.org/wiki/Constitution_of_Serbia#PART_TWO_-_HUMAN_AND_MINORITY_RIGHTS_AND_FREEDOMS

[22] *Constitution of Bulgaria*. Available at: 22 http://www.vks.bg/english/vksen_p04_01.htm

[23] *Constitution of Slovakia*. Available at: http://www.sudnarada.gov.sk/data/files/527_constitution-of-the-slovak-republic.pdf

public enterprises and local government agencies are absolutely prohibited"[24].

6.2.6. Prohibition on the incitement of hatred

This prohibition, apart from the prohibition against racial discrimination, has several specific formulations that come, however, under a common wording of "fomenting of enmity (hatred, intolerance, discord)". Thus, the incitement of "racial" intolerance is prohibited in the constitutions of such states as, for example, Serbia, Macedonia, Poland, Albania, Abkhazia, Ukraine, Sweden; "national (ethnic)" intolerance in Serbia, Georgia, Macedonia, Poland, Albania, Ukraine, Sweden; "religious" intolerance in Serbia, Georgia, Macedonia, Albania, Abkhazia, Ukraine; local (regional) in Georgia and Albania.

6.2.7. Prohibition on the violation of guaranteed human rights

This prohibition is rarely used. For instance, Article 5 of the Constitution of Serbia stipulates that "Activities of political parties aiming at forced overthrow of constitutional system, violation of guaranteed human or minority rights, inciting racial, national or religious hatred, shall be prohibited"[25].

6.2.8. Prohibition on parties that provide for the secrecy of their own structure or membership

The prohibition on parties and associations that provide for the secrecy of their structure and membership ("are of secret character") is applied in Poland, Albania, Spain, and Italy.

In an inverse form a similar prohibition occurs in Part 5 of Article 51 of the Constitution of Portugal, "Political parties shall be governed by the principles of transparency, democratic organisation and management, and participation by all their members"[26].

---

[24] *Constitution of Greece*. Available at:
http://www.hri.org/docs/syntagma/artcl50.html#A29
[25] *Constitution of Serbia*. Available at:
http://en.wikisource.org/wiki/Constitution_of_Serbia#PART_TWO_-_HUMAN_AND_MINORITY_RIGHTS_AND_FREEDOMS
[26] *Constitution of Portugal.* Available at:
http://www.wipo.int/wipolex/en/text.jsp?file_id=206670

6.2.9. Prohibition on a certain basis of a party

This is a rare, almost unique, type of prohibition; furthermore, "bases" to be prohibited vary from party to party. Thus, parties formed on the "ethnic" and "racial" basis are prohibited under the Constitution of Bulgaria, on the "religious" basis in Bulgaria and Portugal, on the "regional" in Portugal.

For example, Part 4 of Article 51 of the Constitution of Portugal says, "No party shall be formed with a name or manifesto that possesses a regional nature or scope"[27].

6.2.10. The inverse prohibition – the requirement for publicity of party financing

This requirement is an inverse prohibition – prohibition against secrecy in party financing. Used in the Constitutions of Albania and the Federal Republic of Germany. For example, Part 3 of Article 9 of the Constitution of Albania spells out that "The sources of financing of parties as well as their expenses are always made public"[28]. The same requirement can be regulated by a proviso; thus, Part 2 of Article 29 of the Constitution of Greece says, "The financial support of parties by the State and the publicity of electoral expenses of parties and parliamentary candidates may be provided by law"[29]. This matter is regulated in a similar way in Portugal.

6.2.11. Prohibition on forced membership in parties and associations

This prohibition is one of the most demonstrative. For example, the Constitution of Lithuania (art. 35) stipulates that "No one may be compelled to belong to any society, political party, or association"[30]. The prohibition is rare, though, and not outright. For example, the Constitution of Iceland specifies that "nobody can be forced into joining any public

---

[27] *Constitution of Portugal*. Available at: http://www.wipo.int/wipolex/en/text.jsp?file_id=206670

[28] *Constitution of Albania*. Available at: http://www.osce.org/albania/41888?download=true

[29] *Constitution of Greece*. Available at: http://www.hri.org/docs/syntagma/artcl80.html

[30] *Constitution of Lithuania*. Available at: http://www3.lrs.lt/home/Konstitucija/Constitution.htm

association"[31]. Such an obligation, however, may be prescribed by the law, if so required, for a public association to operate in public interest or for the defence of rights of others.

6.2.12. Prohibition on party liquidation without legal proceedings

This prohibition is established not for parties but it has a direct bearing on them as it is established in their favour, thereby it will be considered in this chapter, too. It boils down to a very simple thing: parties and, more broadly, associations may be dissolved only in a judicial procedure. Yet, various interpretations of the term "party liquidation" make the whole matter more obscure

Thus, the Constitutions of Georgia and Spain speak about "prohibition of activities", "suspension or prohibition of the activity of public or political associations shall be possible only under a court decision, in the cases determined by the Organic Law and in accordance with a procedure prescribed by law"[32]. This clause provides also for "suspension of the activity".

The approach of Estonia is more mercantile (art. 48): "Only a court may terminate or suspend the activities of, or fine, an organisation, union or political party, for a violation of the law"[33]. This clause specifies that the grounds for "suspension of the activity" are violations of the law, and the perpetrator is a juridical person – a party. The relevance and, more importantly, effectiveness of such a measure as a fine will be considered below.

The Constitution of Andorra speaks about the "dissolution" of a party (art. 26): "The suspension of their activities and their dissolution is the responsibility of the judicial organs"[34]. The Basic Law for the Federal Republic of Germany recognizes "unconstitutionality": "Parties that, by

---

[31] *Constitution of Iceland.* Available at: http://www.concourt.am/armenian/legal_resources/world_constitutions/constit/iceland/icelnd-e.htm

[32] *Constitution of Georgia*. Available at: http://www.wipo.int/wipolex/en/text.jsp?file_id=194553#LinkTarget_3072; *Constitution of Spain*. Available at: http://www.lamoncloa.gob.es/lang/en/espana/leyfundamental/Paginas/index.aspx

[33] *Constitution of Estonia*. Available at: http://www.president.ee/en/republic-of-estonia/the-constitution/index.html#II

[34] *The Constitution of Andorra*. Available at: http://www.wipo.int/wipolex/en/text.jsp?file_id=187171

reason of their aims or the behaviour of their adherents, seek to undermine or abolish the free democratic basic order or to endanger the existence of the Federal Republic of Germany shall be unconstitutional. The Federal Constitutional Court shall rule on the question of unconstitutionality"[35]. What practical implications the recognition of unconstitutionality can have is not specified.

The analogous prohibition in Denmark consists of three parts: (3) "No association shall be dissolved by any government measure; but an association may be temporarily prohibited, provided that immediate proceedings be taken for its dissolution. (4) Cases relating to the dissolution of political associations may, without special permission, be brought before the Supreme Court of Justice of the Realm. (5) The legal effects of the dissolution shall be determined by Statute" (art. 78)[36].

The Constitution of Malta refers to "unlawful associations" and to illustrate this instance we shall cite again the already mentioned article "Article 117. (1) It shall be unlawful to establish, maintain or belong to any association of persons who are organised and trained or organised and equipped for the purpose of enabling them to be employed for the use or display of physical force in promoting any political object. (2) The provisions of this article shall be enforced in such manner as may be provided by Parliament"[37].

In Iceland "People are entitled to form associations for any lawful purpose without having to seek authorization. No association may be dissolved by an executive measure. It may, however, be banned temporarily, in which case an action must immediately be brought for dissolution of the association" (art. 73)[38].

6.3. Prohibitions relating to political activities

This part provides a brief outline of prohibitions related not to parties proper but to political activities in general. Noteworthy is the following:

---

[35] *The Basic Law for the Federal Republic of Germany*. Available at: https://www.btg-bestellservice.de/pdf/80201000.pdf

[36] *Constitution of Denmark*. Available at: http://www.ilo.org/wcmsp5/groups/public/---ed_protect/---protrav/---ilo_aids/documents/legaldocument/wcms_127469.pdf

[37] *Constitution of Malta.* Available at: http://www.constitution.org/cons/malta/chapt0.pdf

[38] *Constitution of Iceland.* Available at: http://www.concourt.am/armenian/legal_resources/world_constitutions/constit/iceland/icelnd-e.htm

"Religious communities and institutions, or religious convictions, may not be used for political purposes". (Bulgaria. Article 13 (4))

"No one may be deprived, for political reasons, of legal status, citizenship, name" (Italy. Article 22).

It is obvious that the lawmaker always strives to clearly define the conditions for political activity in order to avoid political conflicts in a society. Conflicts arise, as a rule, when religious motives are used or somebody is ousted from public and political life (the topic of marginalization frequently occurring in the Resolutions of the General Assembly of the United Nations).

Prohibitions this way or another related to "political crimes" constitute a special, quite large, group.

For example, the Constitution of Greece prohibits punishment for political crimes: "The death sentence shall not be imposed for political crimes, unless these are composite" Article 7 (3); 47 (3). Amnesty may be granted only for political crimes, by statute passed by the Plenum of the Parliament with a majority of three-fifths of the total number of members. (Article 62) "During the parliamentary term the Members of Parliament shall not be prosecuted, arrested, imprisoned or otherwise confined without prior leave granted by Parliament. Likewise, a member of a dissolved Parliament shall not be prosecuted for political crimes during the period between the dissolution of Parliament and the declaration of the election of the members of the new Parliament"[39].

The Constitution of Luxembourg contains analogous provisions: "The death penalty on political grounds and civil death and branding are hereby abolished" (Article 18). "The death penalty, abolished in political matters, shall be replaced by the penalty immediately below it, until such time as this matter has been covered by the new law" (Article 118). The Constitutions of Italy (Article 10) and Portugal (Article 33 (4)), holding the political activity in great veneration, specify that "The extradition of a foreigner for political offences is not admitted"[40].

---

[39] *Constitution of Greece.* Available at: http://www.hri.org/docs/syntagma/artcl80.html

[40] *Constitution of Italy.* Available at: http://legislationline.org/download/action/download/id/1613/file/b4371e43dc8cf675b67904284951.htm/preview; *Constitution of Portugal.* Available at: http://www.wipo.int/wipolex/en/text.jsp?file_id=206670

Conclusion

Thus, a great number of constitutional provisions are meant to regulate activities of parties or associations, yet they do not seek to stipulate conditions for their activities while welcoming political and party diversity. The prohibitions we have reviewed are not ubiquitous and the majority of them are outside the judicial practice.

This Chapter, devoted to the study and analysis of the sources of national constitutional law, likewise the previous one, was meant to provide an overview of legal regulation of far-right and dangerous (Nazi) parties; it also seeks to establish the criteria that would allow us to ban parties. The original hypothesis that the examined parties are socially dangerous, or, to be more general, criminal, may constitute the basis from where to proceed, since, as was shown, the most frequent prohibitions on parties occurring in national constitutions are prohibitions against violence, incitement of enmity, including racial discrimination. Also, upon the examination of national constitutional texts, it becomes clear why the General Assembly of the United Nations should show deep concern and call for ‘constitutional measures’: only two constitutions of those under study provide for the prohibition on Nazi parties.

CHAPTER VII

DIAGNOSTICS AND LIQUIDATION OF PROHIBITED PARTIES: THEORETICAL AND LEGAL ASPECTS

This Chapter aims to put forward an outline of a practicable model of the liquidation of socially-dangerous parties, and this model will be based both on the available theoretical developments in social sciences and also on the available acts of international public law. The authors will try to bridge the gaps in the theoretical research, legal base, even analogies, and the corresponding judicial practice by suggesting their ideas and alternate solutions.

Liquidation of a party through legal proceedings is something out of the ordinary in both the political life of a country and also the national judicial practice. We have already shown that national constitutions resort to various formulations of the process ("prohibition on the activity", "cessation of the activity", "dissolution", "admitting it unconstitutional", "admitting it unlawful"), which allows for a conclusion that there are no universally accepted approaches to the solution of this problem, nor is there a common opinion of what to call parties that have been recognized as socially dangerous: should they be "prohibited", "criminal", "unconstitutional" or something else?

On closer examination, we find out that the problem is not monolithic, but constitutes a tangle of problems. As is usual in such cases, it is essential to understand which thread to pull first. This allows for different methodological approaches. We may catalogue the instructions given by international organizations, first and foremost, by the United Nations, and try and apply them to a particular case revealing their drawbacks in the process. We can take a well-developed appropriate political theory and attempt to examine, again in the test mode, how well it is applied in practice. We can assume a teleological approach, that is, first define the purpose of the liquidation of a socially dangerous party and then, with the liquidation in view, find the appropriate legal means. But at first, as we believe, we should investigate the subject – parties, and the possibility to have them liquidated.

7.1. Parties as a particular case of associations

The previous chapter, while examining the texts of national constitutions where prohibitions against parties were completely disregarded, investigated the corresponding prohibitions on associations. It was then that it was suggested that it was not altogether methodologically correct to place the instructions and prohibitions against parties in the constitutional chapter devoted to fundamental rights and freedoms.

Indeed, at first glance liquidation of parties looks like the grossest violation of human rights, since freedom of association is part of the classic list of fundamental human rights. There is no doubt that the issue of violation of human rights will arise at every court proceeding related to party liquidation. Ex facto, it may seem that the only legal instrument for passing a judgment is a thoroughly elaborated mechanism of applying a universal "human" proviso that allows for limiting the fundamental rights and freedoms. We shall cite Part 2 of Article 29 of the Universal Declaration of Human Rights, "In the exercise of his rights and freedoms, everyone shall be subject only to such limitations as are determined by law solely for the purpose of securing due recognition and respect for the rights and freedoms of others and of meeting the just requirements of morality, public order and the general welfare in a democratic society"[1].

The procedure of "weighing" threats and searching for eligible measure of restricting rights is fairly well established in courts; it is also described in detail in the corresponding legal literature, first of all, that of constitutional law and humanitarian law (human rights).

Yet, the compulsory liquidation of non-profit organizations and, in particular, of Nazi parties technically remains a direct violation of freedom of association. To avoid an essentially unnecessary judicial "prelude" on human rights, it is feasible to resort to Item 4 of the 60/143 Resolution: the General Assembly of the United Nations "reaffirms that such acts may be qualified to fall within the scope of activities described in article 4 of the International Convention on the Elimination of All Forms of Racial Discrimination, and that they represent a clear and manifest abuse of the rights to freedom of peaceful assembly and of association as well as the rights to freedom of opinion and expression within the meaning of those

---

[1] *The Universal Declaration of Human Rights*. Available at: http://www.un.org/en/documents/udhr/

rights as guaranteed by the Universal Declaration of Human Rights, the International Covenant on Civil and Political Rights and the International Convention on the Elimination of All Forms of Racial Discrimination”[2].

The General Assembly of the United Nations expressly states that they are not human rights, that “they represent a clear and manifest abuse” of these rights. Owing to this statement, judgments passed in a conducted trial become more substantive.

Moreover, there are a number of instances that distinguish political parties from associations, they differ so greatly that it stands to reason to pose a question if we still speak about human rights (freedom of association) when we speak about parties. The main difference lies in a “human”, yet the right to form parties belongs not to humans, but to citizens, that is, the criterion of universality, inherent in human rights, is immediately lost here. The requirement for citizenship in the country of residence (or a federation, or a union) is, with rare exceptions, universal for party membership; as an example of such an exception we can refer to Article 102 of the working Constitution of Latvia, which states that “everyone” has the right to join parties. Many laws on parties establish other qualification requirements in addition to the citizenship requirement.

The next fundamental difference between parties and associations is that the setting up of the former follows an administrative procedure while the latter lend themselves to the notification requirement. A party cannot just proclaim itself; the State must acknowledge it as such through the registration procedure, which, as a rule, coincides with its incorporation. It is impossible to form a party without incorporation (which is typical of associations); in any case, we cannot cite an appropriate example. Many laws on parties prohibit the word “party” to be used by associations that are not parties.

The third fundamental difference is the requirement for the minimal number of members needed to have a party registered. It is characteristic that the size completely depends on the political will of the lawmaker and, as a rule, is not science-based.

The reverse side of membership is significant, too, since parties, along with trade unions, are large associations, and in this sense, they are valuable, especially in our time of universal individualism, as a largest storage of human capital. Parties are a good illustration of how thousands

---

[2] *Inadmissibility of certain practices that contribute to fuelling contemporary forms of racism, racial discrimination, xenophobia and related intolerance.* 2005. Available at:
http://www.un.org/en/ga/search/view_doc.asp?symbol=A/RES/60/143

of people can reach a certain agreement. This sole instance may make the task of passing a judgment of party liquidation psychologically difficult.

The fourth difference lies in the principal conflict between the nature of interests and the goals set by a party. Estonian laws are a good illustration of this conflict. As a special case of associations (non-profit associations), parties, according to the law, are founded in the "interests of private persons", but the goals they set are "the exercise of state power and local self-governance", which allows us to draw a paradoxical, yet very convincing, conclusion that power in Estonia is exercised in private interest. However, the egoism of parties is a usual matter: nobody gets surprised when parties that win in the election do not appoint experts to ministerial positions and secure these positions for the party elite. The contemporary dictionary defines it as "political guidance", which often is synonymous with incompetence.

The fifth characteristic is that parties are eligible to stand in elections for political office and, as a consequence, they "exercise state and local self-government power". In many countries only parties have the right to stand in elections, while political associations (electoral alliances) are not eligible, though, again, there is no general rule. Standing in elections endows parties with rights and obligations that are uncharacteristic of associations, and also makes the election law binding on them.

This list of principal differences can be further extended, but here we should make a theoretical remark. The standard of "human rights" established after the adoption of the Universal Declaration on Human Rights resulted in two significant "overreaches", quite obvious now: first, the standard reduced all fundamental rights and freedoms to "rights", which blurred the doctrinal division between right and freedoms, and produced such ugly phrases as, for one, "the right to freedom of associations"; second, all rights relate to a human, to an individual. This standard deprived such freedoms as freedom of assembly and freedom of association of their individual and collective nature, and there emerged such formulations as "everyone has a right to the freedom of assembly". The ridiculousness of such wordings is never taken as something curious, though how one person ("everyone") can form an assembly or an association is impossible to understand. It takes at least two.

These deliberations make us pay attention to the fact that the list of sanctions against socially dangerous parties does not contain such one as expulsion from a party in legal proceedings with a possible simultaneous prohibition against engaging in political activity (the latter took place, as was shown, in postwar Italy). Such a sanction is less grave than liquidation of the whole party, yet it is here, as we believe, that the phenomenon of "human rights" manifests itself in full force and effect: it is easier for the State to liquidate a political abstraction, a party, than to curtail the rights of one, though particular, person. The absence of such a sanction (everywhere only the party itself can expel a member from the party, and the mechanism of challenging the decision is fairly well elaborated, even in a legal procedure) can be accounted for only by profound reverence for "human rights". Yet, as the corresponding experience of Estonia shows, people are forced to leave parties, as a rule, for criticizing the leadership, charged with "violating the party rules" and "damaging the image of the party". It seems that this practice is quite common.

That the proposed legal sanction would be feasible derives from the observation that socially dangerous parties are, as a rule, parties of one leader. The Liberal Democratic Party of Russia with the eternal chairman V.V. Zhirinovsky as its head is one thing, and quite another without him. But parties, as a rule, get rid not of the leaders who steer them toward criminal ends, but of those who criticize these leaders.

Let us consider now the possible enforcement actions (sanctions) against socially dangerous parties.

7.2. Purpose of Party Liquidation

7.2.1. Terminology and Goal Setting

As was demonstrated above, there is no unanimity in understanding what to do about parties that can be recognized as socially dangerous. The proposed terms, apart from "liquidation", such as "prohibition", "prohibition on activity", "cessation of activity", "dissolution", "declaration of unconstitutionality", "and declaration of unlawfulness" differ greatly from one another.

The analysis shows that "liquidation" is the most adequate of practically all other terms used to describe the process. First, "prohibition on activities" does not relate to the nature of associations (the association still exists but is not engaged in any activity?). Second, it leaves a gap between "activity" and "existence"; for example, a racist programme posted at the site of the party is difficult to regard as an "action", especially if it had been placed there before the party was prohibited. Moreover, "prohibition" on activities requires constant control over the performance of the party. "Dissolution" actually means a prohibition against assembly, a prohibition on association, but it still fails to solve the problem of the existence of a party as a juridical person and it does not erase a problem of control. But a party, as a non-profit association, has to convene a general assembly (congress) at least to approve the annual report required by the taxing authorities, which is contrary to the logic of "dissolution" and "cessation of activity".

"Declaration of unconstitutionality" is calqued on the logic of constitutional supervision according to which once a law is ruled unconstitutional, it is immediately abolished; it is its euphemism. But in the case of parties this does not hold; and in practice it is nothing but a censure unless the law establishes that "the declaration of unconstitutionality" entails liquidation. The same goes for "declaration of unlawfulness". Neither do the last two terms reflect social danger of extreme right-wing parties: a party can be declared unconstitutional if some of its members are stateless persons, while only citizens of the country can join a party.

The term "liquidation" is preferable when used in respect of parties, first, because it reflects the existence of parties as a juridical person and not as a certain association. Liquidation of juridical persons is a classical case in law. Second, because in those countries where, apart from physical persons, juridical persons are subject to criminal prosecution, liquidation is a punishment, and the feel of punishment cannot be out of place when a socially dangerous party is being liquidated. "Liquidation" fully encompasses "dissolution" but without further control, which is very valuable for the economy of common property resources.

Unambiguousness in the matter of "liquidation" is absolutely essential for us to proceed in the fight against dangerous ideologies and phenomena. Without this clarity it is difficult to understand, for example, what is meant in Sub-Item 3 of Item 9 of the Declaration, "In order to put into effect the purposes and principles of the present Declaration, all States shall take immediate and positive measures, including legislative and other measures, to prosecute and/or outlaw organizations which promote or incite to racial discrimination, or incite to or use violence for purposes of discrimination based on race, colour or ethnic origin".

The indistinct term "to prosecute" means either supplementary retaliation or an alternative to a similar indistinct term "to outlaw" organizations, which is difficult to take as a guideline to sensible action.

The frequently used phrase "socially dangerous parties" is proposed as a new term. Three instances speak for its benefit.

First: the phrase "criminal organizations" that has acquired currency in practice. It was used in the Preamble to the 60/143 Resolution[3] of the

---

[3] *Resolutions adopted by the General Assembly at its 60 Session.* Available at: http://www.un.org/depts/dhl/resguide/r60_en.shtml

General Assembly which refers to the "Charter of the Nuremberg Tribunal and the Judgment of the Tribunal, which recognized the Waffen SS organization and all its integral parts as criminal and declared it responsible for many war crimes and crimes against humanity". The principal parameter of criminal act is its recognized social danger. The fact of declaring organizations criminal indicates that organizations can be socially dangerous.

Second: social danger (threat to public security) is an acknowledged restriction on an individual's exercise of his human rights. And, while the above-mentioned Part 2 of Article 29 of the Universal Declaration of Human Rights sets limits in favour of "public order", national constitutions, as a rule, emphasize the "state" character of this restriction. Thus, for example, Part 3 of Article 55 of the Constitution of Russia specifies the extent of the said limitation and speaks about the protection of the fundamental principles of the constitutional system" and about the "insurance of defence of the country and security of the State"[4].

Third: the non-classical separation of "political crimes" illustrated by national constitutions. "Political crimes are crimes that this way or another affect political power relationship, the state system, the social structure. As a rule, criminal law in countries of the world does not directly separate political crimes from conventional crimes and refers to them as "crimes against the state" or "crimes against the constitutional system". So the term "political crimes" is found largely in scientific and political jargon[5].

Part 2 of Article 14 of the Universal Declaration of Human Rights exhibits a special attitude to political crimes when the right of asylum is limited in the following way, "This right may not be invoked in the case of prosecutions genuinely arising from non-political crimes or from acts contrary to the purposes and principles of the United Nations".

While the Constitution of the Russian Federation in Part 2 of Article 63 speaks not of "political crimes" but of "persecution for political convictions": "The extradition of people accused of a crime, and also the handover of convicts for serving sentences in other States shall be carried out on the basis of the federal law or the international agreement of the Russian Federation".

---

[4] *Constitution of the Russian Federation*. Available at: http://www.constitution.ru/en/10003000-01.htm

[5] *Bol'shoy yuridicheskii slovar'*. 2003, pod redaktsiey A.Ya. Sukhareva, V.E. Krutskikh, Moskva, pp.704. (*Grand Law Dictionary*. 2003, ed. by A.Ya. Sukhareva, V.E. Krutskikh, Moscow, pp.704. (in the original: *Большой юридический словарь*. 2003, под ред. А.Я. Сухарева, В.Е. Крутских, М., сс. 704).

The very fact of distinguishing "political parties" as a separate non-classical group clearly indicates that socially dangerous acts are possible even in the political sphere whose main actors happen to be political parties.

So we believe that the proposed term "socially dangerous parties" is the most adequate to describing parties subject to forcible liquidation for ideological reasons.

We should also add that the term "socially dangerous" lacks formal categoricalness pertinent to the term "criminal" (remember "presumption of innocence") and most adequately corresponds to the verb "condemn" (instead of "try") frequently used in international law.

What are the purposes of the liquidation of socially dangerous parties? The answer to this question has a practical bearing on, in particular, which court will handle the case of party liquidation – criminal or civil? And what is liquidation essentially – punishment or prevention?

Here we should note that there is no scientific penitentiary mainstream in today's world, and in many ways punishment has remained traditional. While the aims of punishment used to vary from retribution ("rectification of social injustice") through general and particular prevention to re-education (all conceivable combinations were possible), and if it was the period of experimenting with alternative penalties, now of all possible punishments only pragmatic ones – fines and confiscation – remain, since they enrich the treasury.

Yet, as was shown, acts of international public law provide a fairly categorical answer to the question why liquidate socially dangerous parties. The purpose of their liquidation is, first, general prevention so that, when they rise to power, they should not commit apartheid and genocide crimes and unleash annexation wars with neighbouring states. Mankind knows from its own experience that propaganda of, in particular, racial superiority cannot help but bring about only such results, and neither does it wish to retrace its steps along this path nor does it want the effects. Socially dangerous parties, and, even more so, Nazi parties, may not have "another chance" – what if this time they succeed and we all will favour them? No way. Tested and scientifically proved.

Party liquidation is the only possible solution in the case of a party founded on socially dangerous principles. If citizens have formed a party with a view to establishing a regime of racial superiority, no other measures but party liquidation can force them to change their minds – they did not start it for this purpose. It is impossible to "re-educate" a party and reorient its members toward different, non-criminal, goals: this would be contrary to the very idea of freedom of association. So if the purposes are found criminal, liquidation of a party must be inevitable. And as was already demonstrated this can be done only in judicial procedure, which nobody puts to doubt. But different trials – criminal and civil – under equal objective circumstances can lead to different results.

In a civil trial, a claim in a suit for liquidation of a party may be upheld, partially upheld or denied – in a civil procedure the court is bound by the plaintiff's claim. In criminal proceeding, different instances become crucial, namely:

- Admissibility in national law of prosecution of crimes committed by juridical persons;
- Commitment of the crime provided for in criminal law;
- Sentencing, where liquidation actually is the last sanction of the law for a juridical person. Lesser sentences have already been mentioned – fines and cessation of activity. By the way, such a measure as a "warning" is not found in any text;
- The notorious state "political will" embodied in the final opinion of procurator.

As we can see, it is highly problematic, if not impossible, to liquidate socially dangerous parties through prosecution. First of all, because, conventionally, solely physical persons are subject to prosecution. (Here we should add that though the acts of the United Nations do refer to the fact that the Nuremberg Judgment recognized the SS organization as "criminal", this is not so. It is true that the Charter of the Nuremberg Tribunal allowed for declaring organizations criminal, and the prosecution demanded it, but the judges, unwilling to break the classicalness of law, convicted only groups of persons, not organizations).

Furthermore, here we have a certain administrative paradox: a socially dangerous party cannot be liquidated because it cannot possibly be registered. To identify the criminal nature of a party's purposes is impossible without a thorough expert examination of the party constitution, yet the laws on parties, as a rule, do not specify that register officials should conduct such an examination, and as often as not they altogether disregard party constitutions. The registration of a party, as a rule, consists of fulfilling a number of formal, statutory requirements and it differs slightly from registration (creation) of a juridical person. A refusal to register a party is not uncommon, but typically it is due to the unwillingness of other parties to have another political rival, and less frequently the refusal is dictated by some ideological considerations.

Apart from general prevention, can party liquidation pursue other goals, in particular eradication of socially dangerous phenomena proper, such as, for example, the already examined racial discrimination?

7.2.2. Criticism of the aim "elimination of racism, racial discrimination, xenophobia and related intolerance"

The task of the "necessity of speedily eliminating racial discrimination throughout the world, in all its forms and manifestations, and of securing understanding of and respect for the dignity of the human person" was set at the end of the Preamble to the UN Resolution[6]. This Declaration, as was shown, was developed by the General Assembly of the United Nations in a series of topics under the general title of "Global efforts for the total elimination of racism, racial discrimination, xenophobia and related intolerance and the comprehensive implementation of and follow-up to the Durban Declaration and Programme of Action".

It is noteworthy that the consistency and continuity of determination, first shown in the 1963 Declaration, to "eliminate" racism, racial discrimination, xenophobia and related intolerance has remained unflinching.

The title of this series of Resolutions speaks of "total elimination", and the Preamble to the 65/240 Resolution of 24.12.2010[7] emphasizes the importance of "urgently eliminating" these persistent and violent trends. The resoluteness of the task of "elimination", on the one hand, and the increasingly frequent calls for criminalization of entire types of public activities, on the other hand, set a tough problem of striking a proper attitude to this line of action. On the one hand, the activity of the dissemination of ideas and practices of racism, racial discrimination and related intolerance is deemed criminal though it has not been universally recognized as criminal. On the other hand, expert criminologists have long ceased to set themselves a task of "eliminating" crime; it is a question of "combating" it and containing crime within bounds acceptable for the society (doctors do not speak of the "elimination" of a disease, though this analogy is more relevant). Strictly speaking, the point is to preserve and use such a reserve as social, and, for that matter, state security. We have already pointed to the scarcity of this resource.

---

[6] A/RES/1904 United Nations, Resolution. Available at: http://www.un-documents.net/a18r1904.htm

[7] *Resolutions adopted by the General Assembly at its 65 Session.* Available at: http://www.un.org/depts/dhl/resguide/r65_en.shtml

The "resource" constituent is a common theme in the above-mentioned Resolutions. For example, Item 37 of the 61/149 Resolution of the General Assembly of 19.12.2006[8] speaks of the "centrality of resource mobilization", "especially in mobilizing the necessary political will", and the Preamble spells out "the absolute necessity and the imperative nature of the political will for the achievement of the commitments undertaken in the Durban Declaration and Programme of Action". Scarcity of resources and political will (also a resource?) should be "supplemented" by scarcity of scientific thought, of which virtually identical Resolutions under the same title adopted by the General Assembly are an indirect proof. Nevertheless, the question we have posed – can racism, racial discrimination, xenophobia and related intolerance be eliminated speedily and completely in principle? – requires an answer.

Just as criminologists believe that it is impossible to eliminate crime, so do human rights defenders, who think that it is impossible to eliminate discrimination. And the reasons why discrimination cannot be eliminated are even simpler than those why crime cannot be eliminated. Although the cited Resolutions, echoing the Universal Declaration of Human Rights, persist in reiterating in the Preambles that "All human beings are born free and equal in dignity and rights", inequality of people is primary and equality secondary.

The problem of discrimination as unequal treatment refers us to the concept of equality, which has been thoroughly investigated in philosophy of law.

"First, total equality is impossible: in real life our expectations are too great to meet. Equality can be achieved only to a certain extent and for a certain period of time. Second, real life tends to set conditions for opposing relations. What is this opposition? Real equality is secondary to *social inequality*. The latter constitutes an immediate corollary of homogeneous actual inequalities massively reproduced in the community on different grounds. Inequality is inherent in the very nature of human actions, in the dynamics of social relations, in the unsteadiness of position or status in the community. Inequality comes in various forms. The most conspicuous forms are political inequality based on relations of authority and hierarchy (relations of authority), moral inequality perceived as virtual injustice or imperfection. Inequality is not purely destructive and not an inauthentic form of interdependence of people. Since all social structures are natural hierarchies (all people cannot at the same time rule, govern,

---

[8] *Resolutions adopted by the General Assembly at its 61 Session.* Available at: http://www.un.org/depts/dhl/resguide/r61_en.shtml

dominate and intimidate), as determined by the whole body of social institutions, inequality is not a vice of social life but a form of its reproduction, a form of the functioning of social institutions. Therefore, equality should be regarded as an instance of inequality and as management thereof in a particular social space-time with the help of concrete means. Law is one of these means, and objectively the most important at that"[9].

"Real equality has an essential property: its related social relation is, so to speak, "elementary". This means that a particular relation depends exclusively on the engaged subjects, on a particular "configuration" of claims and efforts that is formed inside this relation, and by no means imposed upon as an established and – even more so – legalized measure. It depends on the capacity real people have when acting in the community. Social space along its horizontal line is broken, and this independence of particular relations and the necessity to form a relation in every particular circumstance determine the meaning of real equality of subjects entering these relations"[10].

Yet, the Durban Declaration contains a chapter "Strategies to achieve full and effective equality, including international cooperation and enhancement of the United Nations and other international mechanisms in combating racism, racial discrimination, xenophobia and related intolerance", that is, "full and effective equality" is regarded an achievable goal.

As was already pointed out, discrimination is a special type of inequality; it is unequal treatment of one another in particular ("elementary") situations, so this type of inequality, being an unquantifiable factor, is far detached from the conception of measure.

The Council Directive 2000/43/EC ("racial directive")[11] speaks not of equality as such but of the principle of equality. Article 2 of Chapter I specifies, "For the purposes of this Directive, the principle of equal treatment shall mean that there shall be no direct or indirect discrimination based on racial or ethnic origin" that is, "equality" as understood by the Council of the European Union is absence of discrimination. A broader

---

[9] Malakhov, V.P. 2007. *Filosofia prava*, 2nd izdanie, Moskva, p.145. (Malakhov, V.P. 2007. *Philosophy of Law*, 2nd edition, Moscow, p. 145). (in the original: Малахов, В.П. 2007. *Философия права*. 2-е издание, М. р. 145).

[10] Malakhov, V.P. 2007. *Filosofia prava*, 2nd izdanie, Moskva, p.145.

[11] Council Directive 2000/43/EC of 29 June 2000 implementing the principle of equal treatment between persons irrespective of racial or ethnic origin, *Official Journal L 180*, 19/07/2000 P. 0022 – 0026. Available at: http://eur-lex.europa.eu/LexUriServ/LexUriServ.do?uri=CELEX:32000L0043:en:HTML

understanding is provided in Item 3 of the Preamble to the Directive, "The right to equality before the law and protection against discrimination for all persons constitutes a universal right recognised by the Universal Declaration of Human Rights, the United Nations Convention on the Elimination of all forms of Discrimination Against Women, the International Convention on the Elimination of all forms of Racial Discrimination and the United Nations Covenants on Civil and Political Rights and on Economic, Social and Cultural Rights and by the European Convention for the Protection of Human Rights and Fundamental Freedoms, to which all Member States are signatories".

The European Council assumes a more realistic approach: instead of "full and effective equality" it speaks of "the right to equality before the law" and instead of "elimination of discrimination" of the right to "protection against discrimination".

A much more modern position of the European Council on the issue of equality is closer to philosophy of law than that of the United Nations with its "speedy and total elimination". The text of the Directive, for example, clearly reflects the situational nature of equality, "direct discrimination shall be taken to occur where one person is treated less favourably than another is, has been or would be treated in a comparable situation on grounds of racial or ethnic origin".

Manifestation of racial discrimination can be divided into two groups: "situational" (particular) and "regulatory" (general), that is, embodied in law. It is obvious that, contrary to "situational" discrimination, "regulatory" racial discrimination is easily subject to "speedy and total elimination" since it is easier objectified and discerned, and in principle it is subject to "elimination" – abolition of legal acts. Item 1 (c) of Article 2 of the Convention specifies the obligations for states in the "regulatory" racial discrimination, "Each State Party shall take effective measures to review governmental, national and local policies, and to amend, rescind or nullify any laws and regulations which have the effect of creating or perpetuating racial discrimination wherever it exists".

The same instruction is contained in Article 4 of the Declaration, "All States shall take effective measures to revise governmental and other public policies and to rescind laws and regulations which have the effect of creating and perpetuating racial discrimination wherever it still exists. They should pass legislation for prohibiting such discrimination and should take all appropriate measures to combat those prejudices which lead to racial discrimination".

This immediately poses three questions as to the performance: the presence of the notorious "political will" (discretionary change of legislation), real independence of constitutional courts and admittance of initiators of changes in legislation to judicial procedure (forcible change in legislation through intervention of court, the bringing of a lawmaker to political responsibility).

The fact that "regulatory" racial discrimination takes place is reflected in the Preamble to the Declaration which states that its manifestations are "still in evidence in some areas of the world, some of which are imposed by certain Governments by means of legislative, administrative or other measures, in the form, inter alia, of apartheid, segregation and separation, as well as by the promotion and dissemination of doctrines of racial superiority and expansionism in certain areas".

This allows us to draw a conclusion that in principle only "regulatory" discrimination is subject to "speedy and total elimination", while the "situational" discrimination was, is, will and can be contained only within the bounds acceptable in the community.

7.2.3. The purpose of preventing (eliminating) Nazism

We believe that Nazism is altogether a different case. The question of the possibility in principle to eliminate Nazism was posed, in particular, at the constituent conference held by the International Human Rights Movement "World without Nazism" in Kiev.

The debate went on around the phrase "human rights" and if it should be part of the name of the movement. As is the case of "law-enforcement" agencies, the very name of which speaks of virtual impossibility to eliminate both crime and discrimination; otherwise law-enforcers and human rights defenders would be called "liquidators" of sorts. We believe that such a "human rights defending" approach cannot be assumed towards Nazism. First, Nazism is not such a common reality as discrimination, which sometimes can happen unintentionally. Second, when speaking about the threat of Nazism, we can distinctly outline "the rise of Nazism" to power, the stages of which are clear-cut. The goal set by Nazi during the first stage was to win power, preferably in a legitimate way, to establish a one-party dictatorship (or a dictatorship of several allied parties) and, in the final run, to found a new Nazi state different from the existing one in its format. According to certain researchers into Nazism, in particular, to Roger Griffin, this 'distinguished" state, as a rule, proves to be the "revival" of the "golden age" statehood of a particular ethnos. And this Nazism, having won power democratically, cannot be eliminated democratically, for Nazism eliminates the very democracy by establishing a dictatorship, and a one-leader dictatorship at that.

Thus, when speaking about Nazism, it is feasible to speak not of its elimination (few are those who succeeded in defeating it alone) but of it inadmissibility, prevention, since the stages of its development are easily diagnosed and during this time the interested subjects can take appropriate counteractions. Yet "elimination" remains topical in respect of Nazi parties. Thus, for example, the Ukrainian Nazi party "Svoboda" (Freedom), as we believe, should have been liquidated as long ago as 2007, after the Party Congress approved the draft of the National Constitution of Ukraine[12] and the party's Programme[13] in 1995. It was these documents that allowed for diagnosing Svoboda as a Nazi party. The Nazi coup in Ukraine took place at the beginning of 2014, that is, 7-19 years had passed from the declaration of the intentions to their practical implementation – which seems to be an ample time for a political decision to be made and appropriate measure to be taken.

7.2.4. Setting the task of liquidation of socially dangerous parties: The mandate problem

The above-reviewed UN acts set the tasks of "combating" socially dangerous associations and of their formal elimination. As was stated above, it is about the permissible violation of human rights, to be more exact, about freedom of association; and for further analysis it is of utmost importance to study the following "mandate", that is, whom the UN chooses, and authorizes, to deal with the "elimination" of these associations; strictly speaking, who is charged with the task.

Item 7 of the 60/143 Resolution of General Assembly of the United Nations "emphasizes the need to take the necessary measures to put an end to the practices described above, and calls upon States to take more effective measures to combat those phenomena and the extremist movements, which pose a real threat to democratic values".

Item 8 of this Resolution is devoted entirely to the obligations of states, which are more broadly defined. We repeat – the General Assembly of the

---

[12] *Proekt Natsional'noy konstitutsii Ukrainy, prinyatoy s'ezdom nazistskoy partii "Svoboda"*. Available at: http://www.svoboda.org.ua/pro_partiyu/prohrama/konstytutsiya/(*Draft of the National Constitution of Ukraine proposed by the Congress of the Nazi party Svoboda*). (in the original: *Проект Национальной конституции Украины, принятой съездом нацистской партии «Свобода»*).

[13] *Programma Vseukrainskogo ob'edinena Partii Svoboda*. Available at: http://www.svoboda.org.ua/pro_partiyu/prohrama/ (*Programm of All-Ukrainian Party Svoboda*). (in the original: *Программа ВО Свобода*).

United Nations "reaffirms that, according to article 4 of the International Convention on the Elimination of All Forms of Racial Discrimination, States parties to that instrument are, inter alia, under the obligation:

a) To condemn all propaganda and all organizations which are based on ideas of racial superiority or that attempt to justify or promote racial hatred and discrimination in any form;
b) To undertake to adopt immediate and positive measures designed to eradicate all incitement to, or acts of, such discrimination with due regard to the principles embodied in the Universal Declaration of Human Rights and the rights expressly set forth in article 5 of the Convention;
c) To declare as an offence punishable by law all dissemination of ideas based on racial superiority or hatred, incitement to racial discrimination, as well as all acts of violence or incitement to such acts against any race or group of persons of another colour or ethnic origin, and also the provision of any assistance to racist activities, including the financing thereof;
d) To declare illegal and prohibit organizations and organized and all other propaganda activities that promote and incite racial discrimination and to recognize participation in such organizations or activities as an offence punishable by law;
e) To prohibit public authorities or public institutions, national or local, from promoting or inciting racial discrimination".

The instruction that may be called "the mandate for elimination" goes together with "the mandate for combating", thus, Item 26 of the 65/199 Resolution of the General Assembly of the United Nations "stresses that such information is important for the sharing of experiences and best practices in the fight against extremist political parties, movements and groups, including neo-Nazis and skinhead groups, as well as extremist ideological movements".

Item 24 of the "Racial Directive" says that "Protection against discrimination based on racial or ethnic origin would itself be strengthened by the existence of a body or bodies in each Member State, with competence to analyse the problems involved, to study possible solutions and to provide concrete assistance for the victims".

The cited documents show that the states themselves have a mandate over the said activity, though the lack of "political will" has been frequently noted. Such an approach assumed by the United Nations is understandable – it is States that are members of the United Nations; on the other hand, what is clearly felt is the absence of a special competent agency and a fairly indefinite attitude to subjects that can hardly be blamed for the lack of "political will", that is, human rights organizations.

Article 10 of the Declaration says that "the United Nations, specialized agencies, States and non-governmental organizations shall do all in their power to promote energetic action which, by combining legal and other practical measures, will make possible the abolition of all forms of racial discrimination. They shall, in particular, study the causes of such discrimination with a view to recommending appropriate and effective measures to combat and eliminate it".

An amazing wording: whom these subjects shall "assist"? Who is this main actor who bears all burden of "combating and eliminating"? Here we should note that "non-governmental organizations" also share the responsibility of taking "legal and practical measures", which, should we wish, can be translated as an appropriate mandate.

The Document of the Moscow Meeting of the Conference on the Human Dimension of the CSCE specifies:

"43. The participating States will recognize as NGOs those which declare themselves as such, according to existing national procedures, and will facilitate the ability of such organizations to conduct their national activities freely on their territories; to that effect they will

(43.1) - endeavour to seek ways of further strengthening modalities for contacts and exchanges of views between NGOs and relevant national authorities and governmental institutions;

(43.2) - endeavour to facilitate visits to their countries by NGOs from within any of the participating States in order to observe human dimension conditions".

(43.3) - welcome NGO activities, including, inter alia, observing compliance with CSCE commitments in the field of the human dimension".

Even less does it look like a mandate.

Item 23 of the Preamble to the "Racial Directive" also can be equivocal: "Member States should promote dialogue between the social partners and with non-governmental organisations to address different forms of discrimination and to combat them". It is not clear whether member states should "promote dialogue" with non-governmental organizations or should they act in concert with non-governmental organizations in distinguishing "different forms of discrimination" and in "combating them".

And finally, there is the collision that has never been sorted out. It is the interference of a certain state into the internal matters of another state. On the one hand, the mandate is clearly detailed in the same Moscow Document. We shall repeat:

"The participating parties emphasize that issues relating to human rights, fundamental freedoms, democracy and the rule of law are of international concern, as respect for these rights and freedoms constitutes one of the foundations of the international order. They categorically and irrevocably declare that the commitments undertaken in the field of the human dimension of the CSCE are matters of direct and legitimate concern to all participating States and do not belong exclusively to the internal affairs of the State concerned".

On the other hand, the format of this interference has always been strictly political and not legal; and the Council of Europe has become the authority to submit grievances to, to be more exact, it is the Parliamentary Assembly of the Council of Europe. The European Court of Human Rights is also an institution at the Council of Europe, but the established "individual vs the state" format does not stipulate that other states except the one accused can take part in legal proceedings. The international character of the European Court of Human Rights is determined by the international body of its judges, but the indictment is wobbly (one of the solution to this problem could be the setting up at this court of a special prosecutor's office for human rights).

However, the United Nations gives more detailed instructions for States in Item 14 of the 68/150 Resolution where it encourages States to adopt further measures to provide training to the police and other law enforcement bodies, this call has been already cited.

The call for criminalization of certain social relations and the emphasis on the appropriate training returns us to the question posed earlier: which legal proceedings – civil or criminal – must the case of liquidation of socially dangerous parties be tried in? The Russian experience suggests a certain hybrid model: "The Chief State Prosecutor files a petition to a court for liquidating an all-Russian or international public association. A petition for liquidating interregional, regional, and local public associations is filed by the prosecutor of the relevant subject of the

Russian Federation"[14]. That means that the trial is civil, but the "prosecution" is represented by the State.

On the whole, if we speak about a criminal trial, then, considering the state monopoly in prosecution, only state law-enforcement authorities are the authorized subjects. The criminal trial does not stipulate any other role for non-governmental organizations than to report presumable criminal activities of the said parties or a potential role played by the aggrieved person. To answer this question, we must study the concepts international organizations have of the criminal aspect of the socially dangerous activities under consideration.

7.3. Concepts of Criminal Activity

7.3.1. "Condemnation"

We have already noted that the term "socially dangerous parties" best matches with "condemnation", used in international law, which has a more pronounced political meaning than that of the legal term. Nevertheless, indications of "condemnation" are frequent, and it would be inappropriate to ignore them. Indeed, the examples are plentiful.

Thus, the Preamble to the Declaration says that "the United Nations has condemned colonialism and all practices of segregation and discrimination associated therewith". And "any doctrine of racial differentiation or superiority is scientifically false, morally condemnable". Part 1 of Article 9 of the Declaration runs, "All propaganda and organizations based on ideas or theories of the superiority of one race or group of persons of one colour or ethnic origin with a view to justifying or promoting racial discrimination in any form shall be severely condemned".

The same wording is found in Article 4 of the Convention.

Item 84 of the Durban Declaration goes, "We condemn the persistence and resurgence of neo-Nazism, neo-Fascism and violent nationalist ideologies based on racial or national prejudice, and state that these phenomena can never be justified in any instance or in any circumstances".

Article 3 of the Convention confirms, "States Parties particularly condemn racial segregation and apartheid and undertake to prevent, prohibit

---

[14] Borodin, S.S., Gromyko, S.S. 2007. *Administrativnoe pravo*, Moskva, p. 432. (Borodin, S.S., Gromyko, S.S. *Administrative Law*, Moscow, p. 432). (in the original: Бородин, С.С., Громыко, С.С. 2007. *Административное право*. М., 432 с.).

and eradicate all practices of this nature in territories under their jurisdiction".

These examples by no means exhaust the practice of "condemnation"; as to the practical use of "condemnation" of certain types of public activity, it was already pointed out – it is social danger of the above-mentioned types of activity. In a court of law, one cannot, strictly speaking, resort to the prejudicialness of these "condemnations", but they certainly help to draw the already studied "boundary line of the prohibited".

7.3.2. "Shall Be Considered an Offence"

Still closer to the "borderline of the prohibited" are acts of violence that "shall be considered an offence" as proposed by international organizations. True, such acts cannot be prosecuted criminally, if what is proposed to be "considered an offence" is not embodied in national criminal law: here the same presumption of innocence comes into operation. The instruction "shall be considered an offence" may give us an idea of what the criminal law of tomorrow would be like, yet today it cannot be applied. Examples of such instructions are plentiful. Here are some:

Article 9 of the Declaration: "2. All incitement to or acts of violence, whether by individuals or organizations against any race or group of persons of another colour or ethnic origin shall be considered an offence against society and punishable under law".

Article 4a) and 4b) of the Convention develop this instruction still further.

Item 88 of the Programme of Action of the Conference "calls upon States to criminalize all forms of trafficking in persons," and so forth.

7.3.3. Crimes

Calls for criminalization of any given socially dangerous act reflect the fact that the set of criminal instruments to combat these phenomena on national levels leaves much to be desired. Suffice it to study what exactly international acts consider an offense. Such references are few; thus, the Preamble to the 60/143 Resolution of the General Assembly refers to "the Charter of the Nuremberg Tribunal and the Judgment of the Tribunal, which recognized the Waffen SS organization and all its integral parts as criminal and declared it responsible for many war crimes and crimes against humanity".

Specialist literature frequently offers examples of looser interpretation of this prejudicialness, for instance, "the SS, Gestapo and SD organizations were declared criminal by the International Tribunal, so those who now march along the streets in Riga and Tallinn, as well as administrative officials evoking the murky past, to a large extent fall within the purview of rulings of the Nuremberg trial in respect of war crimes. Unfortunately, the power of supervisor was not delegated to an international institute that could, by reference to the absence of limitation period, consider the phenomenon of glorification of members of criminal organizations in the Baltic States and not only"[15].

A serious problem of criminal prosecution is caused by the fact that the very dissemination of the Nazi ideology and its practices (we should point out that we regard Nazism and Fascism as closely related phenomena and ideologies, and this paper virtually equates them) are not formulated as separate criminal rules. Criminal prosecution of Nazism is conducted (if it is conducted at all) indirectly, through "related" crimes. Thus, the Conference in Item 153 of the Programme of Action "recommends that the Department of Peacekeeping Operations of the Secretariat and other concerned United Nations agencies, bodies and programmes strengthen their coordination to discern patterns of serious violations of human rights and humanitarian law with a view to assessing the risk of further deterioration that could lead to genocide, war crimes or crimes against humanity".

The three listed types of crimes, contrary to that of dissemination of Nazi ideology and practice, are, if we may say so, universally acknowledged.

The Rome Statute of the International Criminal Court in part 1 of Article 5 entitled "Crimes within the jurisdiction of the Court" says, "The jurisdiction of the Court shall be limited to the most serious crimes of concern to the international community as a whole. The Court has jurisdiction in accordance with this Statute with respect to the following crimes:

---

[15] *Pribaltika I geopolitika. 1935-1945. Rassekrechennye dokumenty Slizhby vneshney razvedki Rossiiskoy Federatsii.* 2009, sostavitel' L.F. Sotskov, Moskva, p. 23. (*The Baltic States and Geopolitics. 1935-1945. Unsealed documents of the Foreign Intelligent Service of the Russian Federation.* 2009, compiled by Sotskov L.F., Moscow, p.23). (in the original: *Прибалтика и геополитика. 1935-1945. Рассекреченные документы Службы внешней разведки Российской Федерации.* 2009, составитель Л.Ф.Соцков, с. 23).

(a) The crime of genocide;
(b) Crimes against humanity;
(c) War crimes;
(d) The crime of aggression".

According to the second part of the same Article, "The Court shall exercise jurisdiction over the crime of aggression once a provision is adopted in accordance with articles 121 and 123 defining the crime and setting out the conditions under which the Court shall exercise jurisdiction with respect to this crime"[16].

This provision may be regarded as the outgrowth of the "shall-be-considered-an-offence" topic. The Rome Statute of the International Criminal Court was adopted in 1998, entered into force on 1 July 2002, and the definition of "aggression" was provided in the 3314 Resolution of the General Assembly of the United Nations of 14 December 1974.

The Rome Statute defines the crime of genocide in Article 6, and the crime of apartheid in Point j) of Article 7 "Crimes against Humanity". According to Point h) of Part 2 Article 7 "the crime of apartheid" means inhumane acts of a character similar to those referred to in paragraph 1, committed in the context of an institutionalized regime of systematic oppression and domination by one racial group over any other racial group or groups and committed with the intention of maintaining that regime".

Yet "segregation" that usually goes along with "apartheid" is never mentioned in corresponding texts.

7.3.4. Motive

The Preamble to the 64/148 Resolution of the General Assembly contains a very important theoretical provision – it specifies that the corresponding ideologies and views may serve, first and foremost, as motives of crime. It goes like this, "Underlining the importance of urgently eliminating continuing and violent trends involving racism and racial discrimination, and conscious that any form of impunity for crimes motivated by racist and xenophobic attitudes plays a role in weakening the rule of law and democracy, tends to encourage the recurrence of such crimes and requires resolute action and cooperation for its eradication".

---

[16] *Rome Statute of the International Criminal Court*. 1998. Available at: http://www.icc-cpi.int/nr/rdonlyres/ea9aeff7-5752-4f84-be94-0a655eb30e16/0/rome_statute_english.pdf

This idea needs developing, since these "skinheads" can often be tried in a court of law and found guilty on the count of hooliganism without regard to this motive as an aggravating circumstance, which equates them with ordinary hoodlums, while their ideology receives no public appraisal. The idea is fairly well developed in Item 30 of the same Resolution in which the General Assembly "emphasizes that it is the responsibility of States to adopt effective measures to combat criminal acts motivated by racism, racial discrimination, xenophobia and related intolerance, including measures to ensure that such motivations are considered an aggravating factor for the purposes of sentencing, to prevent those crimes from going unpunished and to ensure the rule of law".

The General Assembly develops it further and Item 11 of the 65/199 Resolution "recalls the recommendation of the Special Rapporteur, made in his latest report to the General Assembly, to introduce into domestic criminal law a provision according to which committing an offence with racist or xenophobic motivations or aims constitutes an aggravating circumstance allowing for enhanced penalties, and encourages those States whose legislation does not contain such provisions to consider that recommendation".

Conclusion

Thus, diagnostics and liquidation of socially dangerous parties must be based, first of all, on the understanding that these parties will be dangerous in future even though they are not perceived as a threat to the existing public order at present. Theoretical studies show that various Nazi factions are capable of "concealing" their true intentions, which, however, become apparent after views and statements of their members and leaders have been examined. Moreover, one should not think that a contemporary neo-Nazi party is an exact copy of a Nazi or Fascist party of the inter-war period. Under the different circumstances in the political and public life, with the production of goods yielding to the production of services, knowledge and emotions that have become both goods and a force of progress, the instruments of political and party leadership as well as the goals set by ultra-Nazi parties have also undergone changes. Physical elimination of political opponents gives way to the idea of emotional and intellectual change, to the idea of manipulating human consciousness.

Moreover, the legal base, both international and national, provides for neither a clear definition of a Nazi party nor proper mechanisms to combat socially dangerous parties.

CHAPTER VIII

DIAGNOSTICS AND LIQUIDATION OF PROHIBITED PARTIES: *MODUS OPERANDI*

It seems that the growing "brown" menace is determined not only by objective factors and the lack of the notorious "political will" but also by the absence of practical technologies of formal expert examination, diagnostics and liquidation of socially dangerous parties, including the well-established judicial *modus operandi.*

8.1. Range of problems in judicial combating socially dangerous parties

The initial conclusion that can be drawn from the listed "starting points" is deplorable – there is no consistent plan for combating far-right radicalism in the world. A great number of problems remain unsolved. Here are some of them:

1) "Nazism" (Fascism) occurs very rarely in the acts of international public law and in national constitutional law. The definition of "Nazism" is missing from both international public law and also the International Conference for combating it. The terms "neo-Nazi" and "neo-Fascism" are not described.
2) The established Nazi regimes defy diagnostics and any criticism, let alone their elimination.
3) National criminal laws lag behind international public law, imperfect as it is. One cannot say that the world fails to understand the danger of the "brown plague", but it lacks instruments and political will to combat it.
4) The tone of international public law suggests that the struggle against "this evil" must be waged by means of criminal prosecution, but in the majority of cases, according to national law,

solely physical persons are subject to criminal prosecution, not juridical persons, and even more so institutions or regimes. Part 1 of Article 14 of the Rome Statute points out directly, "A State Party may refer to the Prosecutor a situation in which one or more crimes within the jurisdiction of the Court appear to have been committed requesting the Prosecutor to investigate the situation for the purpose of determining whether one or more specific persons should be charged with the commission of such crimes". It is obvious that criminal prosecution of "specific persons" will not affect "an institutionalized regime of systematic oppression and domination by one racial group over any other racial group or groups".

5) The role of ultra-right parties in establishing such regimes has not been adequately examined and incorporated into international public law. The context of the human rights doctrine shows parties as associations without due regard to their peculiarities and involvement in political developments.
6) International public law authorizes the regimes themselves to combat "institutionalized regimes of systematic oppression". However, the imperfection of such an approach is well-known and new "countervailers" get introduced, such as the ones described in Point a) of Part 1 of Article 17 of the Rome Statute: "Having regard to paragraph 10 of the Preamble and article 1, the Court shall determine that a case is inadmissible where: (a) The case is being investigated or prosecuted by a State which has jurisdiction over it, unless the State is unwilling or unable genuinely to carry out the investigation or prosecution", that is, the probability that "the State is unwilling or unable genuinely to carry out the investigation or prosecution" is not only taken for granted but it is so high that countervailing measures are regarded necessary.
7) Non-governmental organizations do not have the mandate States have. The role of non-governmental organizations and, more broadly, of civil society is still indistinct. It is further aggravated by the fact that the supremacy of right is still prevalent in the civil judicial procedure of many countries, which, though often unformalized, is a good prohibition on actio popularis. In the full sense of the word, the incompetence of non-governmental organization in criminal trial has been already described.
8) The principle of the renunciation of sovereignty in favour of "human rights" proclaimed by the Moscow Document is an

exclusively political, not legal, dimension, though the Rome Statute proposes certain mechanisms.

8.2. The observation of practices of combating socially dangerous parties

The measures we propose below are subjected to one important aim – to make a judicial procedure for the liquidation of ultra right-wing parties workable. In doing so, we aspire to subordinate the liquidation of socially dangerous parties to the all-embracing struggle against racial discrimination, xenophobia, intolerance, etc., and, ideally, to freeing the liquidation process from the reach of interparty political competition.

This part should be regarded as totally subjective and only one of the possible versions of the solution to the urgent practical problem – liquidation of socially dangerous parties.

We shall proceed in our logic step by step, each time briefly describing probable problems and their solutions, or the ways to avoid them:

1) There is no doubt that the liquidation of socially dangerous parties is administered exclusively in a court of law.
2) Liquidation of socially dangerous parties must be administered in civil proceedings. The drawbacks of criminal procedure have been already examined. Administrative judicial proceedings are also unsatisfactory because, formally, parties are not institutions of public authority.
3) Liquidation of socially dangerous parties in civil proceedings requires the legitimization of a special lawsuit, closest to *actio popularis*. This is an important bifurcation point, since it allows for various approaches. First, there can be a legal act of international public law devoted to *actio popularis.* This seems to be the most preferable. It is the very instrument that non-governmental organizations lack and, instead of simply trying to excite someone's interest with monitoring and shadow reports, to be able to address dangerous phenomena in the community. Another option is to incorporate *actio popularis* in the act devoted to socially dangerous parties; the need for such an act has been already stated. The third option is to incorporate *actio popularis* in the act devoted to such socially dangerous phenomena as racial discrimination, genocide, etc. This approach seems least efficient considering the multitude and lack of consolidation of these acts. This problem has already been considered. The fourth option is to incorporate *actio*

popularis in the act regulating the rights of non-governmental organizations, the need for which is also clearly felt.

4) With due regard to a particular category of the defendant, parties must not have the right to *actio popularis.* The range of claimants should be narrowed down to human rights organizations and physical persons. If the party affiliation of the claimant should be checked is an issue for another discussion. In any case, non-governmental organizations registered as "foreign agents" must not be excluded from this circle of claimants.
5) A separate matter is when a claimant in a projected trial is a foreign state or an international organization, which is a subject of international law. The matter is rather political than legal, so we leave it as a topic of discussion, once again referring to the mandate arising from the Moscow Document. We can only say that recourse to a court of the state the defendant is registered in is the proper form of interference into internal affairs of the state.
6) The specifics of *actio popularis* is that it does not require the proof of the damage done. The lawsuit is filed in the interest of the people (originally, *actio popularis* is "action in the interest of the public"), democracy and public security. The lawsuit filed by the claimant must contain the facts of the defendant's transgressions of the "boundaries of the prohibited" thoroughly examined before. The issue of the period of limitation is a matter of further discussion.
7) The judicial proceedings must apply the rule of shifting the burden of proof to the claimant – a revolutionary measure, legalized by the "Racial Directive". The rationale of the necessity to apply this procedural peculiarity will be provided below.
8) The issue of the extent to which the court is bound by the demands of the claimant deserves special consideration. To answer this question we should consider possible alternative demands, and these demands must be real, not putative (for example, a party is ruled "unlawful" instead of "unconstitutional"). The alternative measures, as the authors believe, can be: expulsion from the party of members who have transgressed the "boundaries of the prohibited", warnings, liquidation of the party. "A warning" means postponed liquidation of a party till the first further transgression by the party of the "boundary of the prohibited" during the time period determined by the court but not less than 5 years. In the case of such a transgression, the court, overruling the objections made by the party, passes a judgment of the party liquidation. Such an

established measure as "suspension of the activity", seems ineffective as it pursues uncertain aims and can be used in competitive struggle by parties pursuing dishonest ends. However, "suspension of activity" may be regarded not as a compensatory remedy but as a measure of restraint – "detention on remand" after a sentence to liquidate a party was pronounced till its entry into legal force or the reversal of the judgment by a superior judicial authority unless the case is not tried by the Supreme Court.

Such a measure as a "fine" cannot be taken seriously at all, especially given the fact that it is ultra right-wing parties that are best financed.

Hence, considering the aforesaid, it seems that the court when passing a judgment must be bound not by the demands of a claimant but by the specified alternatives.

9) Expert examination of the transgression of the "boundary of the prohibited" deserves special attention. The practice of trying the so-called "political" cases when the court requires an expert examination to be submitted is rather a norm than an exception. The purport of any expert examination is to supply the much-needed information, yet the number of judgments in which the court simply incorporates the text of the expert examination into its decision is so big that it poses a question if it is the court's judgment.

   What exactly courts may be unaware of? First of all, of subtleties of politological qualifications, for instance, is it a Nazi party or an "ordinary" ultra-right party? Yet all the previous constructions prove that there is no need for such qualifications, since the court has only to establish the fact of social danger of a party, that is, the transgression of the "boundary of the prohibited", and then to evaluate its scale. The boundary line is drawn quite accurately (though irregularly), so on the whole it should be presumed that courts in general are capable of coping with the problem themselves without resorting to an expert opinion.

10) The final and binding court judgment to dismiss a claim for liquidation of a party must be followed by a moratorium on filing an analogous suit during a certain period of time, for example, two years. It is clear that the next suit must be built on different grounds to make a case – in respect of the previous transgression of the "boundary of the prohibited" the court has already passed its judgment.

11) In our time of total informational forgeries and fakes, we should foresee an occasion when a party may deliberately choose to file a weak suit against itself in order to gain the aforesaid "immunity". To avoid such incidents there must be no restrictions on the joinder of third parties as a plaintiff.
12) When in the course of proceedings the court reveals in the actions of the defendant elements essential to the offence, it must immediately report on them to the law-enforcement agencies.
13) The issue of subjection to a jurisdiction also demands careful consideration. Many factors point to the fact that cases of liquidation of socially dangerous parties must be tried at supreme courts. The main argument here is a shortage of time. Below we shall show that the time of Nazi "expansion" is commensurate with that needed for a case to be tried in three courts, wherefore the issue of prevention may cease to be topical for a simple reason that Nazism has already come to power. The second argument – another parallel to elections. In elections all procedural actions are governed by the pace of the operation, and supreme courts, in essence, act as courts of first appeal when they have to deal with numerous complaints about the decision taken by superior election commissions. The third argument is sooner of philological character: one of the (controversial) synonyms of party liquidation is the pronouncement that they are "unconstitutional", and the issue of pronouncing a law unconstitutional falls within the jurisdiction of either the supreme court or a special constitutional court. Constitutional courts proper are ill-equipped to try a case of party liquidation, as they specialize in abstract control and are not supposed to investigate facts in evidence.
14) A special issue, already discussed, is legal implications of liquidation of a socially dangerous party. Must, for example, deputies of a liquidated party be unseated? What to do about laws adopted with the dominant participation of deputies from the liquidated party? Must ministers representing the liquidated party step down from their posts? How seriously we should take the requirement of the Convention "to regard membership in such organization as crime", if, as was already pointed out, even the Nuremberg Tribunal did not venture to do so?

The fact that these questions do not find elaborate answers in legislature confirms the already mentioned observation that party liquidation is an extraordinary instance. The logic we followed allows us to answer some of these questions. In particular, irrespective of the details of national regulation, deputy factions of a liquidated party must be, at a minimum, be dissolved. The logic here is that if the liquidation of a socially dangerous party is also a prohibition on an association, then this prohibition must extend to any form of an association, including a deputy faction.

15) Court's disposition of the case of party liquidation must be subject to appeal to every national judicial authority (unless the case is tried by a supreme court) and to the European Court of Human Rights. The latter may be reinforced by two instances. First, cases of compulsory liquidation of socially dangerous parties are directly connected with violations of human rights. Second, the very format of appealing to the European Court of Human Rights, somebody vs The State, is crucial when we deal with not just "lack of political will" and "incapability of making investigation" but with the above-mentioned "institutionalized regime".

8.3 Liquidation of ultra-right parties as a constituent part of struggle against racial discrimination

As has been demonstrated, racial discrimination is a unifier for ultra-right parties. So in the matter of liquidating ultra-right parties it is logical to use the same instruments as those used for combating racial discrimination.

The "Racial Directive" is the richest in instrumental solutions.

Item 19 of the Preamble, for example, started (though did not complete) the work on conferring the corresponding mandate on non-governmental organizations, "Persons who have been subject to discrimination based on racial and ethnic origin should have adequate means of legal protection. To provide a more effective level of protection, associations or legal entities should also be empowered to engage, as the Member States so determine, either on behalf or in support of any victim, in proceedings, without prejudice to national rules of procedure concerning representation and defence before the courts". This work cannot be regarded as completed because there is still a conflict between the legal representation as a third party as a plaintiff and national standard of procedure, which must be "without prejudice". Yet, this mandate is far more resolute than the mandate on "cooperation".

Part 2 of Article 7 of the "Racial Directive" formulates this mandate even more precisely, "Member States shall ensure that associations, organisations or other legal entities, which have, in accordance with the criteria laid down by their national law, a legitimate interest in ensuring that the provisions of this Directive are complied with, may engage, either on behalf or in support of the complainant, with his or her approval, in any judicial and/or administrative procedure provided for the enforcement of obligations under this Directive".

Here, as is clearly seen, clearly stated is the primacy of protection of a right – "with his or her approval", which is logical for cases relating to racial discrimination, since in such cases it is not difficult to ascertain the victims of discrimination. In the case of unlawful activities of ultra-right parties, for example, the advancement of racist slogans, the potential victim is hard, or next to impossible, to detect, which makes the authors invoke *actio popularis,* which is totally missing from the instruments used by non-governmental organizations.

And efficacious instrument in legal proceedings relating to the liquidation of socially dangerous parties can be the above-mentioned shifted burden of proof. The transposition of this rule to cases related to the liquidation of socially dangerous parties is well substantiated because cases relating to racial discrimination speak about the same object.

Item 21 of the Preamble to 'Racial Directive" introduces the rule of shifted burden of proof, "The rules on the burden of proof must be adapted when there is a prima facie case of discrimination and, for the principle of equal treatment to be applied effectively, the burden of proof must shift back to the respondent when evidence of such discrimination is brought".

Article 8 of the "Racial Directive" entitled "Burden of Proof", paragraph 1 thereof establishes that "Member States shall take such measures as are necessary, in accordance with their national judicial systems, to ensure that, when persons who consider themselves wronged because the principle of equal treatment has not been applied to them establish, before a court or other competent authority, facts from which it may be presumed that there has been direct or indirect discrimination, it shall be for the respondent to prove that there has been no breach of the principle of equal treatment".

Part 3 of the said article says, "Paragraph 1 shall not apply to criminal procedures", which may serve as an argument in favour of the civil procedure instead of the criminal, – there is no point in ruining the classical presumption of innocence without good reason.

The practical application of "shifted burden of proof" to essentially political judicial proceedings deprives politicians of their much favoured subterfuges, like "I was misunderstood", "I made a blunder", "I found myself in a hostile surrounding and had to defend myself", "I spoke as a private person", etc.

What will the factors that prove that the "boundary of the prohibited" has been transgressed be is discussed below, and now we shall only state that the struggle against ultra-right parties and their elimination as a socially dangerous phenomenon is one of the essential elements of the general struggle against racial discrimination, apartheid, xenophobia and related intolerance, for it allows for the liquidation of collective bearers of criminal ideas – parties, who owing to their nature, actually aim at seizing power in states. Liquidation of socially dangerous parties is the stepping stone on the path of preventing racial discrimination from becoming a state policy that can unleash genocide and war crimes.

8.4. Factual circumstances in legal cases of liquidation of socially dangerous parties

The research shows that in litigation cases of liquidation of socially dangerous parties actual facts may be diverse. If we take a close analogy, Item 15 of the Preamble to the "Racial Directive" says that "the appreciation of the facts from which it may be inferred that there has been direct or indirect discrimination is a matter for national judicial or other competent bodies, in accordance with rules of national law or practice. Such rules may provide in particular for indirect discrimination to be established by any means including on the basis of statistical evidence".

At the same time, if we proceed from the above-mentioned assumption that a court enjoys a relative freedom in choosing a sanction from the proposed alternatives, we should note that the selection of actual facts to be presented to the court virtually predetermines its judgment. If the presented actual facts relate to a party as a whole or were approved by the majority of its members, then it can make a case for liquidation or the issuance of a warning. If it is statements and actions of certain politicians, the court must investigate to what extent these statements or actions of particular members have been approved by the party majority, or how these statements and actions affected the general decisions taken by the party. Here the principle, typical of judicial proceedings for cases dealing with election returns, may apply: the court cancels the results of the election if the violations detected during the election may have affected the results of the election. Accordingly, the decision for a party liquidation may be taken if single and seemingly fragmentary transgressions of the "boundary of the forbidden" are in line with the party ideology and determine the behaviour of the party majority. Here much depends on the post-conflict conduct of the party leadership: if, for example, one of the party members makes a racist statement and the party immediately responds by disavowing it and apologizes to everyone concerned, the party clearly indicates that it does not deserve to be liquidated. The facts presented to the court must cite examples of transgressions of the "boundary of the prohibited", which have been already examined.

8.4.1. Party documents

The main facts confirming the social danger of a party and the ensuing need for its liquidation are undoubtedly party documents, first and foremost, its programmes, party rules, congress resolutions, decisions taken by authorities, and party projected laws. This type of evidence is the most significant since it shows a party as a whole, and conclusions drawn from these documents are binding on the whole party. A tentative analysis of such party documents will be conducted below for the All-Ukrainian Svoboda Union. It seems feasible that party documents in the cases of party liquidation by all means should be examined in court, on the court's own motion or otherwise.

When analyzing party rules, one should determine how democratic or authoritarian (autocratic) a party is. Thus, for example, the Fifth Congress of the Liberal Democratic Party of Russia, held on 2 April 1994, elected Zhirinovsky Chairman for a term of 10 years and endowed him with a right to form the Supreme Council and other steering bodies of the party. Accordingly, new party rules were established to accommodate these changes. On 25-26 April 1998, the Seventh Party Congress, coinciding with Zhirinovsky's birthday, was held in the Column Hall of the House of Unions. Another version of the party rules was duly adopted and Zhirinovsky was unanimously elected Chairman of the Party for the term of another 6 years. A year later, on 25 April 1999, the Ninth Congress again coincided with Zhirinovsky's birthday. The major part of the Congress was a feast. At the suggestion of Sergei Abeltsev, the delegates swore loyalty to the leader of the Party.

In accordance with the degree of leaderism, the emphasis may be shifted from the study of party documents to the study of the political legacy of the leader.

8.4.2. Legal judgments

Of crucial importance here is the question whether the final judgment for the transgression of the "boundary of the prohibited" must be prejudicial in the case of compulsory judicial liquidation of a socially dangerous party.

Irrevocable sentences on cases of "political crimes" and also on non-political cases with the above-indicated motives as aggravating circumstances must be unreservedly prejudicial. In many countries the commitment of a premeditated crime in general, and not only a political one, is a ground to unseat a member and also a ground to deprive a member of the right to be elected. It is the court that is to determine if it deals with a party or with an organized criminal group sheltering itself under the title of a party.

Irrevocable sentences on civil cases should not be unreservedly prejudicial. A good illustration of this is the judgment passed by the Chamber at the Civil Court of the High Specialized Court of Ukraine for civil and criminal cases at the suit filed by All-Ukrainian Svoboda Union against the Editorial Board of the newspaper Communist (Комуніст), an organ of the Central Committee of the Communist Party of Ukraine, demanding the refutation of incorrect information[1].

The excerpt of the newspaper text that was challenged by Svoboda in court ran, "In the Ternopol Regional Council election, Svoboda, an intrinsically Nazi party, won the majority of seats owing to the oligarchs' financing of the campaign. In return for such a support, the leaders of the Svoboda Union headed by Tyagnibok turned a blind eye on the massive electoral fraud". The claimant found that "the information contained in the statements was adverse", and also that "the respondents, by spreading untrue information about Svoboda, had discredited Svoboda in the eyes of its supporters and its members, since it had nothing to do with Nazi, and such an analogy was wrong because Svoboda's Programme contains neither Nazi ideology nor slogans".

It seemed that the litigated case should have focused on the issue of whether Svoboda was a Nazi party. Yet, as was repeatedly pointed out, neither courts nor parties themselves are capable of such diagnostics. As a result, the court of first instance sustained the first claim (the judgment gives not a subtle hint that the Communist party actually tried to prove that Svoboda was a Nazi party), and the High Specialized Court vacated the judgment stating that a "Nazi party" is not an asserted fact but an evaluative judgment, which, according to the law of Ukraine on "Information", is not subject to a "rebuttal with proof". The court, according to the newspaper article, also referred to freedom of speech and the Declaration on freedom of political debate in the media, adopted on 12

---

[1] *Kommunisty vyigrali u "Svobody" v sude*. Available at: http://www.unian.net/politics/702414-kommunistyi-vyiigrali-u-svobodyi-v-sude.html (*Kommunists won at the court against "Svoboda"*). (in the original: *Коммунисты выиграли у "Свободы" в суде*).

February 2004 at the 872nd meeting of the Ministers' Deputies of the Council of Europe; the newspaper even cited the text in question in a very loose interpretation: "the bounds of warrantable criticism of a political figure or a political party to which he belongs are wider than those set for ordinary people. Public officials are bound to expose themselves to close public scrutiny through their speeches and acts and they must accept that."

This judgment passed in October 2012 was interpreted differently by the public and the parties involved. Thus, Eugeny Tsarkov, Ukrainian people's deputy, wrote in his blog that "The High Administrative Court of Ukraine acknowledged the Svoboda Union as a "Nazi organization", which, of course, is far off the mark. In essence, the question of whether the Svoboda Union was a Nazi party or not remained in abeyance. Moreover, the court judgments imply that Nazi parties do not exist at all, since, according to the court, "Nazi" is not a fact but an evaluation, simply put – a curse.

Revealingly, the court never repaired to politological expert examination for help.

This example clearly shows that in civil proceedings judgments cannot, as a general matter, be strictly prejudicial in cases of party liquidation even if it is a question of their social danger.

8.4.3. Disciplinary penalty

Parliamentary discipline is frequently regulated by special laws that endue parliamentary authorities or specially established commissions (for example, on parliamentary ethics) with disciplinary power over other members. One of the common parliamentary disciplinary penalties, for one, is to be ruled out of order for a certain period of time. Parliamentary bodies frequently resort to this measure to punish members for their "non-parliamentary", including racial, statements. Both these statements and the penalties imposed by competent parliamentary bodies can be presented in a court of law as primary evidence.

8.4.4. The use of Nazi attributes

Nazi attributes when worn by members of ultra-right parties always put questions before us – is it an ideological sign, a tribute to a weird fashion, or a psychological derivation? And the second question – how do politicians themselves explain such fetishism and how do parties take it?

Examples of the use of Nazi attributes are plentiful. In 2007, the Minister of Justice of Estonia, a member of the Estonian Reform Party

"Rein Lang celebrated his 50th birthday at the Püssirohukelder restaurant in Tartu. In the invitations Lang noted that the hit of the program would be the play "Adolf" and asked the guests to dress up in the style typical of beer joints of Munich of the 1930s". A Nazi banner was used as a stage prop. "When asked by the weekly newspaper officials to explain the choice of this style, Lang said it was his private business and he would make no comment"[2].

It should be noted that this case is an example of classical dodging the question, which under the shifted burden of proof is impossible.

"A similar incident took place in 2004 when the Executive Secretary of the Estonian Centre Party Mart Viisitamm celebrated his birthday dressed in a Wehrmacht uniform, greeting his guests by the German salute. Viisitamm accounted for his outfit by saying that it was in line with the topical issue of the year – Nazi symbols, T-shirts featuring Hitler's portrait, and the plans to finally unveil the monument in Lihula"[3].

8.4.5. Party members and their participation in other right-extremist and Nazi organizations, "military historical societies" and paramilitary organizations

The prohibition for parties to have paramilitary units is not universal and is easily circumvented by the dominance of a party in any of the legalized paramilitary organizations like the National Guard or the Private Military Company. While the prohibition for professional soldiers to join a party is a common requirement now, a regular army is not the only organization that is armed. And here, as a rule, it is difficult to prove the fact that members of one particular party dominate in a militarized organization. Thus, in particular, when the authors sent an enquiry to the Estonian Kaitseliit military organization about how many their members belong to the Pro Patria and Res Publica Union (*Isamaa ja Res Publica Liit*, IRL), the answer was than no statistics were available.

---

[2] *Rein Lang ukrasil yubiley Adol'fon Hitlerom*. Available at: http://rus.delfi.ee/daily/estonia/rejn-lang-ukrasil-yubilej-adolfom-gitlerom.d?id=16354710 (*Rein Lang decorated his anniversary with Adolf Hitler*). (*Рейн Ланг украсил юбилей Адольфом Гитлером*).

[3] *Rein Lang ukrasil yubiley Adol'fon Hitlerom*. Available at: http://rus.delfi.ee/daily/estonia/rejn-lang-ukrasil-yubilej-adolfom-gitlerom.d?id=16354710

8.4.6. The party response

The response of parties to those actual instances that testify to the adherence of party members to criminal ideas or to their commitment of socially dangerous acts is very important. These reactions constitute independent facts in legal proceedings. Timely condemnations and disciplinary measures down to the expulsion from the party must be regarded as party noninvolvement in unseemly acts of its members. Condemnation and disciplinary measures taken under public pressure especially during the election campaign must be scrutinized in court so as to reveal if they were sincere or forced.

As a very intricate example, we can cite the open letter written by the Chairman of a Russian party, "Fair Russia", to Ilya Ponomarev, member of the State Duma of the Russian Federation, urging him to vacate the seat; by that time Ponomarev had already left the party owing to the political controversies over the events in Ukraine. The example is interesting because the Chairman of the party S. Mironov at that time had no authority over I. Ponomarev, so he tried to influence him rhetorically. This rhetoric was clearly of anti-Nazi character; the party chairman tried to show how wrong I. Ponomarev was when supporting the Right Sector of Ukraine. S. Mironov reasons, "Ukraine has a very old curse – the OUN-B headed by Bandera and his followers, Russia has its own – Vlasov. "Vlasovites of the 21st century still use the same justifications of their acts of treachery as did those who served Hitler. They were allegedly fighting against the existing regime. Yet it turns out that the war is waged not against the government but against its own people, its own country"[4].

8.4.7. The response of allied parties and party internationals

Condemnation and disregard of ultra-right parties by allied parties abroad or by party internationals may be used as a signal that the "front" of the party does not correspond to its content. For example, of great interest is the stand the French National Front took when it refused to cooperate with the British National Party accusing it of its blatant racism.

[4] Sergey Mironov, head of the party "Fair Russia" (Personal page). Available at: https://www.facebook.com/mironov.online/posts/485671674867839

8.4.8. The response of regulatory agencies

In some countries parties are under surveillance of regulatory agencies, competent to take certain decisions against parties. Thus, for example, after the failed August coup of 1991 in Russia, the Zhirinovsky-led party received a warning from the Ministry of Justice after which the members of the Supreme Council of the Liberal Democratic Party of the Soviet Union (later the Liberal Democratic Party of Russia) gave itself a reprimand for the support of the State Committee of the State Emergency[5].

8.4.9. Institution of criminal proceeding

A separate group of facts the courts are to consider with the utmost care. Initiation of legal proceedings against leaders of opposition parties, especially during the election campaign, is a standard method of political struggle in our days. It is characteristic that immediately after the elections these criminal cases, which had been a nine days' wonder, are no longer found in the front-page headlines. Although criminal charges may be dropped for the absence of crime in the act, it is not crime components that are necessary to establish the very fact of a party or a politician to have transgressed the boundary of the "prohibited".

A good illustration of this is the case of the State Committee of the State Emergency when the investigation team had developed a case on six counts against Zhirinovsky, yet the charges were not served[6].

8.4.10. Populism and populist provocations

Populism, as will be shown below, is an essential characteristic of "a legally defined crime" of Nazism, yet hitherto courts have not regarded it as something pertinent to an offence, so they are incapable of diagnosing populism as a social danger and assessing its contribution to it. The populist component of Svoboda's activities will be considered in the Annex, and here we shall cite a vivid example of a populist provocation.

Thus, in answer to the question of his sources of funding Zhirinovsky said, "Let those organizations whose leaders are not sure of tomorrow conceal them", and duly supplied the names of "Stolichny" Bank and the

---

[5] *Novaya Gazeta*, 29.10.1991. Available at: http://www.panorama.ru/works/vybory/party/ldpr.html (*New Newspaper*, 29.10.1991). (in the original: *Новая Газета*, 29.10.1991)

[6] *Megapolis Express*, N 17/92. (*Megapolis Express*, N 17/92). (in the original: *Мегаполис*-Экспресс, N 17/92).

Menatep Concern as his sponsors[7]. Yet the directors of the "Stolichny" Bank stated that they did not maintain any relations with the Liberal Democratic Party, let alone financial. In their turn, the directors of the Menatep Concern noted that Zhirinovsky's statement had done moral and material damage to their association. On either occasion, V. Zhirinovsky explained it in a different way: first, he just made a joke of it; second, he suggested that the Menatep and the Stolichny should start sponsoring his election campaign[8].

8.4.11. Party funding

The topic of openness and transparence in party funding has been paid much attention to lately, and national laws go separate ways, one of which is to reduce party expenditures by establishing an election campaign qualification; the other is governmental funding. Both measures seek to reduce the need of parties for "outside" investments, to make them less dependent from capital. In some countries, prohibitions on party funding by juridical persons are in use. Within the scope of our concern, party funding by criminal structures and radical organizations constitutes a real danger.

Thus, mass media not only in Russia but also abroad showed a keen interest in the financing of the Liberal Democratic Party of Russia. According to the Japanese newspaper Sankei Shimbun, the Liberal Democratic Party received money from the right-nationalist German party, The German People's Union (DVU), with the leaders of which V. Zhirinovsky maintained good relations[9]. The weekly news magazine Stern also reported that the bulk of party money the Liberal Democratic Party had received from the DVU. V. Zhirinovsky and Gerhard Frey have long been on familiar terms. G. Frey's personal worth is 500 m Deutsche marks, exclusively earned through spreading neo-Fascist propaganda[10]. Also, reports in the Press testified to the fact that The Socialist Unity Party

---

[7] *Nezavisimaya Gazeta*, 1993, 16 April. (*Independent Newspaper*, 1993, 16 April). (in the original: *Независимая Газета*, 1993, 16 апрель).

[8] *Nezavisimaya Gazeta*, 1993, 16 April. (*Independent Newspaper*, 1993, 16 April). (in the original: *Независимая Газета*, 1993, 16 апрель).

[9] *Izvestia,* 21.12.1993. (*News*, 21.12.1993). (in the original: *Известия,* 21.12.1993).

[10] *Moskovsy Komsomolets*, 06.01.1994. (*Moscow Komsomol*, 06.01.1994). (in the original: *Московский комсомолец*, 06.01.1994).

of Germany (SED) had financed V. Zhirinovsky from its deposits in foreign banks[11].

The newspaper "Segodnya" (Today) also published copies of fake remittance orders according to which the Liberal Democratic Party had transferred the money through the ProgressBank to the Galaktika Radio Company and the Mayak Radio Station to pay for the election campaign broadcasts. Despite the payment slips, the money never reached the accounts of the radio companies, and the Chairman of the Executive Board of the ProgressBank V.G. Znaiko stated that these remittance orders had not been found among the documents of the Bank. After the news had been published in the newspaper, the accountant at the Liberal Democratic Party (V. Zhirinovsky's sister) promised the Mayak radio station (nothing was said of the Galaktika radio company) to transfer the money, and she also complained about the sponsors, whose unreliability had prevented her from doing it in due time. But, according to V. Kobelev, a Party activist, at the time of the remittance the Liberal Democratic Party had no sponsors, and there was only 200 m received from Tsentrizbirkom on its bank account. Apart from this, the Party had other sources of funding. Thus, the Head of the Ideological Department of the Party, S. Putin stated that enterprises of the Military Industrial Complex had financed V. Zhirinovsky[12]. Also, after 12 December 1993, a party member, Andrei Zavidia, whom V. Zhirinovsky had struck from the roll, stated that his Galand concern had provided three billion rubles for the Party's political campaign and that he was determined to claim the money back in a court of law[13].

The prohibition on funding from abroad is also not uncommon, and this instance may be included in the list of principal differences between parties and associations. The topic of foreign funding shifts the emphasis from social danger to danger for the state, thereby actualizing the "Fifth Column" and "foreign agents" speculations. But there are no international rules to regulate these relations, and Part VI "Non-intervention in internal affairs" of the Helsinki Final Act stipulates a very low threshold non-intervention, "The participating States they will, inter alia, refrain from direct or indirect assistance to terrorist activities, or to subversive or other activities directed towards the violent overthrow of the regime of another participating State".

[11] *Segodnya*, 22.04.1994. (*Today*, 22.04.1994). (*Сегодня*, 22.04.1994).

[12] *Izvestia*, 01.01.1994. (*News*, 01.01.1994). (in the original: *Известия*, 01.01.1994).

[13] *Segodnya*, 29.12.1993; 12.01.1994. (*Today*, 29.12.1993; 12.01.1994). (in the original: *Сегодня*, 29.12.1993; 12.01.1994).

8.5. The Principle of operation tempo

The principle of operation tempo says that for every task there is a time interval outside which the task solution only deteriorates the situation. This principle can be applied to the full extent to the task of the liquidation of socially dangerous parties, first and foremost, Nazi parties.

We have already voiced the idea that Nazism, when risen to power, destroys democracy proper, which makes its liquidation by democratic means impossible, and the liquidation of Nazi parties in a court of law is possible only at the time of rising Nazism, which is characterized by the corresponding phases. In a generalized way, these phases can be described as follows.

Phase 1, which can be regarded both as a pre-party and illegal period. During this phase ultra-nationalists, radicals (Nazi) exist in the format of association (associations). The principal goal during this phase is to come into the limelight of political life. This phase is characterized by illegal political strife, street riots, and aggressive activities deliberately leading to trials to be used as political hustings. During this phase first supporters are recruited and strategies are worked out. This phase can take a long time.

Phase 2 is characterized by the legalization of a party to enable it to stand in election and win seats in the parliament. During this phase the party cooperates with right-of-centre conservative parties, participates in political activities, including legislative, and positions itself as a sole political force capable of overcoming national squalor. Thus, during the interwar period the National Socialist Party Workers Party (NSDAP) presented itself as the sole alternative to the German collapse. Under such circumstances, conservative forces see no other way but to give power to those who are even "higher" than they are. Frequently it happens because the ordinary conservative forces are directly accountable for contributing to the national plight.

The process of overcoming national squalor frequently entails disengagement from international obligations, which ordinary conservative forces cannot afford, thereby opening the road for the populism of ultra-nationalists. In this phase of great importance is the correlation between political ambitions of the ultra-nationalist party and the acknowledgment of this ambition as the sole political alternative by conservative parties, that is, the ultra-right-wing parties heavily rely on the political support of allied parties.

This phase can also be rather long.

Phase 3 is the time for ultra-nationalists to consolidate their position in power, while the very institutions of power get transformed under their onslaught, for instance, the parliament can be dissolved (Reichstag), a "by-election can be held, a "Maidan" can happen. A series of decrees are promulgated, which seemingly legalizes the prosecution of political opponents. For example, when Nazi rose to power in Germany they passed the following laws: the Decree on protection of the German people, which restricted the freedoms of the press and association; the Law on the Protection of People and State, which abolished the fundamental freedoms in the country; the Decree against betrayal of the German people and treasonable intrigues; the Enabling Act giving the government the right to make laws without the involvement of the Reichstag thereby shaping the conditions for the political persecution of rivals and the abrogation of their legislative capacities and activities; the Law for Coordination of the countries with the Reich secured the centralization of governance in the country; the Law for the Restoration of the Professional Civil Service, which allowed for the cleansing of the bureaucratic ranks, ousting all the unwanted officials from the Administration; the Law against other parties' activities; the Law against the establishment of political parties, which resulted in dissolution, sometimes voluntary, of all parties except NSDAP, and had a bad effect on the trade unions movement; the Law concerning the reconstruction of the *Reich*, which made Germany a rigidly centralized country.

This is a very short phase.

Phase 4 is the time of execution of chauvinistic designs both at home and abroad. It is the time for the "winners" to emerge out of the intraparty struggle, the "leader" to seize absolute power in the party, to start intraparty purges, the seizure of the absolute power in the state (the final merge of the posts of the leader of the party and other governmental posts to be held by one person), the outbreak of aggression to gain Lebensraum.

The duration of this phase is determined by the intensity of inter-state repressions and foreign aggression. The "inconspicuous" Nazism can linger for decades.

This analysis of the expansion of Nazism and its consolidation in power shows that the effective legal proceedings are possible only during its first two phases. The third phase is rich in "triggers" but is too short to conduct appropriate prosecution. As a result, the situation gets critical: during the first two phases ultra-nationalism (Nazism) looks relatively "harmless" to institute proceedings against (during the first phase it is not subject to prosecution at all, as a party), the third phase is too short, and during the fourth the democratic judicial instruments cease to function. This leads to a conclusion that it is early diagnostics and prosecution of Nazism that is necessary, which was the topic of this chapter.

8.6. Neo-Nazism

Frequent references to Nazism (neo-Nazism) in international public law without defining its nature make the authors express their opinion on the present state of Nazism, since the prefix: "neo" means "new". What is new in Nazism that required a new name?

The conducted research compels the authors to state that the lack of political will, or any will at all, is inherent not only in the political but also in the scientific communities. One needs courage to diagnose a regime or a party as a "Nazi", and this courage is rare. As a result, instead of diagnosing Nazism, scholars keep coining new names, the need for which seems extremely dubious yet this allows the researchers to avoid diagnosing Nazism as such. Nazism (Fascism) is enshrined in concomitant titles, which complicates the matter of diagnostics still further.

Thus, the scholars note that while during the pre-war period, apart from the terms Fascism and Nazism, there emerged only one, the monarch-Fascism to characterize the dictatorship of A. Tsankov in Bulgaria, the post-war period was rich in such titles that emerged and have remained topical – neo-Fascism, neo-Nazism, right-wing radicals, right-wing extremism, demo-Fascism. During the last decade there emerged such titles as Communo-Fascism, Glamour Fascism, etc. In recent years, there emerged more – Islam Fascism and American Fascism (stemming from the US struggle against part of the Islam realm), NATO Fascism and Global Fascism (resulting from the bombing attacks at Yugoslavia in 1999) and more[14]. This list is far from being complete, which makes the task of passing a sound judgment in court next to impossible, since the defence for the Nazi parties may easily steer the proceeding into the terminological maze, and few are those who understand anything about it.

Yet you cannot say that all "Nazisms" are identical and that, once tested, this diagnostic method can be easily replicated. What are those new properties that the contemporary Nazism has acquired and where has it changed? It seems that the main impediment to diagnosing Nazism is psychological. Nazism is known for its deeds – first of all, its concentration camps and "total war". Without these visible implications of Nazism, it is reasonable to ask a question whether a certain regime is really a Nazi regime.

---

[14] See: *Pravoradikal'nye politicheskie partii I dvizhenia sovremennoy Evropy.* 2011, Sankt-Peterburg, pp.408. (*Right-radical political parties and movements of contemporary Europe.* 2011, Saint-Petersburg, pp. 408). (in the original: *Праворадикальные политические партии и движения современной Европы.* 2011. СПб., 408 с.).

If we try to flesh out the term "neo-Nazism", we shall see that the main difference of contemporary Nazism from the classical Nazism lies in the changed fundamental resource of mankind. M. Delyagin in his work "Global Crisis: General Theory of Globalization"[15] points out that the contemporary fundamental resource of mankind is human consciousness. This concept is crucial for this study, since physical elimination of "subhuman" people is devoid of sense, for to turn a human into a slave capable of producing goods by means of intelligent information technologies is more profitable than to turn a human into a product. Information wars are the reality of today, and information security is a priority of any state. The war for Lebensraum is waged not with tanks, or not only with tanks, but first and foremost by the mass media.

Another possible aspect of "contemporary Nazism" is the transformation of the "golden age" of a nation for which the once Nazi period seems to be such. It is most characteristic of the Baltic States, especially for Latvia and Estonia, which rhapsodize about their "golden age" marked by pro-Fascist dictatorships of K. Ulmanis and K. Päts in the 1920s-1940s. They have nothing else to idealize; that is why the "history rewriting" proves so aggressive. Especially it refers to the period of German occupation.

And the third aspect – the replicated "theory of occupation" and the "continuity theory"; the latter markedly modifies the central myth of Fascism and Nazism. According to the "continuity theory", the "occupied" countries "did not face death, they did not die" but "during the occupation" they were deep in a peculiar "lethargic sleep", likewise Snow White, and were woken up by a kiss given to them by a democratic Prince Charming in the early 1990s. The image of Snow White is borrowed from the *opus magmum* of the "continuity theory" written by L. Mälksoo "Illegal Annexation and the State Continuity: International Legal Status of Estonia, Latvia and Lithuania in 1940-1941 and after 1991"[16].

Accordingly, the central myth of the revival of the "golden age" has been modified into an endless "golden age", the largest part of which Snow White had spent *de jure*, or simply put, asleep. And the "occupied

---

[15] Delyagin, M. 2003. *Mirovoy krizis: obschaya teoriya globalizatsia*, Moskva, pp.768. (Delyagin, M.G. 2003. *The World Crisis: General Theory of Globalization*, Moscow, pp. 768). (in the original: Делягин, М.Г.2003. *Мировой кризис: общая теория глобализации*, М.,768 с.).

[16] *Sovetskaya annexia I gosudarstvennyi kontinuitet.* Available at: http://www.estemb.ru/estonija/istorija/aid-2019(*Soviet Annexation and State Continuity*). (in the original: *Советская аннексия и государственный суверенитет*).

countries" had faced the need to utilize the Soviet period, which resulted in such glaring logical discrepancies that without serious brainwashing of their own people theoreticians stood no chance to succeed. Such brainwashing took place and was a success, if we look at it from the viewpoint of Nazi interests.

These three positions of "contemporary Nazism" should be considered in topical diagnostics.

Conclusion

The authors offer a catalogue of facts and factual circumstances of a party's activity that clearly testify to its socially dangerous nature, ranging from party documents and legal judgments to the funding of its activities. Noteworthy is yet another fact – the attitude to a certain party assumed by allied parties and party internationals, which sometimes best reveals the genuine positions of the party under examination.

Thus, without excluding the traditional view on the nature of a party based exclusively on whether its programmes and speeches contain racist statements, the authors of this book suggest examining parties more closely, by analyzing all aspects of their activities separately and in their relations with allied parties. Only this approach will allow for appropriate diagnostics of socially dangerous parties and for taking certain steps to liquidate them.

CONCLUSION

Right radicalism is not a new phenomenon in the public and political life of Europe. Feeding on xenophobia, fears, intolerance and the urge for national revival modeled upon past (historical) patterns, right nationalism gradually takes up a firm position and already shapes the agenda in many European countries. Furthermore, it has a legitimate image, partly because members of far-right parties try on the image of respectable gentlemen or because other parties and the political establishment do not acknowledge them as dangerous and do not regard them as a threat. In particular, in the countries of Central and Eastern Europe, cooperation of right and far-right parties ensures the legitimacy of the latter. Integrated into the existing party and political system, far-right parties have gained an opportunity to propagate their ideas to the entire society. Since many of them are of radical character, far-right parties are easily recognized and stand out from other parties.

The identity crisis is the heart of the debate about the path the European society should take and this debate is orchestrated by far-right parties. It is they who turned their minds to this problem and tied it with the pressing problem of the population gaining easier access to various resources and their distribution. Thus, they carved out a niche and immediately occupied it; political parties used to appeal to social justice, tolerance and multiculturalism and did not relate the loss of national identity and cultural struggle to the redistribution of common wealth. Nevertheless, in times of socio-economic crises the question of who, and to what extent, deserves certain benefits becomes thornier. Once deprived of them, states and individuals in these states immediately start fighting to regain them. Those who carry political clout have the opportunity to manipulate this redistribution and to manage the problems of access to this wealth. The most obvious distinction, both between states and between various communities inside these states, is their different cultural codes made up from traditions, language, religion and other markers separating communities from one another. Having tied the problem of the loss of national identity of titular majority with the idea that it should have free and unlimited access to state resources and that it is the cultural code of this community that constitutes the foundation of the state itself, the far-right could return to the ancient idea of national superiority, thereby getting a new lease of life, for they appeal not only to the idea of state and national revival but also to the idea of return to traditional values. Thereby far-right parties could fend off accusations of racism though the anti-racist theme is mirrored in their rhetoric aimed against certain ethnic (national) communities.

This can mean to say that the far-right offer the society the so-called regressive utopia that, requiring no other sources for its development but natural fears, enables a person to get rid of them and also of the impact of outside forces, even of its own history at that. Moreover, right radicals keep announcing that it is they who are the bearers of traditional knowledge of the causes of troubles and of their solutions, that is, they are not only the bearers of traditional knowledge but also the bearers of an innermost knowledge of the true inwardness. In this sense, contemporary far-right parties are genetic successors of inter-war far-right parties, who possess technologies of producing myths and utopias; the very idea of raising problems of justice or injustice of the state structure, the state and public order, superior civilization, superior and inferior peoples is largely conventional and utopian. Every point in historical space-time has its own truth, and its actual state is governed by many factors. History has proven that utopian thinking and the relying on it in shaping social, economic and others policies entail not only transformation of the whole political system but also more global catastrophes, for these ideas are also connected with the efforts to found a more perfect society and state while drawing upon the existing patterns. The very idea to define and reanimate the model that existed in the remote past is utopian and fraught with danger.

In this context, far-right parties may be regarded as both utopian and regressive, that is, as setting a goal to reproduce the former perfect state. So when far-right parties purport to form an ethnically (nationally) homogeneous society they can only accomplish this purpose in the contemporary world by methodically pursuing a tough policy of ousting the "unwanted" elements. This requires political power, that is, the establishment of such a political regime that will allow for pursuing such a strategy. Unfortunately, it has proven possible, for many European Constitutions explicitly indicate that nationalism has found its way into constitutional texts that are the basis of state formation and development[1].

---

[1] Eremina, N., Seredenko, S. 2014. Konstitutsionnyi natsionalizm v sovremennoy Evrope: novye ugrozy, *NB: Problemy obschestva I politiki*, N 3, pp. 1-42. Available at: http://e-notabene.ru/pr/article_11170.html (Eremina, N., Seredenko, S. 2014. Constitutional Nationalism in Contemporary Europe: New Threats, *NB: Problems of society and politics,* N 3, pp.1-42). (in the original: Еремина, Н.В., Середенко, С. Н. 2014. Конституционный национализм в современной

Obviously, such a policy will not lead to the regularization of international relations and to stable national and public development, on the contrary, it will contribute to the tension and public disintegration.

But this explains why it is in the states where the search for national identity and the awareness of its crisis are more pronounced that the far-right parties and movements are more firmly established, as is the case in countries of Eastern and Central Europe.

Although the leitmotif of all far-right parties is the struggle against nonethnic population, countries of Eastern (e.g. Poland, Latvia and Estonia) and Western (e.g. Germany, the United Kingdom, France) Europe differ in their interpretation of "nonethnic population", for immigration movements in East European countries are not comparable with those in West European countries. Far-right parties in East-European countries struggle not against immigrant (Islam) communities but against residents of other nationalities, for examples, Russian-speaking people and gypsies, while the West-European countries focus on anti-Islamism.

Today far-right parties, apart from their ideology aimed at the national unity of the state cleansed of all nonethnic elements, are equipped with new instruments. In particular, the mass media, first and foremost, the Internet, are playing a great role. The support of the mass media is of key importance during election campaigns of all levels. Moreover, they publish magazines and have their sites to propagate their ideas.

Despite the evident political success of right-wing radicals over the past two decades, they are either perceived as part of the political establishment or as parties not directly involved, so other political actors and the population do not seemed to be concerned. The analysis of international and national law, however, indicates that these movements have been greatly underestimated as parties capable of forming a political trend. In this sense, far-right parties are very difficult to interpret from the point of view of the danger they constitute to society and state. Moreover, the definition of a fascist party and its ideology proposed by R. Griffin is used in this work as a working instrument to identify the true nature of a party. Such markers as palingenesis, "golden age", national humiliation help to determine the position of a party. In the framework of legal dimension, owing to the established boundaries of the prohibited and the permissible, we can see that we still lack the appropriate instrument to fight these parties.

Европе: новый уровень угроз, *NB: Проблемы общества и политики*, N 3. сс.1-42).

Neo-Nazi parties have already become well-established phenomena in contemporary political life. In some cases they determine the orientation of the state policies. The latest obvious example of such dangerous activities is the All-Ukrainian Svoboda Union, which has become a peculiar curator of Ukrainian political processes.

This study also shows that there is no international consensus on which ideology should be proposed to counter the far-right, socially dangerous ideology. The component parts of the opposition to fascism have been examined by M. Kantor[2],

"Democracy has been discredited by the market. The principles of liberalism are difficult to set against fascism because it is the liberal opposition that has fostered the fascism of today. When an oligarch on the run musters an opposition to autocracy, it only exacerbates the social paradox. Socialism has been done away with. The opposition to fascism, represented by the Communist International, is no longer possible, not only because Stalin destroyed Komintern (later Komintern got assembled by itself) but also because such principles as "man to man – a friend, comrade and brother" and "proletarians of all countries, unite!" were destroyed by liberal and democratic ideology. One cannot match them against fascism. Humanist art no longer exists. Figurative, humanist art was deliberately destroyed by the Western civilization in the course of liberal market reforms, to be substituted for by the glamourous avant-garde. Religion has ceased to dominate human consciousness, in fact, it means practically next to nothing. The struggle for rights has superseded all ideas of duty, including moral duty. The fascism of the last century was defeated by the union of democracy, socialism, humanistic art and religion. All the components of this victory have been deliberately destroyed. Today we have nothing to set off against fascism".

What this new opposition to Nazism will be made of, if it happens at all, remains unclear.

2 Kantor, Maxim. *Poslednyaya skrepa*. Available at: http://www.gazeta.ru/comments/column/kantor/6038901.shtml(Maxim, Kantor. *The last tie*). (in the original: Кантор, Максим. *Последняя скрепа*).

ANNEX

TENTATIVE DIAGNOSTICS OF NAZI PARTIES: CASE STUDY OF THE ALL-UKRAINIAN SVOBODA UNION

The Judgment of the Nuremberg Tribunal morally compels us to have a party diagnosed as a Nazi party immediately liquidated. However, the social consciousness consigned the Nazi parties to oblivion after the defeat of Nazism in 1945 when the Nuremberg Tribunal and the laws on denazification adopted by the Control Council were to close the chapter on the history of Nazism. The reality, however, demonstrates that Nazism has proven more robust than it was thought to be.

As has already been shown, the liquidation of socially dangerous parties does not necessarily require that they be diagnosed as Nazi parties, it is sufficient to prove their willful transgression of the "boundary of the prohibited". At the same time, as follows from the cited example of the All-Ukrainian Svoboda Union, it may well be the task for the court to diagnose the party as a Nazi, but the Ukrainian court in its time as good as abandoned its duties. Still, the problem can be solved; and the diagnostic procedure for its solution is provided below.

The proposed technique to be applied for diagnosing a Nazi party is predicated upon the criteria of "the necessary and the appropriate", that is, a minimal set of markers is selected, which, taken together, constitute a "formally defined crime" of Nazism. Here we must realize that it is not party documents, but public declarations and blatant calls like "drown the Yids in the blood of the Moskals" (this call is very characteristic since pejorative ethnonyms are used for both Jews and Russians) that will trigger legal proceedings. It is in the light of such calls or acts that Party documents emerge full blown, and, expressing the collective will of the party, they constitute the basis for analysis.

The diagnostic technique is applied to the Draft National Constitution of Ukraine (the Proposed Constitution) and the Programme of the All-Ukrainian Svoboda Union (Svoboda's Programme); and Svoboda's Programme can be regarded, with great reserve, as an explanatory memorandum for the Proposed Constitution. Svoboda was chosen, first, because of the topicality of events in Ukraine and, second, because Nazism in Svoboda's performance is naïve, "pure" and undisguised (though never declaring itself as such, as was already pointed out). Third, the diagnostic method applied to this case allows us to "continue" the debate started in the Ukrainian court on whether Svoboda is a Nazi party.

The actual pattern of the events in Ukraine is intricate, and lacks no "triggers". We shall exemplify only one fact directly relevant to the topic of the liquidation of socially dangerous parties and associations. According to the State Agency RIA Novosti, on 28 March 2014 the Ukrainian security service agents held a special operational night conference for the events around the Verkhovna Rada of Ukraine (Supreme Council of Ukraine) and they discussed the possibility to ban the radical "Right Sector" Movement. According to the Agency, among others present at the conference was Andrei Parubiy, Head of the Council of National Security, Oleh Tyahnybok, a deputy and the leader of Svoboda. During the meeting, Arsen Avakov, Minister of Internal Affairs, considering the growing radicalization of the Right Sector, proposed to impose an outright ban on the organization. "O. Tyahnybok took no definite stand, and A. Porubiy seconded A. Avakov's proposal, saying that such a decision would clear those present of the charge of radicalism", says the member of the Batkivshchyna Party to the RIA information agency[1]. Such a scramble of spiders in a jar allows us, inter alia, to surmise that the phase the Ukrainian Nazism is going through is between Phase 3 and Phase 4. (See Chapter VIII).

In the proposed pattern of practical diagnosis "Nazism" proper is regarded, according to R. Griffin's definition, as "populist palingenetic ultra-nationalism". Accordingly, the diagnosis requires three main markers – palingenesis, ultra-nationalism (aggressive nationalism), and populism. The hypertrophied role of the government, totalitarianism, glorification of Nazism, special concepts of Lebensraum and militarism are used as optional markers.

The authors also find it important to note that the markers relating to the above-mentioned conventional category of "esoteric" will not be considered in this action-oriented annex for several reasons. First, the title of these markers shows that they are clandestine, and the detecting of them requires certain investigation, which sometimes cannot be conducted.

---

[1] *Siloviki rassmatrivayut vopros o zaprete "Pravogo sektora"*. Available at: http://ria.ru/world/20140328/1001375442.html(*Law enforcers discuss if to forbid "Right Sector"*). (in the original: *Силовики рассматривают вопрос о закрытии "Правого сектора"*).

Second, the esoteric "component" of Nazism sooner relates to the entire regime and not to the party as such. The Ahnenerbe, for one, was a "research institute" founded by Heinrich Himmler, Head of the "Black Order" of the SS, and did not bear a direct relation to the NSDAP. From the above-said we can draw a demonstrable conclusion that the presence and the exposure of "exoteric" components of Nazism in the party ideology presume the "esoteric" component, for in the majority of cases, and Svoboda is no exception, Nazis do their best to conceal their Nazi nature from the "uninitiated".

The texts adduced below are checked for the presence of the above-indicated "exoteric markers", and if such markers are in evidence, Svoboda can be classed as a Nazi party.

We repeat that factual material relating to Svoboda is in great abundance, so the authors find it justifiable not to use all the cited types of proof (for example, several ultra-right-wing parties refused to cooperate with Svoboda), but only two party documents that are necessary and sufficient to expose Svoboda as a Nazi party.

1. Palingenesis

Nazism is based on the myth of the resurrection of the former might (genuine or putative) of a nation. "Resurrection" should be understood literally as the rising from the dead, the national tragedy and humiliation. The very term "palingenesis" was borrowed by R. Griffin from geology, where it means recurrent "induration" and "paroptesis".

From the viewpoint of palingenesis, the most substantive is the Preamble to the Proposed Constitution of Ukraine proposed by Svoboda, which features both the "golden age", the "national tragedy" and the "continuity", that is, the connection between the present state and the past.

1.1 "The Golden Age"

The text of the Preamble to the Proposed Constitution of Ukraine runs as follows, "We, citizens of Ukraine, aware that the Ukrainian nation is a successor to the rich spiritual and material culture of Tripillians, Scythians and hundreds of succeeding generations of Ukrainians, that the present Ukrainian State stands in direct continuity with the Kievan Rus, the Principality of Galicia-Volynia, the Cossack Hetmanate, Ukrainian People's Republic, Carpathian Ukraine and the Ukrainian Power restored by Act of 30 June 1941, that Independent Ukraine emerged as a result of over 300 years' struggle for national liberation".

"We are aware that the Ukrainian Nation had been under the 300-year-old yoke of colonialism; that it had passed through the genocide during the Golodomor, the famine that brought about drastic demographic losses; that throughout hundreds of years its language and culture were being demolished, that it was subjected to cruel communist repressions".

"Aware of its duty and responsibility before the Creator perished in the struggle for the independence of Ukraine, before the present generation and generations to come, Striving to establish the ideals of justice and supremacy of law in the Ukrainian State, believing that the State is the pride and the matter of honour for all freedom-loving Ukrainians, and freedom is a means to attain happiness and promote the general welfare, guided by our own consciousness and God's will, relying on the glorious historical heritage of the government by the people and the perfect and well-developed Ukrainian law of the Hetmanate, agree to develop a national, indivisible, lawful and fair Ukrainian State that shall be a protector of rights and freedoms of the Ukrainian Nation on the whole and every Ukrainian in particular".

It is clear that "the golden age of the nation" can be both genuine and putative, in the latter case it is the "rewriting of history" that Nazism resorted to, which is the subject of our separate study. To illustrate this, we shall cite Article 23 of the Proposed National Constitution of Ukraine, "The national coat of arms of Ukraine is a Tryzub (Trident), the emblem of the Kievan State of Grand Prince Vladimir the Great".

1.2 The national tragedy

According to the Nazi logic, the "golden age" of a nation shall end in a national tragedy, or even in national degradation – the breakdown of a nation. And the national tragedy must always have an external agency to blame – a blind natural force like the eruption of the Vesuvius volcano is not taken into account. As a result, there emerges a freaky psychological hybrid of a hero-victim. The victim status seems to be necessary for a Nazi party, first, to get rid of the responsibility (the victim is not held responsible for self-defence) and, second, to legitimize their right to Lebensraum in their fight against aliens, dissentients and other states. If a usual pattern of political landscape maps the changes a society undergoes, parties emerge in response to the needs of the society for externalizing these conflicts; it is typical of Nazi parties that, nominally, they externalize not a topical but a decades-old conflict, they raise the topic of the recent historical degradation, and in this sense have a right to call themselves revanchists.

From Svoboda's viewpoint, the national tragedy is everything that connects Ukraine with Russia. Following the Baltic States, Ukraine became one of the largest manufacturers of Russophobia. The studies show that the more dubious the "golden" age" is, the more pompous the national tragedy should be, to enable people to say not "ah, how well we fared!" but "how well we would be faring but for….". Apart from the Preamble to the Proposed Constitution of Ukraine, the whole Part VI of Svoboda's Programme is devoted to the "national tragedy".

The priority steps to achieve the goal of sustainable development are as follows:

"2. To recognize the fact of the occupation of Ukraine by Bolshevik Russia during 1918-1991, which resulted in an unprecedented genocide against Ukrainians.

3. To compel the Verkhovna Rada of Ukraine, the United Nations, the European Parliament, the parliaments of the world to recognize the 20th century Ukrainian genocide that killed 20.5 million Ukrainians as a crime against humanity (rule of terror, plunder and violence during the war waged by Bolshevik Russia against the Ukrainian People's Republic in 1918-1921; dekulakization and forced collectivization; man-made famine of 1921, 1932-1933, 1947; several waves of physical destruction aimed at the Ukrainian elite in the 1920s-40s and the 1970s; killings of civilians during the war, violent uprooting and deportation of Ukrainians to foreign lands; the Vistula Operation; torture in prisons and the humiliation of the political abuse of psychiatry until the collapse of the Soviet Empire; the plundering of the national economy, historical and cultural values; sacrilege and destruction of Ukrainian churches; persecution on ethnic and religious grounds; systematic destruction of Ukrainian culture and language; total Russification).

5. To renew criminal investigation into the 1932-1933 Holodomor which was recognized by the state as genocide against the Ukrainian people, the crime to which no statutory of limitation can be applied; to hold a public trial of communism; to obtain a court order to ban the communist ideology as misanthropic and one that has caused irreparable damage to the Ukrainian people.

6. To make public denial of the Holodomor as genocide against the Ukrainian nation an offence.

9. To demand from Moscow an official recognition, apology and compensation for the genocide against the Ukrainian people; to compel Russia to return the savings of the citizens of Ukraine (amounting to 83 billion karbovanets by 1991); to insist that the rightful share of the

Diamond fund, gold-and-exchange holdings, foreign property of the former USSR be returned to Ukraine.

10. To pay compensations to repressed Ukrainians and their descendants in amounts commensurate with their suffering.

11. To provide Ukrainians from Kuban, Chełm Land, Nadsyannya, Podlasie, Lemko Regions who were evicted from their lands with the status of deported peoples entitled to social protection".

"Genocide of the Ukrainian people" could not help but result in a "demographic crisis". To overcome this crisis, Item 3 of Part III proposes, in particular, to "implement a "Reproductive Health of the Nation" program; to ban abortions, except due to medical necessities or rape, established in legal proceedings; to equate illegal artificial abortion to attempted murder".

1.3. "Cleansing"

The idea of "resurrection" is closely linked with the idea of "cleansing", for the fire that burns the phoenix must engulf everything that is redundant, alien, harmful, including all the political and national "scum", from Svododa's viewpoint, "Yids, Moskals, Poles, homosexuals, migrants, corrupt officials, drug addicts, and communists. Part I of Svoboda's Programme entitled just like that – "Power and Society: Radical Cleansing and Fair System" – spells out the measures to be taken:

1. To lustrate the authorities; to bring down the former agents of the KGB and government officials who held executive posts in the Communist Party of the Soviet Union
2. To promulgate lists of the agents of the KGB who were or are in public service of Ukraine and hold other important public posts.
3. To fill the vacancies with young specialists, graduates of Ukrainian universities, selected on the principle of patriotism and professionalism, after their completion of special government administrative courses.
4. To set a mandatory polygraph examination (lie detection screening) policy for government employees and candidates for elective offices to find out if they have been involved in corruption, collaboration with foreign intelligence services and whether they have dual citizenship.

Item 7 of the Programme serves the same purpose, to be exact, to separate "the clean" from "the unclean":

"Introduce the "nationality" point in passports and birth certificates. The nationality shall be determined in accordance with either one's birth certificates or parents' birth certificates, durante bene placito".

Item 14 further develops this topic proposing to "compel candidates for all elective offices to specify in their curricula vitae their nationality, all previous nationalities (since the Soviet times), party and public posts, record of convictions (both expunged and unexpunged); those candidates that have concealed certain facts shall be deregistered or unseated if such non-disclosure should be found after the election".

The "cleansing" must also be conducted in the economic sphere: Item 12 of Part II prescribes to "check the legality of the privatization of large enterprises (where the yearly average number of employees is over a thousand persons, or the yearly gross income from sales of products exceeds UAH 50 m.) and to transfer the illegally privatized objects into state ownership and labour-collective ownership.".

Item 8 of Part III makes it hard for drug addicts and representatives of the LGBT community by intending to "prohibit the advertising of tobacco products and alcoholic beverages in any manner throughout the territory of Ukraine; advocacy of drug addiction (including the so-called "soft drugs") and sexual perversions shall be criminalized".

Item 12 of Part IV proposes to "take stricter anti-immigration measures and improve the system of detention and deportation of illegal immigrants".

The already mentioned Part VI entitled "Historical Justice: State Succession and Overcoming the Consequences of the Occupation" proposes to:

Item 7. Abolish and ban the use of derisive imperial-Bolshevik symbols, commemorations of dates, monuments and names in honour of the butchers of Ukraine; prohibit the erection of any imperial monuments and the use of symbols that glorify the history of the occupier countries.

Item 8. Set up a special investigative office to search for criminals who were destroying the Ukrainian nation, arrest them and bring to justice.

Item 15. Revoke special pensions for minions of the Soviet regime, the executives of the Communist party, Komsomol and punitive authorities of the USSR.

Surely the "cleansing" theme is treated differently in the Proposed Constitution as compared with the Programme, but still the former contains a reference to "cleansing" sports elite: Article 39 spells out: "It is prohibited to contract with foreigners or persons destitute of nationality for their participation in Ukrainian sports events and in international competitions on behalf of Ukraine".

1.4 The rewriting of history

The two counter flows, the writing of an alternative history and the struggle for the purity of "true" history, when meeting, generate attempts to legally prohibit "perversion of history". This confrontation on the global scale has already gone too far. The typical methods here are contemporary political appraisals presented as "historical facts", which resulted in universal politicization of history.

"Rewriting of history" in the palingenesis context of our concern follows the two main lines: the framing and gilding the "golden age" and, respectively, the framing and exacerbating of the "national tragedy". Here we should note that though the world community is aware that "something wrong is being done about the history", yet these two markers have not been clearly defined as applied to Nazism. For example, Article 98 of the Durban Declaration specifies, "We emphasize the importance and necessity of teaching about the facts and truth of the history of humankind from antiquity to the recent past, as well as of teaching about the facts and truth of the history, causes, nature and consequences of racism, racial discrimination, xenophobia and related intolerance, with a view to achieving a comprehensive and objective cognizance of the tragedies of the past".

A clear-cut programme of rewriting history is spelled out in Part VI of Svoboda's Programme:

"Item 12: A state education programme "The Truth about the Ukrainian genocide" shall be developed and deployed. A separate course unit "The History of Ukrainian genocide in the 20th century" shall be introduced in all schools.

Item 13: The struggle that was waged until the end of the 1950s by the Organization of Ukrainian Nationalists (OUN) and the Ukrainian Insurgent Army (UPA) shall be recognized as the national liberation struggle of the Ukrainian people. UPA soldiers and OUN underground fighters shall be recognized as veterans of the national liberation struggle for the independence of Ukraine.

Item 16: The truth about the Ukrainian liberation struggle in the 20th century shall be spread by means of public advertising, public parliamentary hearings, documentary and feature films, book publishing, etc.; also a special a course in the history of the Ukrainian liberation struggle in the 20th century shall be offered in all schools.

Item 17: A National Memorial Museum dedicated to the Ukrainian valour (armed struggle for independence of the Ukrainian Nation) shall be established.

Item 19: The 14th October (the date of a religious holiday Pokrov (The veil of Our Lady), patron saint of Ukrainian Cossacks, the day of the creation of the UPA) shall be declared a national holiday "the Day of Ukrainian Weaponry"; the so-called "Defender of the Motherland Day" (of the Soviet Army)" holiday celebrated on the 23rd February shall be cancelled".

1.5 A New State

Both Nazism and Communism build a new state, a state different from the existing one. For Communism, the lines from "The International" marching song spell it loud and clear:

> "The earth shall rise on new foundations. We have been naught we shall be all". (Adaptation of Charles H. Kerr translation from the original, for The IWW Songbook (34th Edition), https://www.marxists.org/history/ussr/sounds/lyrics/international.htm).

Nazism is more "sparing" of the existing state and not unwilling in principle to adapt the institutions of the existing state to its needs, without pressing for "changing the foundations". Of principal importance is the revival of the former grandeur and transition to the would-be grandeur. From the Preamble to Svoboda's Programme:

> "The main goal of the All-Ukrainian Svoboda Union is to build a powerful Ukrainian State based on the principles of social and national justice; a state that will take its rightful place among the leading countries and will promote sustainable development of the Ukrainian nation".

The analysis of the Draft of the National Constitution proposed by Svoboda (the Proposed Constitution) shows that the Ukrainian State is not the same as Ukraine, since the Ukrainian Nazis contemplate a more profound institutional reform. For instance, the Verkhovna Rada of Ukraine shall become the National Rada, and the range of legal authority extends indefinitely:

"Article 6. In Ukraine, the principle of the rule of law is recognised and effective. The Constitution of Ukraine has the highest legal force; the others legal sources are statutory instruments, the national legal tradition, common law (common sense), equity law, judicial precedents, international agreements and conventions ratified by the National Rada of Ukraine. The norms of the Constitution of Ukraine are norms of direct effect".

Part VII of the Proposed Constitution ("Final and Transitional Provisions") contains an outline of the institutional reform:

6. "Within six months the National Rada of Ukraine shall bring the legislation in line with the Constitution of Ukraine. The National Rada of Ukraine shall adopt constitutional laws on "the President of Ukraine", "the Government of Ukraine", "the National Rada of Ukraine", "the Administrative-Territorial System", "Court Organization", "Local Governance", The Ukrainian Code of Elections, Referendums, and Plebiscite".

Some instances point to the fact that not all citizens of Ukraine will remain entitled to citizenship in the future:

"Article 9. Citizens of Ukraine are those who were born in its territory. Ethnic Ukrainians who arrive in Ukraine to take up permanent residence and work also become citizens of Ukraine. Persons without citizenship who have lived in Ukraine not less than ten years, have a good command of the Ukrainian language, know the history of the Ukrainian state and the Constitution can, in an exceptional instance, become citizens of Ukraine. These persons cannot be granted citizenship if they have been criminally liable. The Government must conclude agreements with neighbouring countries on the readmission of immigrants. Dual citizenship is prohibited. A Ukrainian citizen who has concealed the fact that he is a citizen of another state is deprived of the Ukrainian citizenship".

The theme of "persons destitute of nationality" (and the Proposed Constitution keeps reiterating it) is clearly borrowed from the Baltic States, where in the early 1990s Russian-speaking residents of Estonia, Latvia, and Lithuania, were massively robbed of their citizenship. In this sense, indicative is the play with "Ukraine" and "The Ukrainian State" – not all residents will be citizens. Addressing the issue of dual nationality is contemplated as an initial measure (many residents of Ukraine have both passports of Ukraine and Russia) to oust all Ukrainian non-citizens from the political life of the country[2].

As a trigger here, we can adduce O. Tyagnybok's statement that persons who openly advocate for the split of Ukraine and who support "the Russian occupation of the Crimea" must be deprived of Ukrainian citizenship. The first on the list was V. Kolisnichenko, deputy of the Verkhovna Rada. "This rascal dares to say such improprieties which no Ukrainian politician, let alone a Ukrainian citizen, can utter. He couldn't care less about Ukraine. All this constitutes a compelling reason to deprive him of his credentials and the Ukrainian citizenship", remarked the fuehrer of Svoboda. "People's enemies cannot be citizens of Ukraine, and, for that matter, have a seat in the parliament and be in public service", O. Tygnybok summed up[3].

"A new state" does demand "new citizens", hence, Article 10 specifies that "foreigners and persons destitute of nationality shall not be allowed to obtain title to land".

1.6 Variations – continuity

We have already shown that the myth of resurrection has taken the form of "continuity" (other terms used in the Baltic States, for example, are: legal continuity, state continuity, juridical continuity, legal identity). The myth of phoenix yielded to the Snow White tale, which added new flavour to the Ukrainian anthem "Ukraine is still alive and kicking". Yet the structure of the state continuity, apart from being controversial as it is, is intricate, and the authors working on the National Constitution of Ukraine and the Programme never sorted it out. Item 1 Part VI of Svoboda's Programme formulates the idea of continuity:

"The Constitution of Ukraine shall specify that the legal continuity of the modern Ukrainian State was founded in Kievan Rus, continued by the Galicia-Volyn Principality, the Cossack Republic of the Hetmanate time, the Ukrainian People's Republic and the West Ukrainian People's Republic, Carpatho-Ukraine and Ukrainian Power restored by Act of June

---

2 *Ukraina khochet lishit' russkikh grazhdanstva*. Available at: http://newsland.com/news/detail/id/373037/(*Ukraine wants to deprive Russians of citizenship*). (in the original: *Украина хочет лишить русских гражданства*).

3 *Furer ukrainskoi Svobody prizval lishat' grazhdanstva vragov naroda*. Available at: http://baltija.eu/news/read/37383 (*Fuhrer of Ukranian "Svoboda" called to deprive "people's enemies" of citizenship*). (in the original: *Фюрер украинской Свободы призвал лишать гражданства врагов народа*).

30, 1941, and that Independent Ukraine emerged as a result of over 300 years' struggle for national liberation".

The authors of these documents equate legal succession (a classic of law) with "legal continuity", which is inadmissible. Legal succession is the transfer of powers from an individual who formerly held them to another who undertakes current responsibilities to execute those powers, while "legal continuity" is the extent of legal existence of one and the same person. "The continuity was founded", a phrase from the Proposed Constitution, is ridiculous, for how can one found continuity is impossible to understand. So the Nazi Ukraine appears to have an extremely dubious format of statehood, which is typical of palingenesis.

Thus it is obvious that the marker of palingenesis is in evidence in Svoboda's policy papers. The concept of the golden age and that of continuity, according to the leaders of this party, automatically grant ethnic Ukrainians, contrary to other ethnic minorities inhabiting the territory of Ukraine, the right of citizenship so that they could exercise their rights of freedoms.

2. Ultra-nationalism (aggressive nationalism)

Examples of manifestations of aggressive nationalism are plentiful in both Svoboda's Programme and the Proposed Constitution, so only brief comments will be provided at the end of this part. Only relevant provisions from both documents are cited:

Svoboda's Programme:

"Part I.

8. All manifestations of Ukraine-phobia shall be prosecuted.

9. A bill on the proportional representation of Ukrainians and national minorities in the executive bodies shall be submitted to the popular vote.

11. The presidential term of office shall be shortened to four years (one and the same person can serve a maximum of two consecutive terms). The President must be a Ukrainian citizen by birth, who has lived the past 20 years in Ukraine, has attained the age of 35 years, has a command of the official language, has not been convicted or prosecuted for anti-Ukrainian misconduct.

16. Deputy immunity from prosecution of criminal and economic offences shall be abolished. Deputies of all levels shall not be held liable for their political stand, statements and voting patterns in councils and their bodies (except cases of anti-Ukrainian, anti-State, Ukraine-phobia activities).

IV. 6. Massive return of ethnic Ukrainian to Ukraine shall be encouraged. Conditions of exemption shall be set for the Ukrainians and their descendants born abroad who wish to return to Ukraine.

7. Bilateral agreements on the legalization of Ukrainian migrant workers shall be concluded. Ukrainians working abroad shall be protected by all possible means.

16. Ukrainian university students shall take priority over foreign students in getting accommodation in dormitories.

17. Foreign students' registration papers shall be checked regularly; educational institutions shall submit lists of expelled students so that their timely departure could be monitored.

Part V. 1. The law "on the protection of the Ukrainian language" shall be adopted to substitute for the law "on languages in the Ukrainian SSR". A State Language Policy Committee responsible for the protection and spread of the Ukrainian language shall be instituted.

2. The use of the Ukrainian language in the mass media shall be regulated according to the number of the Ukrainian population: not less than 78% of their area and air time.

3. Simultaneous translation into the official language of foreign language programs and films on radio and television shall be provided; the translation shall be done at the expense of mass media owners.

5. Public officials and candidates for elected offices shall take an exam in the Ukrainian language; only Ukrainian shall be the language spoken at work and during public meetings.

7. The language of tuition in all schools and educational institutions without exception shall be Ukrainian unless otherwise specified; licenses shall be terminated if the language of tuition is foreign without proper accreditation. No textbooks in foreign languages shall be either provided by or financed from the State budget if the institution has no appropriate accreditation.

8. The best traditions of Ukrainian education must be encouraged. The practice of mechanical modeling upon foreign practices (such as, for example, the Bologna process) shall be stopped.

12. A State programme for patriotic and physical education of the young generation shall be introduced; leisure and recreation for children and young people shall be provided for; networks and youth patriotic organizations, sports clubs, summer camps shall be promoted.

14. Ukrainian scientists working abroad shall be encouraged to return.

17. Soviet propaganda literature shall be removed from children's public libraries. The state budget shall finance only those libraries,

museums, video and audio libraries, etc. that purchase national literature, fine arts, music, films, etc.

21. Licenses of those media outlets that violate the language legislation, demean the national dignity of Ukrainians, spread disinformation or anti-Ukrainian propaganda shall be terminated.

22. All mass media shall inform the citizens of all their owners (the Press in every issue, TV and radio in daily broadcasts).

23. The import duty on foreign printed, audio and video products shall be increased. Retransmission of foreign radio and television programmes, video and audio duplication, music and film rentals shall be taxed. The received funds shall be channeled for the development the national information space.

28. Ukrainian-language software (first of all, for accounting, warehousing, education, office administration, etc.) for government agencies, educational institutions shall be developed and sold in Ukraine. All institutions shall use exclusively Ukrainian software products.

Part VII.

5. An efficient national programme to create and promote a positive image of Ukraine in the world shall be developed and implemented; the large Ukrainian Diaspora through special state programmes can contribute to lobbying the Ukrainian interests in other parts of the world".

The text of the Proposed Constitution is even more radical in its aggressiveness:

"Title 1. The Rights of the Ukrainian Nation and Obligations of the Ukrainian State".

Article 1. Sovereignty unconditionally belongs to the Ukrainian nation exercising it directly or indirectly through its representatives or a referendum. Any attempts to usurp the entire sovereignty or its part made by an individual or by a group of individuals shall be prosecuted. For crimes against the Ukrainian nation, the Ukrainian State and especially grave crimes against a person and citizen capital punishment is instituted.

Article 2. The basis of Ukrainian statehood is the National Concept, the concept of sovereignty of the Ukrainian (titular) nation in Ukrainian territories. Citizens of Ukraine develop the Ukrainian State that shall constantly pursue the interests of the Ukrainian nation as a whole and every Ukrainian in particular. The Ukrainian State shall create proper conditions for adequate spiritual and cultural development of the nation and for high living standards.

Article 3. Ukraine is a national, indivisible, legal, social and just Ukrainian State with presidential government. The Ukrainian State vindicates honour and human dignity of its citizens and guarantees the exercise of plenary rights and freedoms of Ukrainian people. The Ukrainian State ensures the equality of Ukrainians in their rights and before the law irrespective of their social status, religion and sex. The development of the Ukrainian State is carried out on the basis of national and social solidarity, historical justice, power hierarchy and personal responsibility of prominent public officials and citizens for the discharge of their duties. The Ukrainian State shall be the core of spirituality of the Ukrainian nation and the whole European civilization.

Article 7. The Ukrainian language is the only state (official) language in Ukraine. The State ensures comprehensive development and functioning of the Ukrainian language throughout the whole territory of Ukraine in all spheres of state and public life. The use of a different language due to ignorance or unwillingness to speak Ukraine at work and in public meetings constitutes the ground for unseating a deputy, for dismissing a public official from office. The Academy of the Ukrainian Language is set up to control the integrity of the official language. Citizens of Ukraine constituting national minorities have a right to establish cultural organizations, societies, Sunday schools to study their national tongues in released-time classes.

Article 8. The Ukrainian State shall take measures to unite the Ukrainian nation though developing its national consciousness, the unique ethnic culture, by preserving its customs, by safeguarding and multiplying the cultural values of the Ukrainians. The Ukrainian State shall encourage the return to Ukraine of ethnic Ukrainians working and living abroad. With this aim in view, the Ukrainian State creates favourable conditions for their settling in their Homeland.

Article 17. The State guarantees the right to freedom of association in political parties and public organizations whose activities are aimed at the public good of the Ukrainian nation. Communist ideology is banned in Ukraine. Any anti-Ukrainian activities and the setting up of anti-Ukrainian parties, organizations and movements are also prohibited.

Article 18. Information space is the heritage of the Ukrainian Nation and is part of national security. The Ukrainian State shall protect the national information space and allocate sufficient means for its development and functioning. Censorship is prohibited in Ukraine. Every individual can freely speak, write, and publish subject to the condition of his own personal responsibility for the abuse of this freedom in accordance with the norms of Ukrainian law. Citizens have a right to information.

Anti-Ukrainian propaganda and encouragement of amoral and manifestly unlawful behaviour, violence, sexual perversions, and everything else that counters the spirituality of the Ukrainian nation are prohibited.

Article 20. The Ukrainian State conducts foreign policies aimed at serving the interests of the Ukrainian nation, its security, and territorial integrity. The Ukrainian State considers the interests of the Ukrainian Diaspora. Ukraine may join military alliances and blocs only as a response to a threat to its independence, territorial integrity and the Ukrainian nation as such.

Article 22. Everyone can do what he chooses as long as it does no harm to others. The borders of freedom are determined by rules of morality and Ukrainian law. No one can be forced to do what contradicts the rules of morality and Ukrainian law.

Article 25. Laws as a source of law must be legal and based on common interests of Ukrainians and the whole Ukrainian nation.

Article 39. The State shall provide for the health of the Ukrainian people.

Article 40. Tuition in all educational institutions shall be given in the official language.

Article 42. Citizens have a right to hold peaceful meetings and take part in demonstrations, of which they shall inform the executive authorities or bodies of local administration in advance. Anti-Ukrainian meetings and demonstrations are prohibited.

Article 52. Deputies do not enjoy immunity. A deputy of the National Rada of Ukraine cannot be brought to court for his political stand, statements and the way he voted in the National Rada of Ukraine. This rule is not applied in the case of anti-Ukrainian, anti-State activities of a deputy.

Article 58. This Constitution authorizes the National Rada of Ukraine to

d) hear annual speeches made by the President to the Ukrainian nation.

Article 70. No person except a natural born Ukrainian citizen who has resided in Ukraine for the past twenty years prior to the day of election, who has attained the age of thirty five years, who has command of the state language and communicates in the state language, who has no criminal record and has not been held administratively liable for anti-Ukrainian misdeeds, and who has not been disqualified shall be eligible to the Office of President.

Article 71. The President of Ukraine assumes office on the second day after the official announcement of the election results from the moment he takes the oath to the people at the ceremonial meeting of Ukrainians in the capital of Ukraine, "I (name and surname) by the will of Ukrainians as the President of Ukraine, do solemnly swear allegiance to the Ukrainian nation. I pledge in all my undertakings to protect the sovereignty, independence and integrity of the Ukrainian State, to provide for the welfare of the Ukrainian people, to protect their rights and freedoms, to abide by the Constitution of Ukraine and Ukrainian law".

Article 94. A citizen of Ukraine who has attained the age of thirty years, has taken a degree in law and has at least five years experience in law, who is legally capable to act, has lived for the past ten years in Ukraine and who uses and communicates in the official language is eligible to the post of Judge".

As it is, "Death penalty for the offences against the Ukrainian nation" serves as a good indicator of the utmost aggressiveness of the Ukrainian nationalism – and that it should have occurred in Article 1 of the Proposed Constitution! Continual references that the Ukrainian language should be the language not only known but also used by public officials bespeak of the determination to have all posts filled only by ethnic Ukrainians. The all-round prohibition against everything that is anti-Ukrainian is another evidence of its aggressiveness.

Utter helplessness in describing the National Concept is a common weak point with all ultra-nationalists – apart from the official language and a couple of folk dances, they can offer nothing else. And the National Concept is presented sometimes as a philosophy, sometimes as a teaching or even an ideology.

For instance, the President of Azerbaijan issued a decree on 29 December 2006 that says, "The founding father of the independent Azerbaijani statehood, Heidar Aliyev, having made us a gift of such a profound philosophic conception as Azerbaijanism, repeatedly instructed us to protect the Azerbaijani language, the history of Azerbaijan, the Azerbaijani culture and the national spirituals values. In our country much work is being done in the framework of the ideology of Azerbaijanism, yet a strong need is felt for a single center to systematically coordinate this work"[4]. But what this "Azerbaijanism" is about remains unclear.

Similarly, the ultra-national party "Union of Pro Patria and Res Publica" in Estonia failed to describe the "Estonian Cause". The slogans have it like this, "Every day you contribute to the cause. Your work, your

---

[4] Zafar, Guiyev. 2011. Azerbaydzhan posle Alieva, *Regnum*. Available at: http://www.iarex.ru/books/book58.pdf. (Zafar, Guiyev. 2011. Azerbaijan after Aliyev, *Regnum*). (in the original: Зафар, Гулиев. 2011. Азербайджан после Алиева, *Regnum*).

studies, your family, your hopes and your dreams – this is what the Estonian Cause is about"[5]. In what way the "Estonian Cause" differs from the "Azerbaijanism" or the Ukrainian "National Concept" remains unclear. This does not purport that there is no difference between the indicated nations; rather, this is the indicator of helplessness of philosophic thought of ultra-nationalists.

Summing it up, we see that neither the Ukrainian National Concept, not the Azerbaijani "profound philosophic conception", nor the "Estonian Cause" has any other content than the establishment of racial discrimination.

The political instruments of extreme right and ultra-nationalists are made of statements, declarations, and demands which help to sustain the degree of their political radicalism. The signal marker here is populism.

3. Populism

Populism presupposes an appeal to all strata of society and a promise of speedy resolution of complex social problems. Populism feeds on the commonplace sense and the eternal pursuit of justice (economic, social, political, and historical), on the provision of the sovereign remedy for all problems, on swearing allegiance to the people, on demagogic promises that can never be kept, on defamation of political rivals.

Two instances are indicative of populism. First, populism flourishes in times of social and economic recession, that is why the promises that a populist party gives (for instance, to cancel the end-results of privatization, to reduce interest rates, to introduce new taxes, for example, on luxuries, to introduce an interest rate on financial loans) can not be fulfilled, since they cannot be financed. For one, the demand made by Svoboda to impose criminal sanctions on the National Bank for conducting an anti-social policy in the country raises many questions: exactly who bears the responsibility for the decisions taken (you cannot just arrest the whole bank that performs tasks but does not generate them), what the evidential basis that would allow for acknowledging the National Bank the main bearer of responsibility for the impoverishment of the population must be like, and so forth. Or, for example, of great interest are ordinances that afforded territorial communities the right to veto. Among demagogic statements are the numeric data the origin of which is not substantiated or demands to initiate certain actions without providing the mechanisms of

[5] Election poster.

the realization. Or, for instance, declarations about obtainable housing prices when the programme does not specify what an "obtainable price" is.

Svoboda's Programme reveals all the traditional properties of populism by proposing to:

"I. 29. Establish direct grassroots democracy in local communities: referendums, plebiscite, general assemblies, etc.; to hold local referendums on vital issues; to introduce a mechanism of veto to override decisions taken by local governments.

II. 15. Transfer back into to State ownership the privatized enterprises whose owners have failed to meet their social, investment and other obligations.

29. Cancel the criminalized value added tax; introduce a single social progressive income tax with a standard rate of 20%; minimum income wages shall not be taxed; establish progressive taxes on luxuries (real estate, luxury items, etc.); transfer at least 30% of the revenue from sumptuary taxes for the reduction in the user prices of essential consumer goods.

32. Restrict by law the extortionate interest on bank credits for the population and enterprises of Ukraine.

33. Criminalize the anti-social monetary and other policies conducted by the National Bank of Ukraine, which leads to the impoverishment of large sections of the population.

35. Bridge the social gap between the rich and the poor by stimulating the development of the middle class (small and medium-sized entrepreneurs, highly-paid experts, including such public sector workers as doctors, teachers, etc.), which constitutes not less than 60% of the working population.

43. Establish parity of purchasing and selling prices for agricultural products; supply the needs of food with exclusively domestic agricultural products (except for products that do not grow in Ukraine).

55. Compel construction companies to build social housing at affordable prices under the State program.

58. Abolish the unfair pension reform, establish the retirement age dependent on life expectancy; the scale of pension shall be directly dependent on the length of service; the allowed relation between the maximum and minimum shall be fivefold for the pay-as-you-go pension system.

59. Adjust the minimum subsistence level to actual needs; regularly review the size of the minimum subsistence level to maintain its relevance.

V. 24. Channel every sixth hryvnia from foreign film rental revenue for the development of the domestic film industry; impose taxes on advertising broadcast during foreign film exhibitions in behalf of the national cinema".

The Proposed Constitution also contains a list of declarative statements that question tallying, mechanisms of marketing arrangements, and a real understanding of what is offered:

"Article 16. Citizens of Ukraine of various nationalities are equal in their rights. The proportion of the Ukrainian population and representatives of ethnic minorities going to secondary and higher education institutions, working in bodies of legislative, executive and judicial institutions of all levels, serving in the Armed Forces of Ukraine and working in law enforcement agencies, educational and cultural spheres, health care, owning businesses, industries shall correspond to the ethnic composition of the population of Ukraine that is established during the All-Ukrainian census. Governmental subsidies granted to physical or juridical persons also should be distributed proportionate to the ethnic composition of the population of Ukraine".

By way of comment we should note here that "the ethnic composition of the population of Ukraine" has been the subject of severe debate since the promulgation of the results of the first All-Ukrainian census in 2001. The census data and also the scanty official comments aroused lots of questions.

The All-Ukrainian census was carried out from the 5th to the 14th of December 2001. At the end of December of the same year Head of the Federal Public Statistic Service Alexander Osaulenko announced the provisional statistics according to which 48,860,000 persons had completed the questionnaires. The verified data were published in January 2003, according to which the population of Ukraine constituted 48,457,000 persons (51.7 m according to the 1989 census), that is, 403 thousand less than in the preliminary data. As to the ethnic composition of the population of Ukraine, the Ukrainians prevail in most regions (37.54 m, or 77.8% of all the population), the rest 22.2% constitute ethnic minorities, including 8,334,100 Russians[6].

Thus, against the background of the drastic reduction in population (3.2 m persons since 1989), the number of Ukrainians grew by 0.3%. The proportion of Ukrainians in the whole country had still grown by 5.1% (72,7% from the total population size in 1989, 77.8% in 2001). It was the other way round with the Russians: their number reduced sharply by

[6] Malakhova, E. *Skol'ko russkikh na Ukraine?* Available at: http://www.antropotok.archipelag.ru/text/a192.htm. (Malakhova, E. *How many Russians are there in Ukraine?*). (in the original: Малахова, Е. *Сколько русских на Украине?*).

26.6% over 12 years. Its ratio in the size of population amounted to 17.3% in 2001 as compared with 23.1% in 1989[7]. Leaving these scandalous census results without comments, the authors point out that Svoboda relies on this maximum percentage of ethnic Ukrainians in Ukraine that the census had identified.

"Article 21. Legislative, executive and judicial powers are generated on the basis of universal, direct, fair and secret voting. All adult citizens of Ukraine who are not dispossessed of the political and civil rights have the right to vote. (Remember that the standard wording established by the Council of Europe is "free and fair elections", not "fair voting").

Article 24. Civil rights and freedoms of person and citizen are laid down in the Constitution of Ukraine and they can be neither canceled nor trimmed. In the case of the need for rights and freedoms other than those recognized in the Constitution, Ukrainians may exercise them according to the rules of morality and Ukrainian law".

Svoboda's Programme and the Proposed Constitution contain a large number of provisions modeled on socialist ones. It is obvious that Svoboda, by showing contempt for the socialist past but having no financial resources to keep these promises, resorts to these provisions exclusively with demagogic aims in view. So in this context, such references to socialism are also taken as populism.

"Article 32. Everyone has the right to labour and the six month unemployment cost-of-living benefits. All employees shall receive a share of revenue of each enterprise. The State shall establish a Central depositary to organize record keeping and (by/sell) transactions in securities. All employees who are co-owners of an enterprise are deemed employed for life. Their dismissal is allowed only in cases stipulated by law. Employees take part in managing the enterprise in person or through their representatives.

Article 33. The Ukrainian State shall render financial and organizational aid to persons who wish to conduct entrepreneurial activities. Social and economic policies conducted by the Ukrainian State are aimed to develop the middle class in Ukraine.

Article 35. Citizens have a right to social protection. The State shall provide targeted aim to disabled people and orphans. The size of such aid cannot be below the subsistence minimum wage. The right to such aid is guaranteed by state social security out of insurance premium payments; a system of institutions to care after the disabled shall be instituted.

---

[7] Malakhova, E. *Skol'ko russkikh na Ukraine?* Available at: http://www.antropotok.archipelag.ru/text/a192.htm.

Article 36. The State guarantees seniority and disablement pensions. A uniform set of rules governing pensions shall be introduced with the exception of the President of Ukraine. Deputies of all levels and government personnel who have abused their power lose the right to age pension.

Article 37. All citizens have a right to shelter. The Ukrainian State and bodies of local government provide needy citizens and those who need social protection with free housing for occupation. Such housing cannot be privately owned.

Article 38. Everyone has the right to health care. Free emergency medical care is provided in state and communal healthcare institutions.

Article 28. Property acquired by unlawful means is subject to confiscation, and its owner to torts liability.

Article 40. Students who show good performance receive stipends in the amount of minimum subsistence income. The Ukrainian State shall guarantee to the graduates their first employment.

Article 43. Moral and material damage that a person suffers because of the faulty or unlawful decisions made by bodies of state power, local government, court and actions by officials shall be compensated for by the part at fault.

Article 51. Deputies of the National Council of Ukraine shall not enjoy any privileges or benefits.

Article 94. Judges of local courts are elected by Ukraine citizens for a term of five years. Judges of the Supreme Court are elected at the congress of judges of Ukraine for a term of ten years.

Article 100. Judges are removed from office:

a) as a result of a plebiscite;

b) as a result of an impeachment".

Thus, after considering the obvious indicators of populism in the two documents elaborated by Svoboda we see that this political organization set itself formidable tasks to acquire broad political influence in the country as it touches upon all the most important issues of social, economic, political, cultural, etc., life. And the party does believe that harsh measures and regulations can solve all the existing problems in the country. To do this, it intends to reallocate financial resources and redirect financial flows. Svoboda tries hard to emphasize its support of vulnerable segments of population. Considering that the financial position of almost all Ukrainian population has deteriorated in the past two decades, the appeal to the people's perpetual pursuit of justice still remains for Svoboda the basic argument in their campaign to win supporters. By no means will these promises ever be kept because they are too radical, difficult to implement and to massive. If we look at Svoboda' policy papers, we will see that the sum of the social obligations exceeds the capability to meet them manifold.

Apart from the above-indicated and analyzed three main markers of Nazism allowing for diagnosing the party as a Nazi party, we pointed out a series of optional markers that contribute to the diagnostic procedure.

4. Optional Markers

4.1. The central role of the State, the state as a "single mechanism"

The Svoboda Programme pays great attention to the issue of Ukrainian statehood, emphasizes that it consists of territorial communities and bodies of local governance, and demands:

"I.30. To strengthen the influence exerted by local self-governments on life sustenance of society by establishing residents-and-neighbourhood committees and other community associations (calqued on the Nazi blockführer?).

II. 11. To adopt a law on strategic enterprises and strategic industries; ban the privatization of strategic enterprises and transfer the ones previously privatized back to state ownership; exert the state control over natural monopolies.

32. Exert state control over banks (State-owned banks shall constitute at least 30% of the banking capital of the country).

III. 5. Restore and transfer back to State ownership health resort complexes; prohibit the functional conversion of health resorts; ban the privatization of all health resort lands throughout the territory of Ukraine.

IV. 5. Confiscate the property and the capital acquired by perpetrators of the law on citizenship of Ukraine.

Part VII speaks about foreign policies and defence, where the key theme is European Ukrainian centrism and a strong State:

VII. 1. Define the European Ukranian centrism the strategic direction of the State according to which Ukraine aspires to become not only geographical, but also the geographical centre of Europe".

The provisions spelled out in the Proposed Constitution confirm the positions outlined in Svoboda's Programme and emphasize the link between "nation-state" and the hypertrophied role of the State.

"Article 11. The Ukrainian State shall protect the land, which is the main wealth of the Ukrainian nation.

Article 12. The Ukrainian Nation has a right to live in an ecologically balanced environment.

Article 15. The Ukrainian Nation shall display concern about the growth of Ukrainian population. The implementation of the programme "Reproductive health of the nation" is financed by the State Budget of Ukraine.

Article 20. Foreign military bases are not allowed in the territory of Ukraine. It is prohibited to set up armed formations by any persons or groups of persons. The Ukrainian State allows and controls the setting up and activities of militarized formations.

Article 32. Property or industry that carries strategical importance for Ukraine shall stay state-owned. Binding the state and the nation, Party Svoboda proclaims its own foreign policy ambitions".

4.2. Lebensraum, territorial claims, external enemies, and militarism.

Part IV of Svoboda's Programme entitled "The citizenship and migration. Right to a homeland and the protection of living space" makes use of the term "Lebensraum". Svoboda's Programme proposes the following foreign political actions in this context:

"VII. 2. To withdraw from all supranational entities initiated by Moscow: the Commonwealth of Independent States (CIS), the Common Economic Space (CES), the Eurasian Economic Community (EurAsEC), etc.

3. To give real content to the only real geopolitical project in which Ukraine plays the leading role – Georgia, Ukraine, Azerbaijan, Moldova Regional Cooperation Group (GUAM); to involve the Commonwealth countries of the Black Sea-Caspian Basin in this group.

4. To direct foreign policy efforts to building a closer political and economic cooperation with natural allies – the countries of the Baltic and Black Sea geopolitical axis (Sweden, Norway, Finland, Lithuania, Latvia, Estonia, Poland, Bulgaria and, eventually, Belarus and others); initiate mutually beneficial agreements between these States and Ukraine in all strategically important sectors: trade and customs policies, energy security, transit trade, defence, etc.).

6. To complete the delimitation (established by the Treaty) and demarcation (the setting of border marks) of the state border of Ukraine, including the sea border; define the boundary unilaterally in the case of

prevarication on the part of its neighbours, Russia, in particular; to ensure adequate border control; to introduce visa regime for Russia.

7. To demand from the States that declared the safety and inviolability of the borders of Ukraine in Exchange for nuclear disarmament (Budapest, 1994) adequate, not nominal, safeguards; to conclude bilateral agreements with the United States and Great Britain on immediate full-scale military assistance in the event of armed aggression against Ukraine.

8. To file a request with the General Assembly and the UN Security Council to assess Russia's statements about the possibility of pre-emptive nuclear strikes without declaring a war.

9. To re-establish the nuclear status of Ukraine owing to Russia's violations of the Budapest memorandum, with Russia being one of the guarantors of Ukrainian security; to restore the tactical nuclear-missile arsenal; to request assistance in the development of the Ukrainian nuclear program from the United States and Great Britain.

10. To start real, not declarative, actions that ensure the integration of Ukraine into European security order: cleanse the government and power structures from agents of Moscow; to neutralize Russia's territorial claims; to delimit and demarcate the boundary; to extinguish hotbeds of separatism; neutralize all of the territorial claims against Ukraine, to ensure the withdrawal of Russian military bases from the territory of Ukraine; to immediately start reforming and developing the Armed Forces and the Navy of Ukraine.

11. To demand from NATO member countries favourable terms, clear guarantees and specific accession dates for Ukraine to join the Alliance; to develop and implement a parallel plan of security and defense of Ukraine.

12. To develop its own missile attack warning system and methods of counteraction either alone or together with other countries; to fully restore the country's air defense system to protect the air space; to reinforce the air defence to protect the strategic facilities and heavily populated areas; to appeal to Western countries with request for a lease of mobile air defense systems for anti-aircraft and anti-missile shield deployment in exchange for timely information about the Ukrainian radars in Sevastopol and Mukachevo, thereby testing the actual readiness of NATO member countries to cooperate with Ukraine in the field of defence and security.

13. To allocate budget funds estimated at 5% of the gross domestic product to the Armed Forces of Ukraine to bridge the technological gap, given the urgent need for reform and modernization of the army; to reform the Ukrainian Armed Forces, including the Navy and the Air Force, to equip them with state-of-the-art ships, aircraft, air defence systems, to reweapon aircrafts and war-ships.

14. To restore the prestige of the military service; to raise salaries of the military personnel; to solve the housing problem by granting State soft loans.

15. To develop the military-industrial complex to manufacture all kinds of arms for the Armed Forces of Ukraine and make participation of Ukraine in the global arms market effective; to integrate scientific research institutions of the Armed Forces into the military-industrial complex of Ukraine; to establish priority for the research into high-precision weapons; to establish beneficial military technical relations with other States.

16. To ensure strict control over the pricing and the budget military sales revenue; to channel all proceeds from arms sales exclusively for national defense; to discontinue the practice of reckless destruction of the state-of-the-art military equipment at the request of other States or its sales to the prejudice of Ukraine.

17. To develop and systematically implement by 2017 a new program of reform of the Ukrainian army to ensure real national defense capability; to create a high-tech professional army based on contract principles; to establish a National Reserve of the Armed Forces of Ukraine.

18. To institute an integrated system of recruiting and training of reservists (the Swiss model); to restore the system of basic military training and civil defense at secondary schools and military art divisions at universities.

19. To establish an effective counter-intelligence service to ensure the safety of the Ukrainian underground against raiding forces of potential aggressors.

20. To reorganize and strengthen the coast guard of the Black Sea coast; to set up ground-launched antiship and antisubmarine defence systems in areas of strategic importance along the Black Sea and the Azov Sea coasts; deploy modern anti-aircraft and anti-missile systems to provide cover for the coast guard and Marine Corps of the Navy. Increase the strength of the army in the Crimea, retool its modern missile-artillery and armour for rapid deployment to combat potential aggression".

The Proposed Constitution also contains clearly militaristic provisions.

"Article 4. The Ukrainian State shall protect the sovereignty of the nation, its borders and territorial integrity. For this purpose, the Armed Forces of Ukraine, judicial and law-enforcement agencies are held responsible. Failure to perform this task entails criminal responsibility of the Chief Executive Officers of the State. The Ukrainian State shall ensure real sovereignty of the Ukrainian nation through the reinstatement of its nuclear power status, the achievement of energy and information independence.

Article 45. Protection of the Ukrainian State, its territorial integrity, the sovereignty of the Ukrainian nation shall be the duty of all citizens. All mentally sane Ukrainian persons with no criminal background are eligible to acquire and to possess firearms and cold arms.

Article 46. Defence of homeland is the duty of all citizens of Ukraine. All students of specialized secondary schools and institutions of higher education must learn the basics of using the firearms in four months. All higher education institutions shall have a military arts division".

This focus on military training, arms production and readiness to speedy militarization is supplemented with the attributes used by Svoboda.

4.3. Glorification of Nazism, external attributes

"VI. 14. The veterans of the Organization of Ukrainian Nationalists – Ukrainian Insurgent Army are to be granted the due benefits and shall be compensated for those they did not receive during the period of independence".

Conclusion

Thus, the analysis of the policy documents of the party allows for establishing a correlation between radical calls, statements of political activists (for which they are usually brought to court) and the concrete political tasks, ideological directions. It is obvious that the three principal diagnostic markers and a number of optional ones in Svoboda's Programme and the approved Proposed Constitution indicate that the party's activities and aims are typical of Nazism. The proposed diagnostic procedure allows for assessing its Nazi nature, that is, its determination to totally transform statehood, to lay down the law based on the idea of superiority of the nation, to deprive minorities of their political and civil rights, to unite the state and the nation by establishing communities that carry out the task of "defence" of the nation at the very bottom of the pyramid.

BIBLIOGRAPHY

Documents

UN documents

1. *A/RES/1904 Resolution*. Available at: http://www.un-documents.net/a18r1904.htm (accessed 10.03.2014)
2. *Charter of the United Nations*. Available at: http://www.un.org/en/documents/charter/(accessed 10.03.2014)
3. *Convention on the Prevention and Punishment of the Crime of Genocide*. 1948. Available at: http://www.un-documents.net/cppcg.htm (accessed 10.03.2014)
4. *Durban Declaration*. 2001. Available at: http://www.un-documents.net/durban-d.htm (accessed 10.03.2014)
5. *Global efforts for the total elimination of racism, racial discrimination, xenophobia and related intolerance and the comprehensive implementation of and follow-up to the Durban Declaration and Programme of Action.* Available at: http://www.un.org/en/ga/search/view _doc.asp?symbol=%20A/RES /66/144 (accessed 10.03.2014)
6. *Inadmissibility of certain practices that contribute to fuelling contemporary forms of racism, racial discrimination, xenophobia and related intolerance.* 2005. Available at: http://www.un.org/en/ga/search/view_doc.asp?symbol=A/RES/60/143 (accessed 10.03.2014)
7. *International Covenant on civil and political rights*. 1966. Available at: http://www.unhcr-centraleurope.org/pdf/resources/legal-documents/international-refugee-law/international-covenant-on-civil-and-political-rights-1966 (accessed 15.04.2014)
8. *International Convention on the Elimination of All Forms of Racial Discrimination*. 1966. Available at: http://www.refworld.org/docid/3ae6b3940.html (accessed 21.02.2014)
9. *Judgment of the International Military Tribunal*. Available at: http://avalon.law.yale.edu/subject_menus/judcont.asp (accessed 11.03.2014)

10. *Nation-State*. Available at: http://www.unesco.org/new/en/social-and-human-sciences/themes/international-migration/glossary/nation-state/ (accessed 10.03.2014)
11. 67/154 Resolution of the General Assembly of the United Nations "Glorification of Nazism: inadmissibility of certain practices that contribute to fuelling contemporary forms of racism, racial discrimination, xenophobia and related intolerance". Available at: http://www.un.org/en/ga/search/view_doc.asp?symbol=A/RES/67/154 (accessed 15.04.2014)
12. Report of the World Conference against Racism, Racial Discrimination, Xenophobia and Related Intolerance. (Durban Declaration and Programme of Action). 2001. Available at: http://www.derechos.org/nizkor/ley/doc/durban.html (accessed 15.04.2014)
13. *Resolutions adopted by the General Assembly at its 60 Session.* Available at: http://www.un.org/depts/dhl/resguide/r60_en.shtml (accessed 12.03.2014)
14. *Resolutions adopted by the General Assembly at its 61 Session.* Available at: http://www.un.org/depts/dhl/resguide/r61_en.shtml (accessed 12.03.2014)
15. *Resolutions adopted by the General Assembly at its 65 Session.* Available at: http://www.un.org/depts/dhl/resguide/r65_en.shtml (accessed 12.03.2014)
16. *Resolutions adopted by the General Assembly at its 66 Session.* Available at: http://www.un.org/depts/dhl/resguide/r66_en.shtml (accessed 12.03.2014)
17. *Resolutions adopted by the General Assembly at its 67 Session.* Available at: http://www.un.org/depts/dhl/resguide/r67_en.shtml (accessed 12.03.2014)
18. *Resolutions adopted by the General Assembly at its 68 Session.* Available at: http://www.un.org/depts/dhl/resguide/r68_en.shtml (accessed 12.03.2014)
19. *Rome Statute of the International Criminal Court*. 1998. Available at: http://www.icc-cpi.int/nr/rdonlyres/ea9aeff7-5752-4f84-be94-0a655eb30e16/0/rome_statute_english.pdf (accessed 19.05.2014)
20. *Statute of the International Criminal Tribunal for the Prosecution of Persons Responsible for Genocide and Other Serious Violations of International Humanitarian Law Committed in the Territory of Rwanda and Rwandan Citizens Responsible for Genocide and Other Such Violations Committed in the Territory of Neighbouring States*, between 1 January 1994 and 31 December 1994. Available at:

http://www.ohchr.org/EN/ProfessionalInterest/Pages/StatuteInternationalCriminalTribunalForRwanda.aspx (accessed 19.05.2014)
21. *The Universal Declaration of Human Rights*. Available at: http://www.un.org/en/documents/udhr/ (accessed 12.01.2014)
22. *United Nations Declaration on the Elimination of all forms of Racial Discrimination*. 1964. Available at: http://www.un-documents.net/a18r1904.htm (accessed 18.02.2014).

European documents

23. *Conference on Security and co-operation in Europe, Final Act 1975*.Available at: http://www.osce.org/mc/39501?download=true (accessed 12.03.2014)
24. *Document of the Moscow Meeting of the Conference on Human Dimension of the CSCE*. Available at: http://www.osce.org/odihr/elections/14310?download=true (accessed 12.03.2014)

EU documents

25. Council Directive 2000/43/EC of 29 June 2000 implementing the principle of equal treatment between persons irrespective of racial or ethnic origin, *Official Journal L 180*, 19/07/2000 P. 0022 – 0026. Available at: http://eur-lex.europa.eu/LexUriServ/LexUriServ.do?uri=CELEX: 32000L0043:en:HTML (accessed 12.03.2014)
26. Council Directive 2000/78/EC of 27 November 2000 establishing a general framework for equal treatment in employment and occupation, *Official Journal L 303*, 02/12/2000 P. 0016 - 0022. Available at: http://eur-lex.europa.eu/LexUriServ/LexUriServ.do?uri=CELEX: 32000L0078:en:HTML (accessed 12.03.2014)
27. *2000/750/EC: Council Decision of 27 November 2000 establishing a Community action programme to combat discrimination (2001 to 2006).* Available at: http://eur-lex.europa.eu/legal-content/EN/TXT/?uri=CELEX:32000D0750 (accessed 12.03.2014)
28. Intergovernmental Conference, *Flash Eurobarometer № 152*, Report, 2003.
29. La Constituion Europeenne: Sondage Post-Referendum en France Terrain 30-31 Mai 2005, *Flash Eurobarometer № 171*, Rapport.
30. Public Opinion in the European Union, *Eurobarometer 64*, Report, 2006.

31. Public Opinion in the European Union, *Eurobatometer 78/Autumn*, 2012.
32. The Draft European Constitution, *Face to Face Interviews, EU 25*, 2004.
33. The European Constitution: Post referendum Survey in Spain, *Flash Eurobarometer № 168*, 2005.
34. *The European Constitution: Post Referendum Survey in the Netherlands*, 2005.
35. *EU Terrorism Situation and Trend Report.* 2011. Available at: https://www.europol.europa.eu/sites/default/files/publications/te-sat2011.pdf (accessed 18.05.2014)
36. *EU Terrorism Situation and Trend Report.* 2012. Available at: https://www.europol.europa.eu/sites/default/files/publications/europoltsat.pdf (accessed 18.05.2014)
37. *EU Terrorism Situation and Trend Report.* 2014. Available at: https://www.europol.europa.eu/sites/default/files/publications/europol_tsat14_web_1.pdf (accessed 18.05.2014)

Constitutions

38. *Basic Law for the Federal Republic of Germany*. Available at: https://www.btg-bestellservice.de/pdf/80201000.pdf (accessed 10.02.2014)
39. *Charter of Fundamental Rights and Freedoms of the Czech Republic*. Available at: http://www.usoud.cz/en/charter-of-fundamental-rights-and-freedoms/ (accessed 10.02.2014)
40. *Constitutional Act of Denmark*. Available at: http://www.ilo.org/wcmsp5/groups/public/---ed_protect/---protrav/---ilo_aids/documents/legaldocument/wcms_127469.pdf (accessed 12.02.2014)
41. *Constitution of Abkhazia*. Available at: http://apsnypress.info/en/constitution (accessed 12.02.2014)
42. *Constitution of Albania*. Available at: http://www.osce.org/albania/41888?download=true (accessed 12.02.2014)
43. *Constitution of Andorra*. Available at: http://www.wipo.int/wipolex/en/text.jsp?file_id=187171 (accessed 10.02.2014)
44. *Constitution of Azerbaijan*. Available at: http://confinder.richmond.edu/admin/docs/local_azerbaijan.pdf (accessed 10.02.2014)

45. *Constitution of Belgium*. Available at: www.legislationline.org/documents/id/9045 (accessed 12.02.2014)
46. *Constitution of Bosnia and Herzegovina*. Available at: http://www.ccbh.ba/public/down/USTAV_BOSNE_I_HERCEGOVINE_engl.pdf (accessed 13.02.2014)
47. *Constitution of Bulgaria*. Available at: http://www.vks.bg/english/vksen_p04_01.htm (accessed 12.02.2014)
48. *Constitution of Croatia*. Available at: http://www.sabor.hr/Default.aspx?art=2406 (accessed 12.02.2014)
49. *Constitution of Cyprus.* Available at: http://www.presidency.gov.cy/presidency/presidency.nsf/all/1003AEDD83EED9C7C225756F0023C6AD/$file/CY_Constitution.pdf (accessed 10.02.2014)
50. *Constitution of Denmark*. Available at: http://www.ilo.org/wcmsp5/groups/public/---ed_protect/---protrav/---ilo_aids/documents/legaldocument/wcms_127469.pdf (accessed 10.02.2014)
51. *Constitution of Estonia*. Available at: http://www.president.ee/en/republic-of-estonia/the-constitution/ (accessed 10.02.2014)
52. *Constitution of Georgia*. Available at: http://www.wipo.int/wipolex/en/text.jsp?file_id=194552 (accessed 10.02.2014)
53. *Constitution of Greece*. Available at: http://www.hri.org/docs/syntagma/artcl120.html (accessed 12.02.2014)
54. *Constitution of Hungary.* Available at: http://www.kormany.hu/download/e/02/00000/The%20New%20Fundamental%20Law%20of%20Hungary.pdf (accessed 12.02.2014)
55. *Constitution of Iceland.* Available at: http://www.concourt.am/armenian/legal_resources/world_constitutions/constit/iceland/icelnd-e.htm (accessed 12.02.2014)
56. *Constitution of Italy.* Available at: http://legislationline.org/download/action/download/id/1613/file/b4371e43dc8cf675b67904284951.htm/preview (accessed 12.02.2014)
57. *Constitution of Ireland*. Available at: http://www.irishstatutebook.ie/en/constitution/ (accessed 14.02.2014)
58. *Constitution of Latvia.* Available at: http://www.saeima.lv/en/legislation/constitution (accessed 10.04.2014)
59. *Constitution of Lithuania*. Available at: http://www3.lrs.lt/home/Konstitucija/Constitution.htm (accessed 10.02.2014)

60. *Constitution of Macedonia*. Available at: http://eudo-citizenship.eu/NationalDB/docs/MAC%20Constitution%20%28amended%20by%20XXX%29%20eng.pdf (accessed 10.02.2014)
61. *Constitution of Malta.* Available at: http://justiceservices.gov.mt/DownloadDocument.aspx?app=lom&itemid=8566 (accessed 14.02.2014)
62. *Constitution of Poland*. Available at: http://www.sejm.gov.pl/prawo/konst/angielski/kon1.htm (accessed 14.02.2014)
63. *Constitution of Portugal*. Available at: http://www.wipo.int/wipolex/en/text.jsp?file_id=179405 (accessed 15.02.2014)
64. *Constitution of the Principality of Monaco*. Available at: http://www.venice.coe.int/webforms/documents/default.aspx?pdffile=CDL-REF%282013%29021-e (accessed 15.02.2014)
65. *Constitution of Romania*. Available at: http://www.cdep.ro/pls/dic/site.page?den=act2_2&par1=1 (accessed 12.02.2014)
66. *Constitution of the Russian Federation*. Available at: http://www.constitution.ru/en/10003000-01.htm (accessed 10.02.2014)
67. *Constitution of San Marino*. Available at: // http://unpan1.un.org/intradoc/groups/public/documents/un-dpadm/unpan040713~1.pdf (accessed 12.02.2014)
68. *Constitution of Serbia*. Available at: http://en.wikisource.org/wiki/Constitution_of_Serbia#PART_TWO_-_HUMAN_AND_MINORITY_RIGHTS_AND_FREEDOMS (accessed 12.02.2014)
69. *Constitution of Slovakia*. Available at: http://www.slovak-republic.org/constitution/ (accessed 12.02.2014)
70. *Constitution of Slovenia*. Available at: http://www.wipo.int/wipolex/en/text.jsp?file_id=180804 (accessed 12.02.2014)
71. *Constitution of Spain*. Available at: http://www.lamoncloa.gob.es/lang/en/espana/leyfundamental/Paginas/index.aspx (accessed 10.02.2014)
72. *Constitution of Ukraine.* Available at: http://www.legislationline.org/documents/ section/constitutions/country/52 (accessed 21.03.2014)

Far-right parties' programmes

73. *English Defence League*. Available at: http://www.englishdefenceleague.org/ (accessed 05.07.2014)
74. *Proekt Natsional'noy konstitutsii Ukrainy, prinyatoy s'ezdom nazistskoy partii "Svoboda"*. Available at: http://www.svoboda.org.ua/pro_partiyu/prohrama/konstytutsiya/. (*Draft National Constitution of Ukraine proposed by the Congress of the Nazi party Svoboda*). (in the original: *Проект Национальной конституции Украины, принятой съездом нацистской партии «Свобода»*). (accessed 05.07.2014)
75. *Programma Vseukrainskogo ob'edinena Partii Svoboda*. Available at: http://www.svoboda.org.ua/pro_partiyu/prohrama/ (*Programm of All-Ukrainian Party Svoboda*). (in the original: *Программа ВО Свобода*). (accessed 05.07.2014)
76. *The British National Party*. Available at: http://www.martinfrost.ws/htmlfiles/bnp1.html#History_and_overview (accessed 05.07.2014)
77. *The British National Party Program*. Available at: https://www.bnp.org.uk/manifesto (accessed 05.07.2014)
78. *The British National Party*. Available at: http://www.northamptonshirerec.org.uk (accessed 05.07.2014)
79. *The Flemish Interest Party Program*. Available at: http://www.vlaamsbelang.org/files/20140318ProgrammaVerkiezingen2014.pdf (accessed 05.07.2014)
80. *The Freedom Party of Austria Program*. Available at: http://www.wien-konkret.at/politik/partei/fpoe (accessed 05.07.2014)
81. *The National Democratic Party of Germany Program*. Available at: http://www.npd.de/ (accessed 05.07.2014)
82. *The National Front Program*. Available at: http://www.frontnational.com/le-projet-de-marine-le-pen/(accessed 05.07.2014)
83. *The Party Program of the "Flemish interest"*. Available at: http://www.vlaamsbelang.org/files/200806_programma.pdf (accessed 05.07.2014)
84. *The Swedish Democrats Party Program*. Available at: https://sverigedemokraterna.se/var-politik/principprogram/ (accessed 05.07.2014)
85. *The UK Independence Party Program*. Available at: http://www.ukip.org/issue (accessed 05.07.2014)

Archive's documents

86. *Pribaltika I geopolitika. 1935-1945. Rassekrechennye dokumenty Sluzhby vneshney razvedki Rossiiskoy Federatsii*. 2009, sostavitel' L.F. Sotskov, Moskva. (*The Baltic States and Geopolitics. 1935-1945. Unsealed documents of the Foreign Intelligent Service of the Russian Federation*. 2009, compiled by Sotskov L.F., Moscow). (in the original: *Прибалтика и геополитика. 1935-1945. Рассекреченные документы Службы внешней разведки Российской Федерации*. 2009, составитель Л.Ф.Соцков).
87. *Riigiarhiiv. State Archives of Estonia, Repository No. R2324*, name No. 1, shelving unit 14.

Other documents

88. *Kommentarii k Ugolovnomu kodeksu Rossiiskoy Federatsii*. Available at: http://novoart7.narod.ru/simple.html. (*Comments to the Criminal Code of the Russian Federation*). (in the original: *Комментарии к УК РФ*). (accessed 06.03.2014)
89. Sergey Mironov, head of the party "Fair Russia" (Personal page). Available at: https://www.facebook.com/mironov.online/posts/485671674867839 (accessed 30.04.2014)
90. *Unite Against Fascism*. Available at: http://www.uaf.org.uk (accessed 12.01.2014)

Dictionaries and encyclopedias

91. *Bol'shoy yuridicheskii slovar'*. 2003, pod redaktsiey A.Ya. Sukhareva, V.E. Krutskikh, Moskva, 704 p. (*Grand Law Dictionary*. 2003, ed. by A.Ya. Sukhareva, V.E. Krutskikh, Moscow, 704 p. (in the original: *Большой юридический словарь*. 2003, под ред. А.Я. Сухарева, В.Е. Крутских, М., 704 с.).

Monographs and articles

92. Breivik zayavil o bor'be s islamizatsiey. Available at: http://www.bbc.co.uk/russian/international/2012/06/120622_breivik_court_last_day.shtml (Breivik said about struggle against Islamization). (in the original: А. Брейвик заявил о борьбе с исламизацией). (accessed 08.03.2014)

93. Barygin, I. N. Kraine-pravye tendentsii politicheskoy zhizni v politiligicheskom I politicheskom diskursah, *in Pravoradikal'nye politicheskie partii I dvizhenia sovremennoy Evropy*, Sankt-Peterburg: Isdatel'stvo SPbGU, 408 p. (Barygin, I. N. 2011. The Far-Right Political Tendencies in Scientific and Political Discourse, *in Far-Right Political Parties and Movements in Modern Europe*, Saint-Petersburg, 408 p.). (in the original: Барыгин, И.Н. 2011. Крайне-правые тенденции политической жизни в политологическом и политическом дискурсах, *Праворадикальные политические партии и движения современной Европы*, СПб., 408с).
94. *Belaya kniga nazizma*. 2013, Moskva: Knizhnyi Klub knogovek, 1126 p. (*The White Book of Nazism*. 2013, Moscow, 1126 p.). (in the original: *Белая книга нацизма*. 2013, М., 1126 с.).
95. Blyakher, L.E. 2005. *Nestabil'nye sotsial'nye sostoyania*, Moskva: ROSSPAN, 207 p. (Blyakher, L.E. 2005. *Unstable social conditions*, Moscow, 207 p.). (in the original: Бляхер, Л.Е. 2005. *Нестабильные социальные состояния.* М., 207 с.).
96. Bogaturov, A. 1999. Sindrom pogloschenia v mezhdunarodnoy politike, *Pro et Contra*, N 4, pp. 28-48. Available at: http://uisrussia.srcc.msu.ru/docs/nov/pec/1999/4/ProEtContra_1999_4_02.pdf (Bogaturov, A. 1999. The Syndrome of "Absorption" in International Politics, *Pro et Contra*, N 4, pp. 28-48.). (in the original: Богатуров, А. 1999. Синдром поглощения в международной политике, *Pro et Contra*, N 4, с. 28-48). (accessed 15.05.2000)
97. Bolotnikova, E.G. 2008. Pravoradikal'nye partii Shvetsii, *Politex*, pp.49-57. Available at: http://www.politex.info/content/view/405/30/ (Bolotnikova, E.G. 2008. Right-wing radical parties of Sweden, *Politex,* pp.49-57). (in the original: Болотникова, Е.Г. 2008. Праворадикальные партии Швеции, *Политэкс*, с. 49-57).
98. Borodin, S.S., Gromyko, S.S. 2007. *Administrativnoe pravo*, Moskva: GUAP, 432 p. (Borodin, S.S., Gromyko, S.S. *Administrative Law*, Moscow, 432p.). (in the original: Бородин, С.С., Громыко, С.С. 2007. *Административное право*. М., 432 с.).
99. Bradley, J.P. 1969. Party Platforms and Party Performance Concerning Social Security, *Polity*, Vol. 1, No 3, pp. 337– 358.
100. *Britain's Deficient Democracy*. Available at: http://www.centreforcitizenship.org/writ2.html (accessed 23.04.2013)
101. MacGarry, J., O'Leary, B. 2008. Must Pluri-National federations Fail?, *Ethnopolitics,* Vol. 8, No 1, pp. 5-26.
102. Carter, E.L. 2005. The Extreme Right in Western Europe: Success or Failure? Manchester: Manchester University Press, 271 p.

103. Delyagin, M. 2003. Mirovoy krizis: obschaya teoriya globalizatsia, Moskva: INFRA-M, 768 p. (Delyagin, M.G. 2003. The World Crisis: General Theory of Globalization, Moscow, 768 p.). (in the original: Делягин, М.Г. 2003. Мировой кризис: общая теория глобализации, М., 768 с.).
104. Downs, W. M. 2002. Regionalism in the European Union: Key concepts and project overview, *European Integration*, 24 (3), pp.171-177.
105. Duck, R.M., Gibson, J.L. 1992. "Putting up with" Fascism in Western Europe: a Comparative, Cross-Level Analysis of Political Tolerance, *The Western Political Quarterly*, Vol.45, No1 March, pp. 237-273.
106. Dzhozvyak, R. Vybory dayuschie Moskve bol'shoy stopor v Evroparlamente. Available at: http://ru.krymr.com/content/25383492.html (Dzhozvyak, R. Elections allowing Moscow to lock the European Parliament). (in the original: Джозвяк, Р. Выборы, дающие Москве большой стопор в Европарламенте). (accessed 11.06.2014)
107. Eatwell, R. 2000. The Extreme right and the British exceptionalism: the primacy of politics, in *The politics of the extreme right*, ed. by P. Hainsworth, London: Pinter, pp.172-192.
108. Eatwel, R. 2000. The rebirth of the Extreme right in Western Europe?, *Parliamentary Affairs,* No 53, pp. 407-425.
109. Edgar, D. 1977. Racism, fascism and the politics of the National Front, *Race and class*, Vol. 19, No 2 October, pp. 113-131.
110. *Elections in Sweden*. Available at: http://newsru.co.il/arch/world/20sep2010/sweden8001.html (accessed 17.01.2014)
111. *Electoral Performance of the BNP*. Available at: http://www.parliament.uk/business/publications/research/briefing-papers/SN05064/electoral-performance-of-the-british-national-party-in-the-uk (accessed 16.06.2014)
112. Eremina, N. 2014. Radical Right Parties in Political System of State: Theoretical and Practical Aspects, *International Relations and Diplomacy*, 2(2), February, pp.102-110.
113. Eremina, N., Seredenko, S. 2014. Konstitutsionnyi natsionalizm v sovremennoy Evrope: novye ugrozy, *NB: Problemy obschestva I politiki*, No 3, pp. 1-42. Available at: http://e-notabene.ru/pr/article_11170.html (Eremina, N., Seredenko, S. 2014. Constitutional Nationalism in Contemporary Europe: New Threats, *NB: Problems of society and politics,* No 3, pp.1-42). (in the

original: Еремина, Н.В., Середенко, С. Н. 2014. Конституционный национализм в современной Европе: новый уровень угроз, *NB: Проблемы общества и политики*, No 3, с.1-42). (accessed 06.08.2014)

114. Eremina, N.V. 2008. Britanskaya natsional'naya partia: factory rosta I sderzhivania, *Politex*, pp. 36-48. Available at: http://www.politex.info/content/view/404/30/. (Eremina, N.V. 2008. The British National Party: Factor of Growth and Deterrence, *Politex,* pp. 36-48). (in the original: Еремина, Н.В. 2008. Британская национальная партия: факторы роста и сдерживания, *Политэкс*, с. 36-48). (accessed 12.06.2009)

115. *European Socialists fret about far-right victory at EU election*. Available at: http://www.euractiv.com/eu-elections-2014/european-socialists-warn-far-rig-news-533048 (accessed 18.07.2014)

116. *Evroparlament*. Available at: http://ria.ru/cj_analytics/20140627/1013817404.html. (*European Parliament*). (in the original: *Европейский парламент*). (accessed 15.07.2014)

117. Ford, R. and Goodwin, Matthew J. 2014. *Revolt on the Right: Explaining Support for the Radical Right in Britain (Extremism and Democracy)*, London: Routledge, 336 p.

118. *49 Poland's fledging far-right party RN to run in European Parliament election*. Available at: http://www.rawstory.com/rs/2014/01/08/polands-fledgling-far-right-party-rn-to-run-for-eu-parliament-election/ (accessed 15.06.2014)

119. Foucault, M. 1982. The Subject and Power, *Critical Inquiry*, Vol. 8, No 4, Summer, pp. 777-795.

120. Fromm, E. 1994. *Escape from Freedom*, Henry Holt and Company LLC, 302 p.

121. Fromm, E. 1992. *The Anatomy of Human Destructiveness*, New-York: Henry Holt and Company, 576 p.

122. *Furer ukrainskoi Svobody prizval lishat' grazhdanstva vragov naroda*. Available at: http://baltija.eu/news/read/37383. (*Fuhrer of Ukranian "Svoboda" called to deprive "people's enemies" of citizenship*). (in the original: *Фюрер украинской Свободы призвал лишать гражданства врагов народа*). (accessed 05.05.2014)

123. Galkin, A.A. 1971. *Sociologia neofashizma*, Moskva: Nauka, 198 p. (Galkin, A.A. 1971. *Neo-fascist Sociology*, Moscow, 198 p.) (in the original: Галкин, А.А. 1971. *Социология неофашизма*, М., 198 с.).

124. Galkin, A.A. 2006. Protivorechia I ugrozy XXI veka, *Politia*, No 2, pp. 6-21. (Galkin, A.A. 2006. Contradictions and Threats of 21st

Century, *Politia*, No 2, pp. 6-21). (in the original: Галкин, А.А. 2006. Противоречия и угрозы XXI века, *Полития*, No 2, с. 6-21).

125. Gobineau, de J.A. *Opyt o neravenstve chelovecheskih ras*. Available at: http://www.e-reading.ws/book.php?book=108557 (Gobineau, de J.A. *The Essay on the Inequality of the Human Races*) (in Russian: Гобино, де Ж.А. *Опыт о неравенстве человеческих рас*). (accessed 28.03.2014)

126. Givens, Terri E. 2005. *Voting Radical Right in Western Europe*, Cambridge: Cambridge University Press, 178 p.

127. Griffin, R. 1991. *The Nature of Fascism*, London: Pinter, 251 p.

128. Griffin, R. 2002. The Primacy of Culture: the Current Growth (or Manufacture) of Consensus within Fascist Studies, *Journal of Contemporary History*, Vol.37, No1 January, pp. 21-43.

129. Griffin, R. 2000. Interregnum or Endgame? Radical Right Thought in «Post-fascist» Era, *the Journal of Political Ideologies*, Vol. 5, No 2, pp. 163–178.

130. Habermas, J. 1998. *The Inclusion of the Other: Studies in Political Theory*, Massachusetts: MIT.

131. Herder, J.G. 1977. *Idei k filosofii istorii chelovechestva*, perevod I primechania A.V. Mikhaylov, Moskva: Nauka, 133 p. (Herder, J. G. 1977. *Ideas for the Philosophy of History of Humanity*, Translation and comments by Mihaylov A.V, Moscow, 133 p.). (in Russian: Гердер, И.Г. 1977. *Идеи к философии истории человечества*, пер. и примеч. А.В. Михайлова. М., 133 с.)

132. Hofferbert, R.I., Budge, I. 1992. The Party Mandate and the Westminster Model: Election Programmes and Government Spending in Britain, 1945–1985, *British Journal of Political Science*, Vol. 22, No 2, pp. 151–182.

133. *How Europe's far-right will and won't flourish in 2014*. Available at: http://www.newstatesman.com/politics/2014/01/how-europes-far-right-will-and-wont-flourish-2014 (accessed 06.06.2014)

134. *Gollandia mezhdu shariatom I ul'trapravymi*. Available at: http://www.forumn.kiev.ua/2012-02-117/117-15.html. (*Holland between the Shariath and the Ultra Right-wing*). (in the original: *Голландия между шариатом и ультраправыми*). (accessed 13.02.2014)

135. Ignazi, P. 2003. *Extreme Right Parties in Western Europe*, Oxford: Oxford University Press, 270 p.

136. Ignazi, P. 2006. *Extreme right parties in Western Europe (comparative politics)*, Oxford: Oxford University Press, 310 p.

137. Ivanova, E.V. 2011. Formirovanie kraine pravogo dvizhenia v Bel'gii na primere partii Flamandskyi Interes, *in Pravoradikal'nye*

politicheskie partii I dvizhenia sovremennoy Evropy, Sankt-Peterburg: Izdatel'stvo SPbGU, pp. 215-231. (Ivanova, E.V. 2011. The making of the far-right movement in Belgium. Case-study: The Flemish Interest Party, *in Right-wing radical political parties and movements in contemporary Europe*, Saint-Petersburg, pp.215-231). (in the original: Иванова, Е.В. 2011. Формирование крайне правого движения в Бельгии на примере партии Фламандский интерес, *Праворадикальные политические партии и движения современной Европы*, СПб, с. 215-231).

138. Ivarsflaten, E, Gudbrandsen F. 2009. *The Populist radical right in Western Europe*. Available at: http://www.nordic-populism.aau.dk/digitalAssets/43/43663_populistright_routledgeregionalsurveys11.pdf (accessed 14.03.2014)

139. Izvestia, 21.12.1993. (News, 21.12.1993). (in the original: Известия, 21.12.1993).

140. Izvestia, 01.01.1994. (News, 01.01.1994). (in the original: Известия, 01.01.1994).

141. Jackson, Paul. 2011. *The EDL Britain`s «New Far Right» Social Movement*, Northampton: The University of Northampton, Radicalism and New Media Research Group, 78p.

142. Kantor, Maxim. *Poslednyaya skrepa*. Available at: http://www.gazeta.ru/comments/column/kantor/6038901.shtml (Maxim, Kantor. *The last tie*). (in the original: Кантор, Максим. *Последняя скрепа*). (accessed 17.06.2014)

143. Kitschelt, H. and McGann, Anthony J. 1997. *The Radical Right in Western Europe: a comparative analysis*, Michigan: The University of Michigan Press, 352 p.

144. Kolerov, M.A. 2009. *Voyna: vneshnyaa politika Rossii I politicheskaya bor'ba, 1999-2009*. Moskva: REGNUM, 332 p. (Kolerov, M.A. 2009. *War: External Politics of Russia and Political Struggle, 1999-2009*. Moscow, 332 p.). (in the original: Колеров, М.А. 2009. *Война: внешняя политика России и политическая борьба, 1999-2009*. М., 332 с.).

145. *Kommunisty vyigrali u "Svobody" v sude*. Available at: http://www.unian.net/politics/702414-kommunistyi-vyiigrali-u-svobodyi-v-sude.html (*Kommunists won at the court against "Svoboda"*). (in the original: *Коммунисты выиграли у "Свободы" в суде*). (accessed 15.07.2014)

146. Kostyuk, R. 2012. Nad Gretsiey zanimaertsya neofashistskii rassvet, *Novyi smysl,* Available at:

http://www.sensusnovus.ru/analytics/2012/09/29/14591.html. (Kostyuk, R. 2012. The Neo-Nazi day is dawning in Greece, *New Sense*). (in the original: Костюк, Р. 2012. Над Грецией занимается неонацистский рассвет, *Новый смысл*). (accessed 13.03.2014)

147. *Kraine pravye v Evroparlamente*. Available at: http://www.russian.rfi.fr/evropa/20140526-kraine-pravye-v-evroparlamente-ili-u-strakha-glaza-veliki (*Far-right in the European Parliament*). (in the original: *Крайне правые в Европарламенте*). (accessed 22.06.2014)

148. Krasinsky, V.V. 2011. Natsionalizm kak element ideologii ul'trapravyh partii I ego ispol'zovanie na vyborah v Germanii, *in Rossiiskii Obschestvennyi Institut Izbiratel'nogo Prava (ROIIP)*, Available at: http://www.roiip.ru/publication/publication227.htm. (Krasinsky, V.V. 2011. Nationalism as an element of ideology of ultra-right-wing parties and its use in elections in Germany, *Russian Institute of Electoral Rights (RIER)*). (in the original: Красинский, В.В. 2011. Национализм как элемент идеологии ультраправых партий и его использование на выборах в Германии, *Российский общественный институт избирательного права (РОИИП)*). (accessed 29.02.2014)

149. Kundnani, A. 2012. Blind Spot? Security Narratives and Far-Right Violence in Europe, *in ICCT Research Paper*, June. Available at: http://www.icct.nl/download/file/ICCT-Kundnani-Blind-Spot-June-2012.pdf (accessed 16.03.2014)

150. Kurnosov, D. 2008. Britanskaya natsional'naya partia: evolutsia I perspektivy, *Politex*, pp. 23-35. Available at: http://www.politex.info/content/view/403/30/. (Kurnosov, D. 2008. The British National Party: Evolution and Perspectives, *Politex*, pp. 23-35). (in the original: Курносов, Д. 2008. Британская национальная партия: эволюция и перспективы, *Политэкс*, с. 23-35). (accessed 12.06.2009)

151. Lasswell, H.D., Kaplan, A. 1950. *Power and Society: A Framework for Political Inquiry*, New Haven: Yale University Press, 295 p.

152. *Leader of British Far-Right Party Acquitted of Race Hate Charges*. Available at: http://www.iht.com/articles/ap/2006/11/10/ europe/EU_GEN_Britain_Far_Right_ Party.php (accessed 09.07.2014)

153. Le Bon, G. *Psikhologia narodov I mass*. Available at: http://lib.ru/POLITOLOG/LEBON/psihologia.txt. (Le Bon, G. *The Psychology of Peoples*) (in Russian: Лебон, Г. *Психология народов и масс*). (accessed 12.03.2014)

154. Lopukhov, B.R. 1985. *Neo-fashizm: opastnost' dlya mira,* Moscow: Molodaya gvardiya, 178 p. (Lopukhov, B.R. 1985. *Neo-fascism: the World Threat*, Moscow). (in the original: Лопухов, Б.Р. 1985. *Неофашизм: опасность для мира,* М., 178 с.).
155. Lyashchenko, V.A. 2003. Biologicheskie aspekty gumanizma, *Zdravyi smysl*, N 4, pp.10-12. (Lyashchenko, V.A. 2003. Biological Aspects of Humanism, *Common sense*, N 4, pp. 10-12). (in the original: Ляшенко, В.А. 2003. Биологические аспекты гуманизма, *Здравый смысл*, N 4, с. 10-12).
156. Malakhov, V.P. 2007. *Filosofia prava*, 2nd izdanie, Moskva: Yuniti-Dana, 336 p. (Malakhov, V.P. 2007. *Philosophy of Law*, 2nd edition, Moscow, 336 p.). (in the original: Малахов, В.П. 2007. *Философия права*. 2-е издание, М., 336 с.).
157. Malakhova, E. *Skol'ko russkikh na Ukraine?* Available at: http://www.antropotok.archipelag.ru/text/a192.htm. (Malakhova, E. *How many Russians are there in Ukraine?*). (in the original: Малахова, Е. *Сколько русских на Украине?*). (accessed 17.07.2014)
158. *Mapping the Extreme Right in contemporary Europe. From local to transnational*. 2012, ed. by Andrea Mammone, Emmanuel Godin, Brian Jenkins, London: Routledge, 344 p.
159. Marx, K., Engels, F. *Sobranie sochineniy*, 2 izdanie, Tom 1, 416 pp. (Marx, K. and Engels, F. *The Works*, 2-nd edition, Vol.1, 416 pp.). (in Russian: Маркс, К. и Энгельс, Ф. *Соч.*, 2-е изд., Т. 1. 416 с.); https://www.marxists.org/archive/marx/works/1843/critique-hpr/intro.htm (accessed 15.05.2014)
160. *Megapolis Express*, N 17/92. (Megapolis Express, N 17/92). (in the original: Мегаполис-Экспресс, N 17/92).
161. Minkenberg, M. 1998. *Die neue radikale Rechte im Vergleich*, USA, Frankreich, Deutschland, Opladen: Westdeutscher Verlag.
162. McClosky, H., Chong, D. 1985. Similarities and Differences between Left-wing and Right-wing Radicals, *British Journal of Political Science*, Vol.15, No 3 July.
163. Monzat, R. 2007. Region, natsia, Evropa: deistvuyuschie litsa istorii v konseptsiyakh frantsuzskih pravyh radikalov, *in Russkyi natsionalizm v politicheskom prostranstve (issledovania po natsionalizmu v Rossii)*, sostavlen M. Laruelle, Moskva: Franko-Rossiiyskyi Tsentr, pp. 18-29. (Monzat, R. 2007. Region, Nation, Europe: Historical Actors in the Conception of French Right-Wing Radicals, *in Russian Nationalism in the Political Space (the Research on Nationalism in Russia)*, comp. by M. Laruelle. Moscow). (in Russian: Монза, Р. 2007. Регион, нация, Европа: действующие

лица истории в концепциях французских правых радикалов, *Русский национализм в политическом пространстве (исследования по национализму в России),* Сост. М. Ларюэль. М.).

164. *Moskovsy Komsomolets*, 06.01.1994. (*Moscow Komsomol*, 06.01.1994). (in the original: *Московский комсомолец*, 06.01.1994).

165. Mudde, C. 2007. *Populist Radical Right Parties in Europe*, Cambridge: Cambridge University Press, 386 p.

166. Mudde, C. 2003. *The Ideology of the Extreme Right*, Manchester: Manchester University Press, 212 p.

167. Myazin, N.A. 2014. *Islamskoe soobschestvo I islamizm v Anglii v XX – XXI kak factory transformatsii britanskikh pravyh dvizheniy ot neofashizma k antidjihadizmu*, Kaluga, 258 p. (Myazin, N.A. 2014. *Islamic community and Islamism in England at the end of XX – the beginning of the XXI centuries as transformation factors of the British right-wing movements from neo-fascism to anti-jihadism*. The abstract of dissertation for the first level of postgraduate degree, Kaluga) (in the original: Мязин, Н.А. 2014. *Исламское сообщество и исламизм в Англии в конце XX – начале XXI вв. как факторы трансформации британских правых движений от неофашизма к антиджихадизму.* Автореферат диссертации на соискание ученой степени кандидата наук, Калуга).

168. Namazova, A. 2001. Konstitutsionnye reformy v Bel'gii v XIX – XX vekah, *Evropeyskyi al'manakh*, Moskva, pp. 29-40. (Namazova, A. 2001. Constitutional Reforms in Belgium in the 19th - 20th centuries, *European Almanac*, Moscow, pp. 29-40). (in the original: Намазова, А. 2001. Конституционные реформы в Бельгии в XIX – XX веках, *Европейский альманах*, М., с. 29-40).

169. *Nezavisimaya Gazeta*, 1993, 16 April. (*Independent Newspaper*, 1993, 16 April). (in the original: *Независимая Газета*, 1993, 16 апрель).

170. Norris, P. 2005. *Radical Right: Voters and Parties in the Electoral Market*, Cambridge: Cambridge University Press, 350 p.

171. *Novaya Gazeta*, 29.10.1991. Available at: http://www.panorama.ru/works/vybory/party/ldpr.html (*New Newspaper*, 29.10.1991). (in the original: *Новая Газета*, 29.10.1991)

172. *Novye pravye v Pol'she*. Available at: http://voprosik.net/novye-pravye-v-polshe/. (*The New Right-wing in Poland*). (in the original: *Новые правые в Польше*). (accessed 12.05.2014)

173. Obucina, Vedran. 2011. Radical Right-Wing *Parties* in Former Communist Countries: Challenges to Liberal Democracy or a Social Economic Protest?, *Anals*, No 8, pp. 93-105.

174. Panebianco, A. 1988. *Political Parties: Organization and Power*, Cambridge: Cambridge University Press, 336 p.
175. *Parliamentary Election 2010*. Available at: http://www.gmu-countries.ru/europa/swed/sweden-encl-vibory.html (accessed 14.03.2014)
176. *Parliamentary Elections 2005*. Available at: http://www.dw.de/15272878 (accessed 11.03.2014)
177. Paxton, O.R. 1998. Five Stages of Fascism, *Journal of Modern History*, Vol.70, No 1 March, pp. 1-23.
178. Pedahzur, A., Brichta, A. 2002. The institutionalization of extreme right-wing charismatic parties: a paradox? *Party Politics,* Vol.8, No 1, pp. 31-49.
179. *Pervye itogi vyborov v Evroparlament demonstriruyut usilenie pozitsii radikalov I polulistov*. Available: http://itar-tass.com/mezhdunarodnaya-panorama/1215406 (*First results of Euro parliament elections demonstrate strong positions of radicals and populists*). (in the original: *Первые итоги выборов в Европарламент демонстрируют усиление позиций радикалов и популистов*). (accessed 11.07.2014)
180. Plyasunov, S. 2013. Slovakia: Neozhidannaya pobeda, *Vsya Evropa*, Available at: http://www.alleuropa.mgimo.ru/slovakiya-neozhidannaya-pobeda. (Plyasunov, S. 2013. Slovakia: Unexpected Victory, *All Europe*). (in the original: Плясунов, С. 2013. Словакия: неожиданная победа, *Вся Европа*). (accessed 12.02.2014)
181. *Poland's fledging far-right party RN to run in European Parliament election*. Available at: http://www.rawstory.com/rs/2014/01/08/polands-fledgling-far-right-party-rn-to-run-for-eu-parliament-election/ (accessed 19.07.2014)
182. *Pozitsii kraine pravykh v Evrope krepnut*. Available at: http://www.dw.de/15272878. (*The positions of the far-right gain strength in Europe*). (in the original: *Позиции крайне правых в Европе крепнут*). (accessed 19.07.2014)
183. *Pravoradikal'nye politicheskie partii I dvizhenia sovremennoy Evropy*. 2011, Sankt-Peterburg: Izdatel'stvo SPbGU, pp.408. (*Right-radical political parties and movements of contemporary Europe*. 2011, Saint-Petersburg, pp. 408). (in the original: *Праворадикальные политические партии и движения современной Европы*. 2011. СПб., 408 с.).
184. Putnam, R.D. 1993. *Making Democracy Work: Civic Traditions in Modern*, Princeton, NJ: Princeton University Press, 258 p.

185. *Rein Lang ukrasil yubiley Adol'fon Hitlerom*. Available at: http://rus.delfi.ee/daily/estonia/rejn-lang-ukrasil-yubilej-adolfom-gitlerom.d?id=16354710 (*Rein Lang decorated his anniversary with Adolf Hitler*). (*Рейн Ланг украсил юбилей Адольфом Гитлером*). (accessed 19.07.2014)
186. Roze, A. 2012. Igra v Nazi, *Rossiiskaya Gazeta*, Available at: http://www.rg.ru/2012/01/23/germany.html. (Roze, A. 2012. A Nazi Game, *Russian Newspaper*). (in the original: Розэ, A.2012. Игра в nazi, *Российская Газета*). (accessed 18.07.2014)
187. Samuel, H. *Marine Le Pen Would Beat Nicolas Sarcozy in presidential election*. Available at: http://www.telegraph.co.uk/news/worldnews/europe/france/8364812/Marine-Le-Pen-would-beat-Nicolas-Sarkozy-in-presidential-election.html (accessed 19.07.2014)
188. Schedler, A. 1998. The Normative Force of Electoral Promises, *Journal of Theoretical Politics*, Vol. 10, No 2, pp. 191–214.
189. *Segodnya*, 29.12.1993; 12.01.1994, 22.04.1994. (*Today*, 29.12.1993; 12.01.1994; 22.04.1994). (in the original: *Сегодня*, 29.12.1993; 12.01.1994; 22.04.1994).
190. Seredenko, S. *Analiz preambuly Latviiskoy konstitutsii*. Available at: http://www.baltexpert.com/2013/12/05/sseredenko_analiz_preambula/. (Seredenko, S. *Analysis of the Preamble to the Constitution of Latvia*). (in the original: Середенко, С. *Анализ преамбулы Латвийской конституции*). (accessed 11.02.2014)
191. Shekhovtsov, A.V. 2008. Novyi pravyi radikalizm: k voprosu ob opredelenii, *in Vestnik SevNTU*, *Zbornik nauk*, Vyp. 91, Sevastopol', pp. 141-144. (Shekhovtsov, A.V. 2008. New right-wing radicalism: definition issue, *in Vesnik SevNTU, Collection of sciences*, Vol. 91, Sevastopol, Published by SevNTU, pp. 141-144). (in the original: Шеховцов, А.В. 2008. Новый правый радикализм: к вопросу об определении, *Вiсник СевНТУ: Зб. наук. праць*, Вип. 91, Севастополь: СевНТУ, с. 141-144).
192. Shekhovtsov, A. *Ukraine: the far-right in parliament for the first time*. Available at: http://www.opendemocracy.net/od russia/anton shekhovtsov/ukraine-far-right-in-parliament-for-first-time (accessed 14.06.2014)
193. Schneider, Heinrich. 1998. Riigiteoreetilisi probleeme: miks nad on tekkinud ja kuidas neid lahendada?, *Juridica*, No 7, pp. 350-361.
194. *Siloviki rassmatrivayut vopros o zaprete "Pravogo sektora"*. Available at: http://ria.ru/world/20140328/1001375442.html (*Law enforcers discuss if to forbid "Right Sector"*). (in the original:

Силовики рассматривают вопрос о закрытии “Правого сектора”). (accessed 20.07.2014)

195. *Sovetskaya annexia I gosudarstvennyi kontinuitet.* Available at: http://www.estemb.ru/estonija/istorija/aid-2019 (*Soviet Annexation and State Continuity*). (in the original: *Советская аннексия и государственный суверенитет*). (accessed 20.07.2014)
196. Sumlenny, S. 2010. Migranty otvetyat za vsyo, *Internet Proekt Expert Online*, Available at: http://expert.ru/expert/2010/42/migranty_otvetyt_za_vse/ (Sumlenny, S. 2010. Migrants will pay for everything, *Internet Project Expert Online*). (in the original: Сумленный, С. 2010. Мигранты ответят за всё, *Интернет-проект «Эксперт онлайн»*). (accessed 12.03.2014)
197. *Swedish democrats*. Available at: http://www.right-world.net/countries/sweden/sd (accessed 16.04.2014)
198. Taggart, P.A. 2000. *Populism*, Buckingham: Open University Press.
199. Tamas, G.M. 2000. O post-fashizme, *Konstitutsionnoye pravo: vostochno-evropeyskoe obozrenie,* No 3 (32), pp. 6-14. (Tamas, G.M. 2000. On post-fascism, *East European Constitutional Review*, No 3 (32), pp. 6–14). (in Russian: Тамаш, Г.М. 2000. О постфашизме, *Конституционное право: восточноевропейское обозрение*, No 3 (32). с. 6–14).
200. *Teoriya gosudarstva I prava*. 1998, ed. by Marchenko M.N., Moskva, pp. 448. (*Theory of State and Law.* 1998, ed. by Marchenko M.N., Moscow, pp.448). (in the original: *Теория государства и права.* 1998, под ред. проф. М.Н.Марченко. М. 448 с.).
201. *The British National Party Gains Strength. 2007.* Available at: http://www.thetimes.co.uk/tto/news/politics/article2023003.ece (accessed 14.04.2014)
202. *The Flemish National Union.* Available at: http://foriz.ru/flamandskij-nacionalnyj-sojuz (accessed 14.04.2014)
203. *The League of the North*. Available at: http://right-world.net/countries/italy/ls(accessed 14.04.2014)
204. *The National Revival of Poland*. Available at: http://www.right-world.net/countries/poland/nop (accessed 14.04.2014)
205. *The Revival of Right Wing Extremism in the Nineties*. 2013, ed. by Peter H. Merkl, Leonard Weinberg, London: Routledge.
206. *The Slovak National Party*. Available at: http://optoshka.ru/styhrmnyhriovteof/(accessed 14.04.2014)
207. *The Swedish Democrats*. Available at: http://www.right-world.net/countries/sweden/sd (accessed 14.04.2014)

208. *The True Finns*. Available at: http://www.right-world.net/countries/%5Bcountry%5D/if (accessed 14.04.2014)
209. Toffler, A. 1990. *Powershift: Knowledge, Wealth and Violence in the 21-st Century*, New-York: Bantam Books, 586 p.
210. Tomin, L.V. 2014. *Sovremennye konflikty: poststrukturalistskiy analiz*, Sankt-Peterburg: Izdatel'stvo GUP, 167 p. (Tomin, L.V. 2014. *Modern Political Conflicts: Post-structuralist Analysis*, Saint-Petersburg, 167 p.). (in the original: Томин, Л.В. 2014. *Современные конфликты: постструктуралистский анализ*. СПб., 167 с.).
211. *Triumf pravykh I kraine pravykh*. Available at: http://www.pravda.ru/world/16-05-2002/807218-0/ (*Triumph of the right-wing and the far-right*). (in the original: *Триумф правых и крайне правых*). (accessed 14.04.2014)
212. Trotsky, L.D. 1930. *My Life*. (-my-life-trotsky.epub), Chapter XVII. Available at: https://www.marxists.org/archive/trotsky/1930/mylife/1930-lif.pdf (accessed 04.02.2014)
213. Tulupov, D.S. 2008. Sovremennaya politika Datskoy narodnoy partii v otnoshenii immigrantov, *Politex*, pp. 58-67. Available at: http://www.politex.info/content/view/406/30/. (Tulupov, D.S. 2008. Contemporary policies pursued by the Danish People's Party toward immigrants, *Politex*, pp. 58-67). (in the original: Тулупов, Д.С. 2008. Современная политика «Датской народной партии» в отношении иммигрантов, *Политэкс*, с. 58-67). (accessed 14.04.2009)
214. *Two years to go to the 2014 European elections*. Available at: http://www.europarl.europa.eu/aboutparliament/en/00191b53ff/Eurobarometer.html?tab=2012_4 (accessed 12.06.2014)
215. *Ukraina khochet lishit' russkikh grazhdanstva*. Available at: http://newsland.com/news/detail/id/373037/ (*Ukraine wants to deprive Russians of citizenship*). (in the original: *Украина хочет лишить русских гражданства*). (accessed 16.06.2014)
216. *V britanskuyu politiku vorvalas' partia grazhdanskih natsionalistov*. 2013. Available at: http://lenta.ru/articles/2013/03/21/ukip/. (A party of civil nationalists has burst into the British politics). (in the original: *В британскую политику ворвалась партия гражданских националистов*). (accessed 07.04.2014)
217. *V Germanii sozdana paria protivnikov evro*. Available at: http://lenta.ru/news/2013/03/11/antieuro/. (*A party to oppose the euro has been founded In Germany*). (in the original: *В Германии создана партия противников евро*). (accessed 07.04.2014)

218. *Varieties of Right-Wing Extremism in Europe*. 2013, ed. by Andrea Mammone, Emmanuel Godin, Brian Jenkins, London.
219. Veugelers, J.W.P. 1999. A Challenge for Political Sociology: the Rise of Far-Right Parties in Contemporary Western Europe, *Current Sociology*, Vol.47, No 4 October, pp. 78-107.
220. Voss, K. 2007. *Support for the Far Right: the Desire for Cultural Preservation in an Increasingly Globalized and Multicultural Europe*. Available at: http//www.icpsr.umich/edu/ICPSR/prize/winners.html (accessed 11.02.2014)
221. *Vybory v Norvegii: Partia Andresa Breivika voshla v sostav pravitel'stvennoi koalitsii*. Available at: http://www.regnum.ru/news/polit/1706441.html. (*Elections in Norway: the Party of Andres Breivik goes into the government coalition*). (in the original: *Выборы в Норвегии: партия Андреса Брейвика вошла в состав правительственной коалиции*). (accessed 07.06.2014)
222. Weber, M. 1921. *Politics as Vocation*. Available at: http://www.sscnet.ucla.edu/polisci/ethos/Weber-vocation.pdf (accessed 12.02.2014)
223. *Western Democracies and the New Extreme Right Challenge*. 2003, ed. by Eatwell R. and Mudde C., London: Routledge, 235 p.
224. *White Power Music: Scenes of Extreme Right Cultural Resistance*. 2012, ed. by A. Shekhovtsov, P. Jackson, Ilford: Searchlight and RNM Publications.
225. Wippermann, W. 1983. *Europäischer Faschismus im Vergleich 1992-1982*, Frankfurt am Main: Suhrkamp.
226. Worsley, P. 1970. The Concept of Populism, *in Populism: Its meanings and National Characteristics*, ed. by G. Ionescu, E. Gellner, London: Weidenfeld and Nicolson, pp. 212–250.
227. Yefremov, A.E. 1970. *Korichnevaya ugroza*, Moscow: Politizdat, 152p. (Yefremov, A.Y. 1970. *The Brown PlagueThreat*, Moscow, 152 p.). (in the original: Ефремов, А.Е. 1970. *Коричневая угроза*, М., 152с).
228. Zafar, Guiyev. 2011. Azerbaydzhan posle Alieva, *Regnum*. Available at: http://www.iarex.ru/books/book58.pdf. (Zafar, Guiyev. 2011. Azerbaijan after Aliyev, *Regnum*). (in the original: Зафар, Гулиев. 2011. Азербайджан после Алиева, *Regnum*). (accessed 07.04.2014)
229. *"Zavoevat' Frantsiyu, a zatem unichtozhit' Evropu": Marine Le Pen I proryv kraine pravyh na evrovyborah.* Available at: http://www.regnum.ru/news/polit/1808594.html *("To conquer France and liquidate Europe": Marine Le Pen and far-right victory*). (in the

original: *"Завоевать Францию, а затем уничтожить Европу": Марин Ле Пен и прорыв крайне правых на выборах*). (accessed 15.06.2014)

230. Zolotova, M. Yu., Kurchanova, E.M. 2011. Evolutsia ideino-politicheskih pozitsii etnoradikalov v sovremennoy Frantsii v kontekste predstavleniya osnovnyh kontseptov ih politicheskogo diskursa, *in Pravoradikal'nye politicheskie partii I dvizhenia sovremennoy Evropy*, Sankt-Peterburg: Izdatel'stvo SPbGU, pp. 324-355. (Zolotova, M. Yu., Kurchanova, E.M. 2011. The evolution of ideological and political positions of ethnic radicals in contemporary France in the context of the main concepts of their political discourse, *in Right-wing radical political parties and movements in contemporary Europe*, Saint-Petersburg, pp. 324-355). (in the original: Золотова, М.Ю., Курчанова, Е.М. 2011. Эволюция идейно-политических позиций этнорадикалов в современной Франции в контексте представления основных концептов их политического дискурса, *Праворадикальные политические партии и движения современной Европы*, СПб., с.324-355).

231. Zuercher, Ch. 1999. Multilulturalizm I etnopoliticheskyi poryadok v postsovetskoy Rossii: nekotorye metodologichskie zamechania, *Polis (politicheskie issledovania)*, No 6, pp. 105-118. (Zuercher, Ch. 1999. Multiculturalism and Ethnopolitical Order in Post-Soviet Russia: Some Methodological Rcmarks, *Polis (Political Studies)*, No 6, pp. 105-118). (in Russian: Цюрхер, К. 1999. Мультикультурализм и этнополитический порядок в постсоветской России: некоторые методологические замечания, *Полис (Политические исследования*), No 6, с. 105-118).